Gustave D'Alaux

Soulouque and his Empire

Gustave D'Alaux

Soulouque and his Empire

ISBN/EAN: 9783337172992

Printed in Europe, USA, Canada, Australia, Japan

Cover: Foto ©ninafisch / pixelio.de

More available books at **www.hansebooks.com**

SOULOUQUE

AND

HIS EMPIRE.

FROM THE FRENCH OF

GUSTAVE D'ALAUX,

TRANSLATED AND EDITED

BY

JOHN H. PARKHILL, A. M.,

OF BALTIMORE.

J. W. RANDOLPH,
121 MAIN STREET, RICHMOND, VA.
1861.

Entered according to Act of Congress, in the year 1861, by
JOHN H. PARKHILL, A. M.,
in the Clerk's Office of the District Court of the United States for the District of Maryland.

TABLE OF CONTENTS.

	PAGE.
AUTHOR'S PREFACE...	17
I. Historical Review—Origin of Haytiën Parties..	21
II. Black Politics and Yellow Politics...	54
III. The yellow *Bourgeoisie*—A negro 24th of February—Guerrier, Pierrot, Riché—Soulouque—A conjured *fauteuil*...	67
IV. Negro illuminism—Devotions of Madame Soulouque—The hunt after *fétiches*...	82
V. Similien...	99
VI. A Haytiën trial of the press...	110
VI. A Negro Solution...	126
VIII. Massacres—M. Maxime Raybaud—Negro Communism...	134
IX. The scruples of Soulouque—A Negro *Impromtu*,	167
X. The Conspiracy of capital in Hayti...	185
XI. A sun-set—The misfortunes of the *piquets*—A voltairian *papa-loi*...	200
XII. Victories and conquests of Soulouque—A sorcery trial—The Empire and the Imperial Court..	220
XIII. The Haytiën Clergy—Ceremony of the Coronation...	251
XIV. The principal of authority in Hayti—The Secret of Soulouque...	270
XV. The Dominican Republic,...	296

INTRODUCTION.

Soulouque and His Empire was published at Paris, in 1856. At that time, Soulouque was firmly seated on his throne—his name a terror to his own wretched people, and a by-word of ridicule to all the world besides. He spent nearly ten years—decorating himself—creating a black aristocracy with the most preposterous titles—ruthlessly slaying all, his suspicions, hatred, or caprice singled out—and, in making a ludicrous war on the Dominicans. The social condition of Hayti was constantly retrograding;. the material interest of the country neglected; commerce driven away by ruinous exactions; and all sinking, rapidly, to a lower level of civilization.

Certainly then ten years of this tragic buffoonery was sufficient; the gew-gaw concern was falling to pieces of itself; a breath of opposition was only necessary to complete the work; and Geffrard gave it. With a few resolute followers, on the 25th day of December, 1858, he made a descent upon Port-au-Prince, in a *row-boat;* and the Empire of Faustin Ist became a matter of history. The Ex-Emperor, with his family, escaped to Jamaica, where he now passes his time, playing billiards and swinging in a hammock.

The success of Geffrard, who is himself a mulatto, is the triumph of the *men of color*. This class is few in number, but it possesses what there is in Hayti, of education, energy, and hope for the future. It is only, by and though it, that the ancient prosperity of the Island can be restored. In this work, President Geffrard has a high mission before him; and we have every reason to believe that he will endeavor to fulfill it. This leads to the inquiry—how can he do it?

Hayti has been, now, under negro domination for seventy years. Previous to this, the agricultural and commercial prosperity of the Island had reached a high degree of development. The population of French Hayti exceeded a half million in 1791; and its annual exports to France alone were more than five millions sterling. It could not have been otherwise, when we consider its favored material resources. Situated under the tropics; possessing a climate and soil eminently fitted to grow sugar, cotton, and indigo; its mountains rich in gold, copper and coal; its rivers, bordered with forests of mahogany, cedar, and dye-woods; and its position on the track of the Great West Indian trade, making it the entrepot for the ships of all nations; are elements of wealth possessed by few countries.

These were all fostered, and industriously developed, by the French colonists, and repaid them with fabulous wealth. All these natural capabilities still belong to Hayti; but, for the want of the life-giving energy of labor, and intelligent interest, have fallen back into their aboriginal condition. The social and individual characteristics of the population are changed. In fact, it is not the same people; it was *French*—it is now *African*. This explains all. To show, in its details, how this change has destroyed the social and material prosperity of Hayti, would take a volume; involving considerations of history, political economy, and ethnology. The space of a few pages does not warrant our entering on such an investigation.

The fact is, however, patent to the world, that the present social, political, and economical condition of the Haytiens, is depraved to that degree, as to predict barbarism, in a few more generations. Indeed, M. d'Alaux says "Hayti will be prosperous in ten years, or cannibal in twenty." This Island lies so near the coast of the United States, its capabilities are so manifest, and its staple products are so necessary, that we cannot remain indifferent to its fate. The practical spirit of the age, will not allow, such a country, to lie waste. How can it be made useful? The answer rises to my mind, at once; *colonize it, with the* FREE *blacks of the United States.*

In this direction, lies the true policy of Geffrard, in putting his country upon a new career of improvement. He seems, already to have recognized this; and, in a measure, to have adopted it. For, it is a fact, that he has invited the immigration of free blacks from the United States into Hayti; indeed, has offered them bounties to come. Several companies of them have gone already, and settled themselves down comfortably on the rich plains of the Artibonite. These pioneers should be followed rapidly by others; and will be, if the advantages of the country become known.

President Geffrard has manifested, in this measure, a correct view of the necessities of Hayti, and a knowledge of the proper means of supplying them. This liberality argues well for the future of the Island under his rule. He knows that the United States' immigrants of color will increase the influence of his class, and thus strengthen his hands to carry forward any plan of reform. This is his political reason. In an agricultural aspect, these immigrants will occupy the waste lands, and introduce upon them improved implements of husbandry and labor-saving machinery. The consequence of this would be an increase of population and production; and, upon these foundations, mercantile and commercial interests would be established. These new economical agencies would then only have to be stimulated to their utmost, to bring back the ancient prosperity.

The Island of Hayti is then *open to the immigration of our free blacks.* The next, and only question now is: Will they go? The fact is, that this class of our population have manifested great apathy in availing themselves of the benefits of colonization. Nearly all the immigrants annually taken over to Liberia, are manumitted slaves, whose expatriation is made the condition of their freedom; and they may be properly called compulsory immigrants. These are from the Southern and Middle States. It is very rare that any Northern free negroes are induced to immigrate. Indeed, it may be affirmed without incorrectness that, as a body, they are opposed to immigration. This result has been produced, in a great measure, by the influence of abolitionists, who are opposed to *every* scheme of colonization beyond the limits of the United States. It can then be scarcely said that there are any voluntary immigrants to Liberia. The few free negroes from the Middle and Southern States, who go over in the vessels of the Colonization Society, are the only exceptions. The conclusion, therefore, is manifest: that if colonization of the free blacks depends upon voluntary immigration, it is impracticable.

The only alternative is, that its beginning and growth, up to a certain point, must be compulsory. This necessity offends the feelings of many persons whose opinions deserve respect. A little reflection however will recall the fact, that forced colonization has been the order of past events. The Puritans formed the colony at Plymouth from necessity, and were forced immigrants; so were the early settlers of Virginia, and the exiled Huguenots of South Carolina. Australia is an example of this in our own day. It has been for years a penal settlement of England; until now it has arisen to the dignity of an important power; and the process of forced settlement has been transferred to Van Deiman's Land and New Zealand. These instances are cited to show that it is no new thing sought to be introduced, but a recognized method by which new States have been founded. We may then safely answer the question: that the free blacks of the United States will not, voluntarily, remove beyond the limits of this country anywhere, either to Liberia or to Hayti.

The two classes of blacks, slave and free, cannot remain together in the same community without producing pauperism and crime in one, and discontent and insubordination in the other. The Southern States are fully convinced of this truth, by practical demonstration. Hence the importance, indeed necessity, of ridding themselves of the free blacks in their midst. The Northern States refuse to receive these pariahs, therefore the alternative of reducing them to slavery, by legislative enactments, is seriously agitated in the South; and, in a few Legislatures, bills to this effect have been already introduced and considered. Popular sentiment will, the more readily, sanction this method of disposing of the difficulty, because of the antislavery agitation at the North, and the growing demand for slave labor at the South.

The colonization of this class, on the Island of Hayti, presents a much preferable way of getting rid of them, and the plan is of easy execution. The Island is only a few days sail from all the Southern sea-ports, and the expense of their transportation would scarcely be felt by the Southern people. The slightly increased taxes necessary for this purpose, would be trebly compensated—by the removal of this element of pauperism, vice and insubordination from all contact with the slave population—by the diminished expenses of criminal administration and patrol regulations—and by cutting off a prominent agency of kidnapping, incendiarism and rebellion, now wielded by abolitionists against Southern society. By this measure, all parties would be benefited—the Southern States, the Island of Hayti, and the free blacks themselves. The plan is simply suggested; there is no space in which to elaborate it.

The importance of redeeming this fertile Island from its present waste, seems to be kept constantly in view by the Author; and he turns to the probability of its being seized by the Americans. It manifestly presents a more inviting and open field to their enterprise than Cuba. According to its size, it is superior in material resources; the whole coast is exposed to attack, and its subjugation would be easy. It is not probable, however, that England

and France would be willing to see the United States hold the Island, nor indeed any part of it. The recent efforts of Mr. Cazeneau to obtain a treaty from Santana, granting important privileges to the United States in Spanish Hayti, were strenuously opposed by the French; and, finally, defeated through their influence. There is evidently much jealousy, on this subject, towards the United States; not, that we have shown any disposition to assume sovereignty over Hayti, but, that it is natural to look, in this direction, for the influences (if any are to be applied) for its salvation from impending barbarism.

In my view, the free blacks of the United States should be made the medium through which the reforming power of our civilization can be brought to bear on the social condition of Hayti. Dr. Livingstone very truly remarks, that "trade is the pioneer of Christianity." This truth is the result of sixteen years of missionary experience among the wild tribes of Africa; and it is confirmed, by the history of commerce, the world over. The patriot and philanthropist, therefore, whether his sympathies are with the black man or the white man in the United States, must favor any feasible plan of colonizing the free blacks *beyond* our limits.

It is objected, that the success of this enterprise would be to build up a black government, so near our Southern States, as to affect injuriously the slave population. If it was, now, first proposed to establish negro rule in Hayti, the objection would have much force. But the Island is, in fact, already under a black administration; and the effect of colonizing our free negroes on it, is limited to improving this new Africa, and benefiting the condition of the immigrants.

I have been induced to translate this work, because of another reason. Reliable information, as to the practical working of emancipation in Hayti, is wanting to American readers. The following history is by a Frenchman, concerning a former French colony; his means of correct information are the most abundant, and his motives for truthfulness the highest. We may therefore accept his picture as drawn to the life. But what a picture! Laocoon writhing in the deadly embrace of the serpent, was not more certainly doomed than are all civilizing interests in Hayti, in the stifling grasp of African barbarism.

We of the Southern States are, specially, interested in this matter. Like questions are being stated, affecting our social institutions; and similar fanatical agencies are seeking a like solution—the solution of cruelty and blood. I desire to warn the Southern people against this result, by holding up, before their eyes, the ludicrous and sanguinary consequences of African domination.

These pages point out the significant fact, *that the white and black races cannot exist together as equals in the same community.* The truth goes further: that even the *yellow* and black castes cannot commingle socially. Government becomes, in such a condition, a question of the dominance of races. All other interests become merged in this one; a war of skins exhausts every element of prosperity, and general ruin settles down upon the unhappy country. Applying these teachings .to the slavery question in our country, the conclusion is irresistible: that the African race here, must remain a servant to the white man, as a necessary condition of the preservation of our civilization and liberties, or be removed altogether beyond the limits of the United States. The latter alternative is scarcely possible, unless the wicked agitators of the land shall, in their madness, hurry events to that crisis, when the preservation of the white race shall demand the *extermination* of the black race. The black man would then have changed his relation, as a loyal servant, happy and secure, under the constant protection of a christian master, to the position of our wild Indian tribes—an outcast and an Ishmael, wasted by the ceaseless aggressions of white civilization.

Transpiring political events seem to portend a great social revolution, growing out of this question. It may result in a distinct confederation of the Southern States. Such a Government would know how to harmonize the social and political interests, so deeply rooted in domestic slavery, by maintaining the present humane relation between the white master and the black servant. Every patriot would deplore the disruption upon which this new Confederation would be consequent; but self-preservation is a law of so supreme a nature, as to consecrate all necessary means to secure its end.

I commend this work to the reader, with the assurance, that the ludicrous and the horrible will spice the subject sufficiently to please the strongest taste. *It is Punch in Dahomey.*

BALTIMORE, 1861.

AUTHOR'S PREFACE.

Ça pas bon, ça senti fumée.—(Emperor Dessalines.)

The subject I am about to treat, considered all together, attracts and embarrasses me. I have to speak of a country, which has journals and sorcerers—a middle class and *fétiches*; and, where the worshippers of snakes have proclaimed by turns, "in the presence of the Supreme Being," democratic constitutions and monarchs "by the grace of God."

What I am about to relate of this country, and, especially, of the Chief who rules it, falls far short still, both of what we know, and could imagine of the subject. But, in this tragi-comedy, the conclusion of which, after all, will be the condemnation or final restoration of one of the five human families, is there then only the interest of curiosity to follow? Here my hesitations begin. The black world, from which we are about to tear the veil, presents, indeed, in the same incident, and often in the same man, such a confusion of contrasts—civilization and the Congo—the touching and the atrocious—the ludicrous and human blood, mingle, penetrate, and jostle in it, with such an improbable and startling brutality—that in remaining scrupulously truthful, I risk authorizing at the same time, the most opposite expectations. Let it, therefore, be well understood, in advance, that the sentiments which guide me in this recital, and the conclusion which is developed from its whole, are equally removed from excess of optimism, and excess of negation.

I do not admit, for example, with some stupid negropholists, that the facial angle is the measure of human duties; and that a broad flat nose excuses certain abominations. But, so far from concluding, however, from these abominations, the original inferiority of the black race, I see in them the proof of its moral liberty ; that is to say, of its perfectibility. If this race can descend to extreme perversity, it can, therefore, attain to extreme virtue; and, we find it, in fact, at these two degrees of the moral scale. I do not deny, however, that the civilizing aptitude of the negro has exceeded but little, up to the present time, certain instincts of imitation ; but every civilization is not necessarily spontaneous. In the case of nine European nations in ten, what is it after all but *progress*—intelligent imitation ? That this imitation is not always intelligent in Hayti—that this France, with crisped hair, exhibits in its borrowed accoutrements, an incoherence burlesque, or savage—proves conclusively this fact : that we cannot go from the river *Gambia* to the banks of the *Seine*, in one day. The essential matter is, that this faculty of imitation is not limited. We recognise, infallibly, the perfectibility of nations, races, and species, only by this sign: and experience confirms this in Hayti. Talents, which would do honor to any country, have been produced among some Haytiëns, who, before and since the emancipation, have lived in our intellectual midst; and, even among those, who have received the radiation afar off.

Although Hayti has been, for the past eight years, in the full reaction of African barbarism, it is repugnant to admit, that so many encouraging symptoms may be only the derision of chance; and that these appeals of the last hour have been uttered, for more than half a century, by the breath of civilization, only to pass away, and be miserably lost on the Ivory Coast. Likewise, it appears to us moreover, that the Empire of Soulouque is to be estimated neither better nor worse, altogether, than many republics of the neighboring continent. If Spanish civilization has forgotten itself, is it at all astonishing that sometimes, Cafre barbarism calls itself to mind? All differences of the past being laid aside, Hayti, has, moreover, an excuse that these republics have not; because, it concealed, beforehand, in its own bosom two elements of strife—namely: a minority of half-whites, whose inclinations and education placed them on a level with French ideas; and a black majority, to which despotism is, at once, an instinctive aspiration, and a necessary transition. Each of these elements, by turns, has found it difficult to acclimate itself in the political atmosphere of the other; hence, a perpetual uneasiness, and sometimes, also, fever and delirium. If the crisis is more violent than ever, at the present time, so much the better perhaps; only decisive symptoms are exhibited; and there are many chances in favor of health. Soulouque, in whom all the reminiscences of original savagery are, accidentally, summed up, seems indeed guided, half by the force of things, and half by his own instincts, to build up on its true foundations, this rudiment of nationality.

These reservations being made, I feel perfectly protected from every accusation of partiality, or systematic hostility. Besides, now that the very basis of the dispute has been decided by emancipation, what interest would there be to remain partial? I will, therefore, take men and facts, just as I find them, and leave each to produce its own conclusion, without disquieting myself to know, whether they furnish reason, to benevolence, for laughter or horror.

SOULOUQUE AND HIS EMPIRE.

I.

Historical Review—Origin of Haytiën Parties.

Most of the well informed Haytiëns, make it a sort of point of honor, to disguise as much from the stranger, as they do from themselves, the antagonism which divides the *sang-mêlée*, or yellow caste, from the black caste. I consider it much more useful to rectify the double misunderstanding whence this antagonism springs, for we do not destroy error by denying it. If, at the present time, Hayti seems condemned to become a branch of the kingdom of *Juida*—if each of the two elements which were civilizers, after their fashion, is often there transformed into an instrument of barbarism—it is especially because the facts, on all sides, are not understood in time. A historical summary of the two great Haytiën parties is indispensable, to the proper understanding of the interests, passions, hopes, and terrors which heave about that pinchbeck and ebony majesty, called Faustin 1st.

The quarrel of these two castes reaches back, even to the origin of Haytien independence. Each one of them claims for itself alone, the work of enfranchisement, and accuses the other of having, from principle, covenanted with white oppression. Both are, at the same time, right and wrong. The truth is, the yellow element and the black element have both, equally, participated in the common work; but each in its time, on its own account, and in the order, and within the limits, assigned it by the force of things. As to the initiative, the honor of it does not belong to either party. We are about to see the revolutionary shock pass, in some sort fatally, from above downward—through every gradation of the old colonial society; and at every pause which manifested itself in the transmission of this movement, the metropolis interfered to accelerate it.

In this case, the real revolutionary initiative belongs to the planters. Not less improvident than the metropolitan aristocracy, although at bottom more logical, they warmly accepted and patronized the ideas, whence sprang 1789. The enfeeblement of monarchical authority was the relaxation, in their favor especially, of a system which excluded them from high colonial positions, and forced their pride, and their habitudes of despotism, to bow before the almost discretionary power of the metropolitan agents. Civic equality, in their estimation, was the complete assimilation of the colony to

France, and the free exercise of the means of action, which their immense wealth appeared to secure them. It was in this sense that they interpreted the convocation of our States-General. Without waiting for the authorization of the Government, the colonists formed themselves into parish and provincial assemblies, and sent to Paris eighteen deputies, who were admitted, some by right, and others as petitioners. Over excited by this first success, these pretensions to political and administrative equality transformed themselves, very soon, among the colonial aristocracy, into open opinions of independence. The provincial assemblies delegated, the direction of the interior affairs of the colony, to a sort of convention, which met together at *Saint-Marc;* and this body, (in which the planters' influence was dominant) declared itself constituted *by virtue of the power of their constituents;* contrary to the advice of the minority, which proposed saying, "In virtue of the decrees of the metropolis."

But, at the side of this aristocracy, were found the whites of the inferior and middling classes, who especially welcomed, in the new opinions, an advent of civil and social equality. These two classes could not hesitate between the feudal oligarchy, which the planters had a glimpse of in their dreams of independence, and a share in the conquests already realized by the metropolitan liberalism; they took a stand for the mother country. The planters very quickly changed their tactics. They pretended to renounce their projects of independence; armed themselves against the metropolitan influence of demagoguic ideas, and thus succeeded in organizing for themselves, out of the dregs of the white population, a numerous party. But Governor Peinier, supported by the sound portion of the colonial middle class, dispersed the insurrectionary Assembly of Saint-Marc.

At this conjuncture, a third element appeared on the scene; and proceeded to take, in relation to the entire white population, the *rôle* which the colonial middle-class had assumed with reference to the planters. Whilst the colonists discussed liberty and equality, the manumitted slaves did not stop up their ears. They had more reason than any of the other classes, to see in the revolution a benefit; because, the suspicious susceptibility of colonial prejudice took delight in rendering the destinction between them especially wounding and harsh, for the reason, that by their color (two-thirds of them being *sang-mêlée*) their education, and their quality as free-men and proprietors, they were brought into immediate contact with the white class. The decree of the 8th of March, 1790, conferred upon them, in fact, some political rights; but this decree excited, in all ranks of the white population, so much dissatisfaction, that the Governor himself concurred in preventing the execution of it. The manumitted slaves had in vain taken up arms in favor of the metropolis, in the struggle, sustained by the Governor, against the colonial aristocracy. The latter, after the victory, did not behave the least well towards them; indeed, he pushed his dislike so far, as to refuse them the right to wear the white pompoon, which served to distinguish the royalist party. The mulattoes abandoned this party; and a new decree, by which the Constituent Assembly repealed the decree of the 8th of March, completed the rupture. I can only recite, from memory, the revolt of the mulattoes, *Ogé, Chavannes,* and *Rigaud.*

A third decree restored, to the manumitted slaves, their rights; new resistance was made by the whites. The demagoguic party rebelled against authority; the aristocratic party, or the independents, offered the Colony to England; the royalists, quite as hostile to the mulattoes as the two other parties, could devise no better plan of holding the planters in check, than by secretly exciting the blacks to revolt; and the mulattoes, who, on their side had again taken up arms, to maintain their rights against the white caste, reaped all the benefit of this intervention of the blacks, among whom they even made numerous recruits.

I will not relate over again this bloody *imbroglio,* in which the three white factions (for, in the colonies, as well as in France, the royalist party itself was already condemned to play the part of a faction,) found themselves, successively, reduced to the necessity of treating, as equal with equal, with the manumitted slaves. One fact is, here, prominent above every other: the new citizens, feeling that their only point of support was in the metropolis, had the address, or the good faith; which is often all one, to remain faithful to it. It thus happened that they became for the time, as to the commissioners charged with pacifying the Island, what the white middle-class had been to Governor Peinier—the only colonial auxiliaries of French influence; so that the final triumph of metropolitan authority resulted, necessarily, in the preponderance of the men of color.

The colored class is severely reproached for neglecting, at the outset, to stipulate any thing in favor of the slaves; and, what is more, for having injuriously affected to separate their interests from those of the black population. Indeed, the mixed-blood, Julien Raymond,* appealing to the generosity of the Constituent Assembly, in behalf of the men of color, made a merit of their composing the criminal police of the colony; and, in this capacity hunting after runaway negroes. He represented the men of color as the real rampart of colonial society; and protested, with force, that they had no interest in exciting the slaves to revolt,

---

* The same individual afterwards asked at the tribune of the Convention the liberty of the blacks, as a natural consequence of the civic equality accorded to his caste.

inasmuch as they owned this kind of property themselves. Ogé, with arms in his hands, held nearly the same language; and, obstinately repelled the proposition, which his companion, Chavannes, made to him, to wit: to excite the slaves in the workshops to rebellion. This is the accusation: that Raymond and Ogé acted, knowingly or not. as very clever abolitionists. Can it be proved, if required?

Could the mulattoes, reasonably, have begun, by proclaiming their *solidarité* with the black caste? But it was this very community of interest, which the adversaries of their civic rehabilitation denounced and developed. These objected, with reason, that the prejudice of skin was the most powerful safeguard of society, and of colonial property; and, that this obstacle being once removed, for the benefit of the enfranchised class, there was no reason why the black tide would not overflow at the same issue. Most of the mulattoes affected to separate themselves from the slaves, that they might serve the common cause better. In proceeding otherwise, the colored class would have necessarily failed, and the negroes would have gained only one thing: that is, to have remained separated from liberty by two removes, in place of one.

But, at first, did the blacks desire liberty? Did they even comprehend the meaning of it? On their part, this is what is denied them; and, at first view, this accusation is much more tenable, than those, from which we are about to exculpate the yellow caste. In their struggles against the mulattoes, the confederated whites armed a portion of their slaves; and the African companies, as they were called, tortured and massacred with fury, these very mulattoes, who nevertheless had come to open the way to the black race. The mulatto party, which in their turn, had armed their own people, gave liberty to the principals; but the new freed men thought they could not better attest their gratitude for this, than by returning their companions to slavery, which act did not provoke the least protestation. At the affair of the *Croix-des-Bouquets*, where fifteen thousand blacks (this time veritable insurgents, for they had been principally recruited from the workshops of the whites) gave the victory to the colored class. Was it still emancipation that they sought? Was it the magic word liberty, which precipitated these unarmed and half-naked Congos, under the horses feet, to which they clung; hurled them on the bayonet points, which they seized with their teeth; and crowded them on the mouths of the loaded cannon, into which they thrust their arms, until they touched the balls, exclaiming in an excess of silly hilarity to be speedily interrupted by the explosion, which scattered them to fragments: "*Moé trapé li!*" (I have caught it, I hold it?) No! it was a bull's tail—an enchanted tail, it is true—which their chief, *Hyacinthe*, who knew his world, brandished through their ranks, for the purpose of turning aside the cannon balls, and changing the bullets to dust.

I leave the reader to imagine what carnage was made of these unhappy creatures. But the sorcerers, who formed the staff of Hyacinthe, immediately, proclaimed with loud cries, that the dead revived again in Africa; and a new human offering rushed joyously to add itself to that bed of corpses.* These credulous heroes—(who can deny them this title?)—were at bottom much less revengers of their race, than devotees to some gloomy African rite brought direct from Cape Lopez, or Cape Negre; and as tradition is perpetuated still from house to house, and in the mysterious conventicles of *Vaudoux*.† The *fête* having terminated, the survivors returned, peaceably, to their labor as slaves, at the order of Hyacinthe, and without demanding their profit in the affair.

In the meanwhile, it is true, the pure negro element, the insurgents of the Northern province,

---

* This belief, in the migration of body and soul, caused so many suicides among the slaves of the Gold Coast, especially the *Ibos*, that the planters were obliged to have recourse to a strange expedient to prevent it. They cut off, either the head, or the nose and ears, of the suicide, and nailed them to a stake. The other Ibos, ashamed at the idea of appearing in their country without these natural ornaments, were resigned not to hang themselves.

† A kind of African *free-masonry*, of which Souloque is one of the high dignitaries. We will see it reäppear in the later events of Hayti.

which the royalist party were already frightened in having let loose, refused to disperse. But, what retained these bands under the authority of Jean-Francois, Biassou, and Jeannot, was much less the thirst for liberty, than the fear of punishment, (which they deserved for their robberies), and the prestige, which the gloomy, and grotesque *paraphernalia* of African sorcery, still exercised over them.

After the example of Hyacinthe, " Biassou surrounded himself with sorcerers, and magicians, and formed his council of them. His tent was filled with little cats of all colors, snakes, bones of the dead, and all other objects, which were symbols of African superstition. During the night, great fires were kindled in his camp; naked women performed horrible dances around them, making frightful contortions, and chanting words, which are only understood, in the deserts of Africa. When the excitement reached its height, Biassou, followed by his sorcerers, presented himself to the crowd, and exclaimed, that the Spirit of God inspired him. He announced to the Africans that, if they fell in battle, they would reappear alive in their old African tribes. Then frightful cries would echo far through the forest; the chants, and the sombre tambours recommenced; and Biassou, profiting by these moments of frenzy, hurled his bands against the enemy, whom he surprised in the dead of night." (Histoire d'Haïti, 1847.)

Jean-Francois and Biassou knew this so well that they proposed to enslave again their innumerable hordes, in consideration of six hundred exemptions. They aimed so little at exercising an apostleship over the race, that they sold, without ceremony, to the Spaniards,* negroes, who were not insurgents—men, women and children, who fell into their power.

They did not act much more liberally towards their own soldiers, who were subjected to a discipline, but little less hard than slavery, and over whom they arrogated the right of life and death. This is not all: for whilst the small party led by the old freed-men—I am far from saying all the old freed-men—strove to show themselves worthy of the social restoration for which they fought, the

---

*The author we are about to cite, reproduces the following letter, in which, Jean-Francois asks an agent of the Spanish Government for authority to sell the young Negroes, who were his prisoners.

TO M. TABERT:

Commandant of His Majesty.

"Humbly praying Mr. Jean-Francois, *Chevalier of the Royal Order of St. Louis, and Admiral of the whole French portion of subjugated Saint-Domingo,* that, having some *very troublesome* subjects, and not having *the heart to destroy them,* we have recourse to *your good will,* to ask that you will allow them to pass, that they may be removed from the country. We prefer to *sell them for the benefit of the king,* and employ the proceeds in making purchases of necessaries for the army, encamped for the defense of His Majesty's rights."

Let us render this justice to the excellent heart of Jean-Francois, *that a civilized person could not have used more hypocrisy.*

black chiefs, on the contrary, seem to have been careful to place in relief the original task of brutality and savagery, with which their caste is reproached.

Jean-Francois, the most cultivated, humane, and hypocritical of the band—Jean-Francois, who died a general officer in the Spanish service, formed a harem for himself of his white female prisoners, and surrendered to his officers and soldiers all those of whom he grew tired.

Jeannot violated the young white girls, in the presence of their families, and immediately afterwards slew them. His standard was the dead body of a white child, borne on the point of a pike. His tent was surrounded by a hedge of lances, each one of which bore the head of a white person, and all the trees in his camp were furnished with hooks, from which hung by the chin other white bodies. He also sawed up his prisoners between two planks, and either amputated the feet of those he found too long, or stretched others *six inches* whom he found too short. When Jeannot would say good humoredly, "I am thirsty," a new head was cut off, the blood squeezed into a vase, some rum added, and he drank the revolting mixture.

I can only speak from memory of Biassou, who contented himself with burning his prisoners over a slow fire, and tearing out their eyes with forceps.

We have reason to be disgusted at certain liberal and humanitarian antiphrases of the epoch in question; but frankly, these traders in black flesh, and carvers of white flesh—these strange regenerators, half satyr, half wolf, seemed to give themselves little care, (as little, as the stupid crowd, by turns, let loose, or terrified by their voice,) to furnish arguments for the Abolition Society of Paris. Besides, upon which side was Jean-François and Biassou ranged? On the side of the emigrants and of Spain; on the side of the old regime and of slavery; against the revolution, which openly prepared the abolition of slavery; but which in proclaiming it could not detach from the enemy either of these two black chiefs, or the body of their army. Such was the fate of the blacks. The latter were only inert brutes, who fought stupidly for the first who armed them, without enquiring after liberty; the former, were but perverted brutes, who fought knowingly against liberty, the voluntary agents of their own degradation—to speak the whole truth, *Negro legitimists!** This term may appear harsh, but we have very deliberately applied it.

Let us, however, look to the bottom of things, and see, if under all this stupidity of courage—this automatic indifference, this savagery, these abomi-

---

*Their chiefs wrote to the commissioners of the Republic, "We cannot conform to the will of the nation, because, since the *world began*, we have only obeyed that of the king. We have lost the king of France, but we cherish the king of Spain, who gives us evidence of his favor by rewards, and never ceases to succor us. Therefore, we cannot recognize you as commissioners until you have found a king."

nations—to see, if under this *negro legitimism*—there were not some real instincts of social reconstruction and of liberty.

And first, generally, as to those nations which are struggling, what is the striking and enviable aspect of liberty? Above all, the right to conquer and not to be vanquished. The blacks who fought with such good will for the planters, achieved liberty after their fashion. In becoming soldiers, they saw themselves rise, by a step, in the human hierarchy; they found themselves assimilated to the liberated class, which, alone had been admitted into the colonial companies. With regard to the blacks transported from Africa, in particular, and who had never read the *social contract,* what could liberty mean to them? Evidently the condition which had preceded slavery; the right to live as they had done in Africa—to have themselves killed for cows' tails, white cocks, and black cats, and to carry in their arms chiefs adorned with plumes, and who have the right of life and death over them.* Among these poor slaves, who seemed to wish only to change their chains, there was therefore not merely an awakening of individual liberty, but what is more, a confused awakening of nationality.

As to the black chiefs, finally, the *ne plus ultra* of liberty, and of human dignity, was evidently to do what the white chiefs did—that is, to have clothes broidered with lace, to own slaves, and to

---

*This is what was practiced in the army of Hyacinthe.

sleep with white women; and this is why Jean-Francois, Biassou and Jeannot sold negroes, violated white women, and wore so much lace. It was, throughout the declaration of the rights of man, but translated into Mandingo, and some little impressed to suit the occasion, with the uncultivated ferocity of the translators. Besides, in point of cruelty, the whites, in their terrible reprisals against the black insurgents, furnished, more than once, to the latter an excuse for the spirit of imitation.

The insurgents of the North were again, from their point of view, very logical, when they called themselves the *king's people*, and united with the counter-revolutionists. The two great fractions of the revolutionary party of Saint-Domingo, were, as we have seen, equally hostile to the abolition of slavery; and is it at all wonderful, that the blacks, seeing they had the same enemies as the king, identified their interests with his?

The confusion, (if there was really here any confusion) was so much the more excusable, because the authority of the king and his agents, revealed itself less to the slaves, as a protector, than as a mediator between them, and the severity or cupidity of their masters. The royal justice being like christian equality, their only point of contact with common right—was it reasonable to expect from it only a revolution, which had, (according to their expression), "assassinated the King of France,

Jesus Christ, and the Holy Virgin." Besides, they knew, from good authority, that the King of Congo, armed himself against the republicans, in the depths of the mountains which concealed this fugitive Africa. Toussaint Louverture, was the very first to believe this a long time. The black chief, Macaya, who, having been dispatched to Jean-Francois and Biassou, for the purpose of converting them to republicanism, but returned converted by them, construed therefore again, in his own way, the declaration of the rights of man, when he explained to Commissioner Polverel, his defection, thus:

"I am the subject of three kings: of the King of Congo, who is master of all the blacks—of the King of France, who represents my father—and of the King of Spain, who represents my mother: these three kings are the descendants of those, who, guided by a star, went to adore the God-Man."

This is not so bad, for a Congo. Altogether, there was only a misapprehension in this matter. And when Commissioner Sonthonax abolished slavery, the transports of thanks and joy,* which

---

*The proclamation of general liberty was published, in all parts of the North where the authority of the Republic prevailed, by municipal officers, preceded by a *bonnet rouge*, borne on the end of a pike, and excited in the people an enthusiasm, which amounted to delirium. The younger Boisrond, a man of color, and one of the intermediary commissioners, instructed by Sonthonax to make this proclamation, saw the country people assembled in mass, and run be-welcomed his proclamation, and the explosions of anger which Commissioner Polverel provoked, by endeavoring to procure some restrictions, (otherwise very proper), upon the enfranchisement, prove that the mass of the black population, fully comprehended the value of liberty.

The greater number of the bands of Jean-Francois themselves, enlightened by Toussaint as to their true interests, followed the defection of the latter, some months later, and became enthusiastic auxiliaries of the republic.

The two oppressed classes, finally remained masters of the field, and each of them brought a decisive concourse, to the common victory. The yellow race, in opening a breach in the prejudice of color, showed the way to the blacks; and this yellow race, in their turn, aided by their black auxiliaries, did not fail in their second rebellion against the whites. It was not until then that the remembrance of their partial antagonism, only became, for the old and new freed-men, a motive of thankfulness and union; for each caste

---

fore him, from village to village. These new and impressionable men appeared doubtful of so much happiness; they made bridges over the streams along his route, of thick oak plank which they had brought on their heads more than three leagues, and covered the earth with leaves from the trees. The name of Southonax was blessed; they called him the *Bon Dieu*. From Port-de-Paix to Gros-Morne, Buisrond was borne *en chaise* formed of men's arms, along a way in direct line, opened in a few hours through the woods, (Madiou', Histoire d'Haïti).

found they had served the interests of the other by combating it. But for the support given by the negroes of the North, to the white factions, the agents of the metropolis would not have been led, in order to make head against this additional danger, to depend, on their part, upon the old free people—to the increase of their importance—and the personification, in them, by turns, of French influence, and the triumph of that influence. Without the support given, by the old free people, to the metropolis against the black insurgents, and their white instigators, Saint-Domingo would have become, the prey of the independents, who appealed to the English, and of the counter-revolutionists, who appealed to Spain; that is to say, of two parties, and of two countries, equally, hostile to emancipation.

This is the reason, why it would have been important for them to have come to an understanding; they did not have time for it. It has been said that the distinction of color would extinguish itself, and that the two classes could never hold together, on this soil, so much shaken, without its sinking under one of them. At the very moment, when their past, and future seemed to be confounded in a common interest, the struggle broke forth anew, this time, general, inexorable, and mortal, between the yellow and black races.

Two events were developed after the emancipation. Some old freed-men, who were themselves owners of slaves, cast themselves, by reason of cupidity and revenge, into the arms of the English. A little later, a few black officers, (until then in the service of the republic, but jealous of the preference, which the mulattoes had obtained, in the distribution of grades, by their superior instruction, and their long services,) imitated the treason of the old freed-men. These shameful exceptions were not blamable to either caste; and besides, the responsibility of them, was reciprocal. But that the least enlightened of the two should be the most suspicious was natural; but the blacks, whose mistrust, the planters had excited by hatred, only saw, in this double treason, that of the men of color. They repeated to the newly liberated slaves, that these latter were the partisans of slavery; that they never desired civil and political rights, but for themselves alone and to increase still more, the distance, which separated them from the blacks. Isolated facts, which seemed to corroborate this accusation, were easily adduced. The newly liberated slaves would give the more willing heed to this, because in the old colonial society, contempt for the enfranchised class was, often, reproduced in the slaves. And what is there surprising in this?

Having to bear the whole burden of the prejudices against color, could the enfranchised class resist the temptation of reaping the benefit of it. It was, only, in withdrawing themselves from the blacks, that they drew nearer to the privileged race. It was useless to say, that their *rôles* were completely changed; and that from the day, the enfranchised class became citizens—that is politically and civilly equal to this race—the prejudice of color, could no longer manifest itself to them but in its wounding features. It was their highest interest to have this only cause of social inferiority forgotten which weighed thenceforth upon them; to efface the very germ of distinctions, which they could not have maintained below, without authorizing them above; to restore, in a word, this African blood, which after all, flowed in their veins. But these half-savage masses could neither see so far, nor so justly; and Sonthonax finally spoiled all, by appearing to notice only in the isolated defections abovementioned, those of the people of color.

The principal mulatto chiefs, Villate, Bauvais, Monbrun, and Rigaud, who did not show themselves less irritated and severe than himself, against the traitors of their caste, were naturally wounded by this partiality. Sonthonax, in his turn, thought he saw in their discontent, much too vividly expressed moreover, the symptoms of new defections; and in order to neutralize the old free people of color, he finally denounced them, openly, as the enemies of the republic, and the blacks; at the same time, he affected to give these last, all his confidence. We can comprehend what frightful echoes, an imputation found in the African masses, which was guarantied by the *Bon-Dieu* Sonthonax himself. More and more embittered and discouraged, by these suspicions, some of the mulatto chiefs, came very near justifying them. Monbrun and Bauvais, by the inefficiency of their operations, seemed to connive at the English; Villate, on his part, provoked an *émeute* against Governor Laveaux, and had him arrested, with the view of putting himself in his place. Toussaint hastened, with ten thousand blacks, to rescue Laveaux, who proclaimed him the "Messiah of the black race," and made him his Lieutenant. A little after, Toussaint was promoted to the grade of General of Division; this, placed, all the colored generals, under the orders of an ex-colonel of the bands of Jean-Francois. One of them, André Rigaud, who had not ceased to give brilliant proofs of his devotion to the republic, was indignant at this injustice; and, while remaining wholly faithful to the metropolis, which had too slowly given him its confidence, he refused to surrender the South, where he commanded, to the authority of Toussaint. It was not merely a question of priority; but the latter, maintained in his distrust, by French agents, by the English, and especially by the planters, who had already adopted this black Caussidière, saw in it but the susceptibility of caste—the contempt of the mulatto for the African. The extermination of what was already called, by him, the aristocracy of skin, became, thenceforth, his fixed idea, and publicly avowed. After bloody turns of fortune, during which, most of the men of color finally grouped themselves about Rigaud, the latter was expelled by his black competitor, who massacred some thousands of the mulattoes.

Such was the first act of that war of color, which continues to this day in Hayti. Was this for the benefit of the mongrel class, who took the initiative in it, as certain negrophilists have repeated with so much affection? The mistake whence this war sprang was, at least, equal on both sides; but it was the black chief alone, (let us state it correctly,) who armed with rancors of caste, threw himself between the old free colored people, and the newly liberated slaves, for the purpose of dividing them. This is not all; in spite of the ferocious obstinancy of Toussaint, in taking skin for a cockade, the blacks of the South, and a part of the West, who, since the commencement of the revolution, had accepted the direction of the men of color and were satisfied with it, remained on the side of Rigaud; and thus formed, in fact, as they continue to do, the majority of what is called the mulatto party.

In short, the aristocracy, the third-estate, the mixed-bloods, every stage of the old colonial society, were successively crushed, the one upon the other; and the metropolitan power, at each crash, aided by a push the fall. It had only to fall in its turn.

Scarcely nominated General of Divison, Toussaint had nothing more pressing than to disembarrass himself of Laveaux and Sonthonax, by having them chosen as deputies. The latter, who already suspected his *protégé*, exhibited a visible hesitation in leaving. Toussaint, played to the life, the scene of Mon. Dimanche; and, while overwhelming Sonthonax with protestations, pushed him gently along by the shoulders to the vessel, which was about to bear away this unfortunate spy. On the arrival of the Envoy of the Directory, Hédouville, Toussaint's projects of independence, were very clearly manifested. These were encouraged by the English, who, in evacuating the country, step by step, before the French Agents and Rigaud, pretended to capitulate only with the black chief; and, even offered by secret treaty to recognize him King of Hayti. Braving, one by one, the orders of the day, issued by Hédouville, he reëstablished worship, and recalled the emigrants; filled with them, the administration, and the staff of the colonial army; sent back to the old plantations, for• five years, the newly liberated slaves; and reduced, by a third to a fourth, the portion accorded to the latter, in the product of their labor. He did not less discover the secret of making the blacks believe, that Hédouville (who, nevertheless, wished to protect them against the complaisance of their chief to the planters,) had as his mission to reëstablish slavery; and the Envoy of the Directory was compelled, by a revolt, to leave the Island, after confiding the interests of the metropolis to Rigaud, of whose ill-success we have already spoken.

Here the same recriminations were reproduced under another form: against Toussaint, who sought the independence of Hayti—and against Rigaud, who fought for the sovereignty of France; against the black chief, who restored, in fact, all the old régime, without other corrective than the substitution of the cudgel,*—even the gun for the whip; against the mulatto chief, who defended republican institutions, whence sprang the emacipation. Which was the true Haytiën?—which the traitor?

A war of words still. Rigaud played a loyal and safe game—whilst Toussaint risked all for all, and cheated; but the stake, on both sides, was the social regeneration of the blacks. The mulatto chief saw it entirely in civil liberty; and, he was as logical as he was honest, in persisting to confound the political destinies of his country with those of France, where no anti-abolitionist tendency was yet manifested. The black chief sought it in national liberty; and, whether his ambition abused it or not, he was, from the point of view given, not less logical, in adopting and strengthening all the interests hostile to the metropolitan power. If Rigaud had succeeded, the expedition of General Léclerc would not have been necessary; and the violent reaction, from which resulted successively, the reëstablishment of slavery; and the definitive

---

* The rights of man above all; but they only employed—at least it was seriously agitated only to employ—a *tricolored* cudgel.

separation of Saint-Domingo, and its isolation from all civilized contact, would not have been justified. In exchange for its name of *Hayti*, this bloody trunk of African barbarism would now be vital with European and French life. But because Toussaint favored the old colonial aristocracy, because he made the estates yield a third, or more, than they did before the emancipation, must it be concluded, as has been written, that he was the voluntary instrument of the planters; and that he had secretly sold, in exchange for their complicity, the liberty of the blacks?—that, in a word, to consummate the usurpation he meditated, he stopped at the strange expedient, of exciting against himself nineteen-twentieths of his future subjects, and driving them into the arms of the metropolis?

This is not debatable. Toussaint was only doubly clever in this matter. Having to deal with two interests, which would have been able, equally, to say they were spoliated—with the metropolis and the planters—ought he not to have endeavored to disarm, at least, one of them? But he cast his right of preference on that one of the two, which could best accommodate itself to his projects of independence, and with which, contact was the least dangerous. This was the case of the planters, who made, as it is seen, a very good sale of their French nationality; and who, lost in an ocean of the black population, strong in the protection alone of Toussaint, could never inspire him with any suspicion. The old colonists brought, besides, to the black nationality, awakened by Toussaint, the principal elements of all organized society—civilization, capital, commercial relations, and influence abroad;—even, by their affinities with the counter revolution in Europe.

But why the reëstablishment of the workshops? Because the old black ruler comprehended, by instinct, what a terrible and dear experience, alone, had taught the whites. The essential character of slavery being compulsory labor, the first proof of liberty, which the old slaves attempted to realize, was unlimited sloth; and Toussaint prevented this last excess, by the contrary extreme. If he suspended liberty, in fact—he fortified it in principle; for he destroyed the principal argument of the partizans of slavery—by proving, that emancipation could be, very readily reconciled with the interests, and the rights, of the proprietors; and in the same way he popularised his project of independence with the latter—by proving, that a black government could make labor produce more than it did under a white administration.

The best proof, that Toussaint did not conspire against the rights of his race, is that he prepared it for the practice of these rights; exciting in it, by religion, the sentiment of human dignity, and moral responsibility, which the servile régime had extinguished; reacting by his exterior* rigorism against the dissolute habits, bequeathed by this régime; rendering instruction obligatory, as well as labor; in a word, endeavoring to civilize the men, and to render the women less savage. He especially knew how to inspire in these old hordes of Jean-Francois, who had, up to this time, only learned liberty by devastation and pillage, an almost superstitious horror of the property of others. It reached that point, that they did not dare to take even the gratifications, which the whites offered them.

This model order, in truth, was only obtained at the price of a frightful despotism; but it is necessary, always, to keep the medium course. With regard to the blacks, who remembered their native Africa, as well as the greater part of those who could only interrogate the souvenirs of slavery, the

---

* "His private life" writes Pamphile Lacroix "is not less edifying. Our young generals, curious and indiscreet, found in the chests of the black Governor, many love-letters, and a great many locks of hair of *all colors*. But his natural hypocrisy served to conceal his faults. He knew, as he once said in one of those discourses which he frequently made in the churches where the people were assembled—he knew that the scandal caused by public men resulted in consequences much more ruinous than that produced by a simple citizen. And outwardly he remained a model of reserve. He recommended good morals; he imposed them; he punished adultery; and, at his soirées, he dismissed married women and young girls, without sparing white ladies, who displayed exposed breasts—"not seeing," he said, "how any honest woman could thus wound decency."

idea of authority was inseparable from that of absolute rule and violence. After the proclamation of general liberty, Commissioner Polverel published regulations for the organization of labor, the principal prescriptions of which glided but timidly between the nettles and briars of the rights of man. "The work of the first legislator of free labor," said Monsieur Lepelletier Saint-Remy, "was received with the laughter and jokes of his new *justiciables.*" "*Commissai Palverel, he too much fool—he know nutting,*" said they, in laughing at the trouble the commissioner of the Republic had given himself to legislate for them. Here is the slave of yesterday, and especially the African of the day before; they would not think they were governed unless they felt themselves oppressed. Here, as in the bands of Biassou and Hyacinthe, the oppressor was a black chief, and this was sufficient for their vague aspirations of liberty. Toussaint founded, in short, the true black policy—that only which was suited to the uncivilized and brutish element of the new people. In fact, we will see, that almost all the negro chiefs successively developed it, as if by instinct; and through every breach, which the times or generous illusions made in this bloody obstacle, savagery overflowed anew.

But the trembling fragments of the colored population, whose education, tastes, and past rôle had initiated them into French manners and opinions; the old slaves of the Southern party, which a political contact of ten years with this class had comparatively civilized, and who, in remaining to the end on the side of Rigaud, had learned to taste the mildness and equity of the French administration—these two fractions of the yellow party, in a word, ought naturally to have found the yoke of the black usurper intolerable. Therefore, they welcomed the expedition of 1802 as a deliverance. On their side, the principal black generals, who, by reason of making all bow under them, were unaccustomed to bow themselves, abandoned Toussaint, one after the other. Here the inevitable result of each black tyranny was again developed.

I only mention from memory the consequences of the expedition of Leclerc; the reëstablishment of slavery, as disloyal as it was imprudent, rekindling that insurrection which solemn promises of liberty had extinguished; the accidents of climate aggravating the faults of policy; the yellow fever carrying off fourteen generals, fifteen hundred officers, twenty thousand soldiers, and nine thousand sailors; famine adding itself to this epidemic, and the dark storm driving, even into the power of the English squadron, the dying remnant of our army; not without frightful struggles, in which all human horrors—those of civilization and those of barbarism—appeared to soil the mutual prodigies of heroism. Independence was proclaimed, and general Dessalines became Chief of the new State, with the title of Governor General for life—which he was not slow in changing to that of *Emperor*.

The men of color could not be suspected, thenceforth, of conspiring against the liberty of the black race; they were washed of this accusation in French blood. It was even one of them, Pétion, adjutant general in the army of Leclerc, and whom we will soon see appear at the head of his caste—who, upon learning of the reëstablishment of slavery, gave the signal for insurrection, carrying with him into the woods, the generals, Clairvaux (mulatto) and Christophe (black). But the antagonism, between the enlightened and the African element, was about to reappear under another form; and it already betrayed itself, secretly, by the very affectation, which the mulatto minority showed, in disseminating and proscribing the distinctions of skin, and in calling themselves *negroes*.* Do not laugh; alas! have we not had, also, our *mulatto negroes?* It was at the death of Dessalines, that this antagonism broke out.

Dessalines in character was Toussaint, doubled by Biassou and Jeannot; but the Biassou and Jeannot element finally got the advantage, so that a regiment killed him, one fine day, by surprise, and without ceremony, as they would kill an enraged

---

*These timid appeals for reconciliation, were translated into official language. Article XIV of the first Haytien constitution, voted by the generals of both colors, but engrossed by the mulattoes, who were only educated, said: "All regard for color, among the children of the same family, of which the chief of the State, is the father, ought necessarily to cease; the Haytiens will only be known, hereafter, under the generic denomination of *blacks*."

wolf. Because this assassination was accomplished in the South-west, where the influence of the men of color predominated—and because the colored general, Clairvaux, gave the signal, they concluded that it was only, a reaction of the mulattoes there against the domination of the blacks. In reality, both castes were engaged in it. They persuaded Dessalines that, he would not be master, until he disembarrassed himself of his old equals—the generals of the war of independence; and Christophe, the second black personage of the Empire, being most endangered, by this system of summary eliminations, placed himself at the head of the conspiracy. The mulattoes felt themselves so little prepared for power, that they were the first to confer it upon him; their ambition was limited, at the time, to obtaining, by the establishment of a parliamentary *régime*, some guaranties against the autocratic tendencies of the black government, and the share of influence which this *régime* would secure to the most enlightened class. But, it was at this very point, that the schism was produced.

Christophe, irritated by the restrictions, which the assembly of *Port-au Prince*, imposed upon the executive power, commanded it to disperse; and marched against it, just at the time, when the constituency decreed him the presidency of the Republic. This negro trick was especially at the address of the men of color; and fear contributed, as much as their democratic susceptibilities, to put arms in their hands. Pétion marched to encounter Christophe, and, after a short struggle, the two influences classed themselves, as in the times of Toussaint and Rigaud.* The Southern portion of the country, (called the South and West divisions) bestowed the presidency upon the colored chief, who, having been twice reëlected and, finally, named for life, employed in the exercise of power, a simplicity and disinterestedness, which we no longer hesitate to call republican.

The North submitted, on its part, to the black chief; who, less than five years afterwards, on the 28th of March, 1811, proclaimed himself King of Hayti, under the name of Henry 1st. This time it was not a monarch after the fashion of the Emperor Dessalines, who from time to time, spread his imperial mantle over the grass and weeds in order to resign himself more at ease, in the midst of his camp, to the tumultuous caprices of the dance, and African orgies. Christophe took his part altogether seriously, and played it, for nearly ten years, with an ease, an aplomb, and a sustained spirit, which did honor to the imitative genius of his race. The old hotel-keeper had a magnificent coronation, and

---

*Rigaud appeared himself, a short time afterwards, in the South, and organized a republic, within that of Pétion. A common instinct of preservation, alone prevented the two colored chiefs, from coming to blows. Rigaud died soon after, and his successor, Borgella, submitted to Pétion.

surrounded himself with princes, dukes, counts, barons, chevaliers and pages.*

He had a grand marshal of the palace, a grand master of ceremonies, a grand huntsman, a grand cup-bearer, a grand pantler, a chancellor and his chafe-wax, a king at arms, chamberlains and governors of chateaux; he had a royal and military order of Saint Henry, Haytïen guards, life-guards, and light-horse, without counting a company of *royal-bonbons.*† The military and civic households of the Queen, Marie-Louise, of the prince royal, and the princess Améthyste (*Madame première,*) were in proportion. Classic etiquette presided over the great and small *levées*, of their black Majesties. At these, hair-powder and the sword were *en rigueur;* and the stools of the duchesses were kept at a distance from the folding chairs of the simple countesses. There was besides much more to laugh at in this innocent negro carnival. Among these poor African helots, who, to manifest their equality, found nothing better than to borrow the hair-powder and laces of the old white aristocracy, there were altogether, more sincere aspirations of social progress, more veritable democratic instincts, as we would say, than there were among the lawyer-workmen, and physicians in blouses, of our yesterday's of revolution.

---

*Dessalines manifested in his savage pride this inspiration, really otherwise royal: "I alone am noble!" he replied scornfully to those of his generals who asked him to create an aristocracy.

†A military school.

II.

Black Politics, and Yellow Politics.

Here are black politics and yellow politics, really now face to face. The planters are no longer behind the first—nor France behind the second. Each one of them, is, henceforth, left to its own instincts, and each is, in the midst of its own preferences. Let us see them at work.

Christophe renewed the tyranny of Toussaint. Like St. Louis, the little black monarch was pleased to render justice under a tree; but he only gave decrees of death. Death was almost the sole article of his code; idleness, disobedience, the smallest theft, the least symptom of discontent, or of monarchical indifference—nothing esaped this punishment. But this *régime* of terror could not suit the enlightened minority, under Christophe, any more than it had done under Toussaint; and, as he felt they were secretly desirous of throwing off his yoke, the suspicious despot was led precisely to make it more aggravating; thus exciting the hostility, against which he sought to defend himself. No tyranny could escape this law. In an expedition against the West, two mulatto officers, passed, with their corps, over to the side of Pétion; and Christophe slaughtered, in retaliation, the numerous colored population, without distinction of age or sex, which were found at Saint-Marc, one of his frontier places. Those men of color, and black adherents of the old yellow party, remaining in the North, were only the more eager to emigrate to the republic of Port-au-Prince; bringing away, gradually, the little civilization, which gave life to the kingdom of Christophe.

With the despotism of Toussaint, which was now no longer mitigated by the European influence of the old planters, Christophe restored, and even exaggerated his system of agriculture, although, like the first black chief, he had no longer preëxistent interests to care for. The plantations were erected into hereditary fiefs, for the benefit of the principal officers; and the blacks were attached to them, under the same conditions, as previously; with this difference only, that wages were substituted for the permanent guardianship, which implied slavery; and, that the new planters, transformed into great feudatories, arrogated the right of life and death, over the old slaves, who thus became serfs. Therefore planting on a large scale was revived more flourishingly than ever. As a temporary organization of labor, this rigorous discipline, I repeat it, was a necessary transition to the blacks; and could be even reconciled with the idea, most of them yet had of liberty; the more so, that the feudality of Christophe being entirely military, the discipline of the workshop, seemed to be the natural continuation of that of the barrack, and the battle field. But there was more in this than the forced labor and temporary engagements, of the system of Toussaint; there was *mortmain*, which, under the form of eldership, fixed immovably, almost the entire property, and the glebe, and, by making the cultivators an integral part of the real estate, deprived them of all certain hope of becoming, one day, free laborers, and proprietors. But we can comprehend how the old slaves, after having tasted, sufficiently, the proud satisfaction which an African can feel, of being tyrannized over only by Africans, they should have finally become sufficiently indifferent to a nationality, which only terminated in an indefinite aggravation of slavery.

Christophe foresaw it himself; to resist this tendency, and, at the same time, to make the remembrances of the old Franco-mulatto alliance operate against his Southern rival, the black tyrant, (whom the agents of England and the United States moreover deceived, as they did Toussaint,) endeavored to revive their hatred against France; putting to death as a spy, the first French envoy, which ventured into his dominions; and not allowing the second French commission to land which presented itself in 1816. By the exaggeration itself of this system, Christophe here again opposed his own object. He could not have taken, in fact, a better method of provoking, sooner or later, an invasion by France; which, having Europe, no longer, on her hands, and being able to choose her own time, would have, infallibly, reëntered into the possession of her old colony.

Pétion adopted, entirely, a different policy. Half from inclination, half from tactics,—and to attract to him the civilizing forces, which his rival alienated—the Southern chief measured his tolerance, by the despotism of Christophe. But, after the geographical division of these two' influences, just as there was left in the North a nucleus too advanced for the black tyranny, there remained in the South, a small party too inexperienced for the mulatto *régime;* and which, by an interpretation, of which negro genius does not possess the monopoly, forthwith construed republican liberty as the right to dance, to sleep, and to eat the bananas of the *"bon Dieu,"* taking them fresh from the trees. The banana is food fallen from heaven; and likewise, will suggest the rights of labor to these socialists of nature. It was not, that there did not exist very sage regulations against the idleness, and unsteadiness, of the cultivators; but, the difficulty was to apply these regulations.

By appearing to adopt, even partially, the coërcive measures of Christophe, would not Pétion have lost, with these distrustful natures, all the benefit of the contrast, he endeavored to establish? The attractions of caste were not to be dreaded, moreover, on the side of the North altogether. A bandit of the school of Biassou, the black Goman, founded a small African State, in the very heart of the republic; about which, all the refractory elements, of the North and South, were imperceptibly aggregated. In order not to furnish recruits to this faction (called the insurrection of the *Grande-Anse*) it was necessary, therefore, to respect the vagabond fantasies of our amateurs of bananas. The *vandoux*—a kind of religious and dancing free-masonry, which was introduced into Saint-Domingo by the Aradas negroes, and greatly feared by the planters—the *vandoux*, grouped them in associations, which were gradually substituted for the rural police, ruining or enriching, at their pleasure, the proprietors, they disgraced or protected. Pétion desired to found a little France, and it was Africa which took possession of it.

Pétion experienced at first fewer mistakes in the establishment of his land system. To create a powerful combination of democratic interests, in opposition to the feudal interests, which the government of the North represented, and threatened to impose; to neutralize, by attaching the army to himself, any possible defection of the generals who, being themselves constituted proprietors of the best plantations, might be reduced, at length, by the guarantees, which the administration of Christophe offered to planting on a large scale,— and, especially, by the perspective of seeing their farm-leases transformed into fiefs; to give the black masses palpable proof, that the yellow class, in calling them around it, intended, not to work them, as Christophe repeated after Toussaint,—but to associate them the better for their welfare and rights ; to interest, in short, these masses for the independence of the country—and to create in them, by a desire for property, the taste for labor, —the obligation of which, his color prevented his imposing too openly ; such were the multiplied objects which Pétion proposed to attain. With this view, he divided the national domain. A part of it was distributed, in small lots proportioned to rank ; first, among the veterans and then, among different classes of the military, and civil functionaries in active service. The remainder was put up to sale, in equal parcels, and at a very low price ; the undervaluing of which, Pétion was the very first to encourage, in order to hasten the political results he sought to obtain. This inducement succeeded beyond all expectation. It was among the industrious cultivators, that these facilities, which were offered to become proprietors, would be availed of. Those, whose competence was insufficient, would engage to farm, with an equal share of the profits, the lots of the military and civil grantees, whose functions and agricultural inexperience, would not permit them directly to work ; and they thus became, in their turn, proprietors in fact. But here again, the evil manifested itself, by the side of the good. Cultivation on a large scale which could only furnish exterior commerce, with advantage, sugar, coffee, indigo, and cotton—that is to say, the chief elements of colonial riches—lost, at length, by this transformation, the small number of diligent arms, it had been able to retain. It was so much the more to be regretted, as Pétion understood, far better than Christophe, the commercial interests of his country. Even, in seeking to show France that, in order to reconquer St. Domingo, she would have, hereafter, a hundred thousand proprietors to exterminate, the mulatto chief did not disguise that the simple possibility of a new Leclerc-expedition, would be equivalent, to a blockade of the Island ; and, instead of fortifying himself against us, in the savage and stupid isolation of Christophe, he hastened to establish the principle of a pecuniary indemnity ; which became the basis of negotiations, from which resulted the friendly recognition of Haytien nationality.

In short, each of these two policies had sacrificed half of its undertaking, for the accomplishment of the other. Christophe, whilst restraining barbarism, trod out the civilizing element ; Pétion opened, on the contrary, a wide door to the civilizing element, and to social progress, but he let barbarism pass through it. The first, based upon his oppressed people, the foundations of a great national prosperity ; the second, made a good bargain of the national riches, in order to give liberty, and immediate benefits, to the masses. Whilst the negro tyrant, finally, deprived the system of extended cultivation, which he had so violently organized, of the security, and commercial outlets, which are its vital guarantees, the mulatto President disorganized it, whilst laboring to create these guarantees. The yellow policy had, nevertheless, an incontestable advantage over the black policy; it was, by doubly serving the cause of independence, that the latter was doubly compromised.

In 1818 Pétion, worn down by profound discouragements, to which were added domestic chagrins, allowed himself to die, they say, of hunger. General Boyer succeeded him, and continued his work. The second, and third years, of his government were signalized, by two decisive events : the pacification of the Grande-Anse; and the submission of the North. In consequence of an attack of apoplexy, Christophe remained half paralyzed; and, on seeing the tiger down, his trembling attendants did not hesitate to fall upon him. A military insurrection burst out at Saint-Marc; then, at the Cap. Christophe endeavored to give his limbs, a momentary elasticity, by having them rubbed, with a mixture of rum and pepper; but it was in vain. Roaring with impotence, he had himself carried into the midst of his guards; harangued them; and ordered them to march on the Cap, which he gave them the right to pillage. These took up the line of march, with all the demonstrations of negro enthusiasm; but meeting the insurgents on the route, they thought it much shorter to return, with these, and pillage the royal residence. Foreseeing this last outrage, Christophe discharged a pistol into his heart.

Two black Generals, Richard, *Duke de Marmalade*, and Paul Romain, *Prince de Limbé*, expected certainly, in conspiring, to gather the heritage of Christophe. But Boyer, to whom the insurgents of Saint-Marc had sent, in guise of an invitation, the head of one of Christophe's chiefs,—Boyer, had only to present himself, to be recognized by the entire North. To crown his good fortune, the Spanish part of the Island, where the colored class was as numerous, as the black class was in the French part, were led to imitate the North ; bringing thus, to the yellow minority, a reinforcement, which went far to counterbalance, and much beyond that, which the fall of Christophe and Romain gave the black majority.

At length, a treaty with France, sanctioned definitely the independence of Hayti. An entirely new path was then opened, before the mulatto government. The exaggerations and the weaknesses, into which it had fallen thus far, proceeding, especially, from the necessities, which the incessant antagonism of the two black governments had caused it—the eventuality of a French invasion—and the too great numerical inequality of the two colors—it was natural to believe that, these three causes having disappeared, or being diminished, the yellow policy would, henceforth, only manifest itself, through its good features. Unhappily, the very opposite happened. Boyer saw his own success turned against himself.

Christophe had exceeded, the rigors of the old system of slavery; and, even, those of his two black predecessors; therefore, the reaction of insubordination and sloth, which followed his fall, were more violent than ever. And when this new tide of emancipated slaves abrubtly broke into their midst, where nothing was organized to restrain it— I leave you to imagine what an inundation it was! Nevertheless, when this first effervescence had quieted a little, so that the division of the soil, in being extended from the South to the North, might interest, the working minority of the old subjects of Christophe, to maintain the new régime—and the peace with France allowed the residue to be relieved from the system of extended cultivation— Boyer thought it was time for his people, to consume a little less rum, and to produce a little more sugar. A rural code was promulgated. The farm-laborers were declared exempt from army service, and militia duty; but whoever could not prove himself possessed of sufficient regular means of living, was required to bind himself as a farm-laborer, for three, six, or nine years, by individual contract; this cut short the tyranny of the dancing corporations. Unhappily, as it is impossible to designate certain things, otherwise than by their proper names, some of the regulating provisions of the code, recalled too literally, the old discipline of the workshops. Secret rancors, which began to agitate the triumphant party, and which four or five successive conspiracies of the black generals revealed, did not fail to develope these analogies. Sonthonax, Toussaint, and Christophe had therefore spoken the truth; and the colored class had, thus far, only flattered the blacks, in order to disarm them, and afterwards oppress them at pleasure!

Boyer recoiled before this sudden awakening of prejudices, which the mulattoes had taken thirty years to dissipate; and they reproached him, too severely, with this confession of weakness. For this cause alone, in fact, that it was no longer grouped about Christophe and the bandit king of the Grande-Anse, the ultra-African party were now found everywhere, sowing their old ferments of ignorance and hate, even in the most docile portions of the masses; only, waiting, perhaps, a provocation, to rise, at the same time, on twenty different points; and this was so much more to be feared, because the spectacle of the black tyranny was no longer present to neutralize the antipathies of skin. To accept this struggle, would have been to risk all; and Boyer preferred to leave this spirit of mistrust and revolt to extinguish itself, gradually, for the want of aliment.

The rural code, therefore, fell into desuetude; he

labored only who wished. Peace even, in rendering useless a military organization, which alone had maintained, until then, a remnant of discipline and unity, in agricultural labor, contributed to disorganize it. Hayti began its career, in the life of nations, by this double contradiction: a government, the defeat of whose interior enemies became a new cause of fear and feebleness; "and a people, which languished and died, by the very law of the development and prosperity of nations— security."

In some cantons, however, the execution of the rural code was begun; but how? A Haytien journal of the time will inform us: "Refusing to be employed by others for wages, they (the farm-laborers) accused, the synallagmatic contracts, of restraining their free choice; and they should have said their fickleness. *In order to free themselves from their obligation, they impoverished the proprietors, disgusted them, drove them to despair—even so far as to induce them to sacrifice their properties.* Then, by the terms of the contracts, their gross earnings, patiently amassed, were hence to be offered to the proprietors, who submitted." In the negro peasant, there is largely, as we see, the material of an European peasant. Easily excited and directed, this spirit of cupidity and cunning might have become later, in the last resort, a powerful lever of social organization; but, in the mean time, there was exhibited sloth for excitement—relaxation of production for policy—and the acceleration of division, for the result.

A supreme, but decisive, expedient remained; it was to invite the energy and capital of strangers, to develope the immense virgin resources of the Island. The constitution of 1805, and all the other constitutions, in succession, had said: "No *white* person, whatever may be his nation, shall put foot on this territory, with the pretence of being master or proprietor; *and cannot for the future acquire any property here.*" After the recognition of Haytien independence, the retention of this article, was nothing less than a ruinous and ridiculous contradiction. Unhappily, in the position in which he was left to act, Boyer was the last person, who dared to declare this logical consequence, from the treaty with France. This treaty, without which, Hayti would probably be now called Saint-Domingo, and which will be, for generations less prejudiced, the great historical title of Boyer—this treaty excited, in the bosom of the ultra-black party, violent recriminations.

The patriots of the school of Toussaint, Dessalines, and Christophe, were, almost as highly indignant, as the patriots of a certain French school, against those "mulattoes" who were allowed to sell (at a very good price, however) a territory which the "blacks" had conquered; and, as each one of these rare parcels of the indemnity was paid, which the government sent, in ringing cash, to Paris, the "black people," condemned as they were to the meagre régime of *assignats* (paper-money), naturally felt the wound renewed. This was not all; did not these constant efforts of Pétion, of Boyer, and of all the mulatto party, to remove the only obstacle, which opposed, thenceforth, white immigration—that is to say, the crossing of the two races, and of consequence the increase of the *sang-mêlés*—did they not betray an after thought of numerical preponderance, and of oppression? But there is no pause possible, in the policy of feebleness; having yielded, on one point, to the prejudices of the ultra-African party, Boyer and his caste were condemned, in advance, to yield on all the others; and, just as we have seen them, justify themselves from the reproach of despotism, by endeavoring to merit the opposite reproach, they found nothing better, in order to escape the reäction of anti-French mistrusts than in taking themselves the same direction.

The hatred of France, at first affected, and finally real; the daily appeals to the national senment against the dark conspiracies of France; the tricks of every kind instigated, by some French and European merchants, who had not recoiled before a sort of civil death, with which, the white race was, and is still, smitten in Hayti; became, from this time, the governmental tactics of Boyer, and of nearly all the men of color. They, therefore, still exhibited that sad and singular spectacle, of a government reduced to strike, itself, the most fruitful part of its work with sterility; and an entire class, condemning itself through fear, to discard the only solution, which could relieve it from its moral oppression. As if it had been said, finally, that not one of the most able combinations of Boyer should escape from this chain of mistakes, the mulatto majority of the East, whose manners, traditions, and interests, were opposed to such a system, were not slow in repenting of the annexation; and only, therefore, became an embarrassment, thenceforth to the mulatto minority of the West, to whom they should have brought a decisive reinforcement.

Nevertheless, Boyer had a powerful auxilliary—*time*. Twenty years of calm, had so softened manners, that armed robbery, and murder, had become unheard of things. The pacific contact of the two castes led gradually to their fusion; and, already, the black party properly so called—the school of Toussaint—was not more than a feeble minority, which became more enlightened every day, carrying with it, into the tomb, the germ of savage susceptibilities; before which, governmental action had been obliged to efface itself. Boyer and the intelligent men who surrounded him, as many of them yellow as black, anticipated, therefore, the time, when they could strike this block of barbarism, without exciting insurrection—vain hope yet! To this society, which decomposed in its birth, there was wanting a last dissolvent; and the third party appeared.

III.

The yellow *bourgeoisie*—A negro 24th of February—Guerrier, Pierrot, Riché—Soulouque—A conjured *fauteuil*.

We must render this justice to the Haytiens—that, if they made absurd constitutions, they excelled in violating them. Pétion himself, in spite of his democratic illusions, was not slow in comprehending, that the more the governmental authority was affected with feebleness, the more necessary it was, not to divide it; and, that unity of action, and direction, was especially the only possible corrective of the excessive tolerance, which the prejudices of the lower caste imposed upon him. A part of the Senate, and behind it, a sufficiently numerous party, which rallied itself afterwards on the momentary schism of Rigaud, wished to oppose these indispensable encroachments. Pétion got rid of it, by an 18th *Brumaire à l'Africaine;* and, in not abusing the dictatorship for a single instant, he manifested that he exercised it, not from taste, but from necessity. The dissentients were finally convinced of it themselves; and the constitution being revised in 1816, granted him all the power he had usurped. Boyer was able to continue in peace, during twenty years, the centralizing system of Pétion. But, at length, an entirely new generation had sprung up; who finding all the offices occupied, became naturally his opponents; and which, having only been able to study its *rôle* of opposition, in the French journals, (see the community of idiom) began to report, these tirades of the *National,* to its public of six hundred thousand negroes, who could not comprehend a word of them; and who, notwithstanding, continued to dance the *calinda,* with the accompaniments of the *bamboula.*

Seeing their success was so indifferent, the actors concluded, very naturally, one of three things: that the *parterre* was stupid—or that it was sold—or that the liberty of applauding was not allowed. To whom was this to be attributed? Evidently to President Boyer, with the governmental concurrence. This unhappy *rafter-president,* who had not a penny; who did not see before him anything more formidable than the ignorance of the masses; and whose whole crime was having wished to transform, too hastily, the slaves of yesterday into citizens—this unhappy Boyer, we say, was therefore accused of "subsidizing" consciences; of plunging the Haytiens into "servilism;" and of "systematically brutalizing" them by ignorance; in order, the better to dominate over their torpor.

The colored class being the most lettered—or almost the only educated class—the new opposition recruited itself extensively in its ranks: it was the inevitable citizen denouncing the government of the citizens. Boyer remonstrated with it, of the danger and ridicule of such a course, with much good sense. Would Africa—pure Africa—who perhaps only slept with one ear closed—would it not finally awaken, at the noise of these mulatto quarrels? But, upon understanding that the government was alarmed, the opposition only redoubled their violence; and Africa, which had been really awakened, learning also that it was frightened, resolved to profit by the occasion. The earthquake of 1842, which destroyed the city of the Cap, and caused one-half of its inhabitants to perish, furnished it, that occasion. The country population invaded the ruins, and, deaf to the hissing of the conflagration, as well as the groans of the dying, pillaged them for fifteen days; rushing, indifferently, on their way, over the mulattoes of the conservative party—of whom the opposition had spoken so disparagingly—and over the mulattoes of the opposition, of whom the government had spoken so little good.* Thus, it was only necessary to agitate slightly this stagnant water, to cause all the depraved and savage instincts to remount to the surface, which for forty years had been fermenting, at the bottom. The opposition only saw in these events, a new pretext for agitation; accusing the government of not having dared to punish these

---

* The black peasants gave as their reason: "The *Bon Dieu* has given us this; yesterday, it was your day; to-day is our day."

abominations; which, was unfortunately too true. But, this ought to have been an additional reason, for not adding to the feebleness of the government.

Two or three, successive *coups d'etat*, destroyed the opposition, in the Chamber. It soon revived, in the country, a conspiracy, under the direction of an aspirant of feeble capacity, Herard-Riviere, commander of artillery; which was engendered by Herard-Dumesle, an ambitious man of talent. The conspiracy broke out in the South, by the publication of what was called the *Manifesto of Praslin*. The signers of this remarkably written document conferred the executive power upon Herard-Riviere; at the same time, naming the form of a provisional government, of which, the former lieutenant of Rigaud, old General Borgella, was the Dupont de l'Eure. But Borgella, whom they had appointed through confidence, marched furiously against the insurrection, which complicated the struggle for a time; a struggle sufficiently bloodless, however; and, in which, more promotions were exchanged, during six months, than gun-shots. It appears that Herard-Riviere might have understood, better than Boyer, how to make them; apparently, because he knew less than Boyer what they cost. But, the latter, yielding moreover, as much to the disgust which killed Pétion, as to the progress of the revolt, embarked, the 13th of March, 1843, for Jamaica, after having addressed his farewell to the country, in language not wanting in dignity.

The two Herards remained, at the head of the government, long enough, to expiate the attacks, which had opened the way to them; namely, by doubling the lists of the army-staff, which, a short time before, they found too crowded-; renewing, in aggravated forms, the financial measures, which they had come to destroy; and, by reviving the *coups d'etat* of Boyer,* against the parliamentary and municipal power, whose entire offence, was having called in question, their recent constitutional theories; in short, by seeing the Spanish party, separate itself from Hayti, which they caressed and used in opposition, and which now forms the Republic of Dominica. But there is no 24*th of February* without a day after; and the next day came.

In the last struggle, of the mulatto government, against the mulatto opposition, the masses, feeling cajoled by both sides, remained almost neutral. The revolution which they had made, in their name, being once accomplished, there succeeded many months of slumber to the republic. It was, at this juncture, that the "peal of Liberty" had assembled at Port-au-Prince only two hundred electors out of six thousand; in some important localities, not even a single one appeared; but

---

* With an improvement which deserves to be noticed. In order to dissolve the constituent and municipal Assembly, Herard-Riviere signified to the members, the necessity of their joining the army immediately : "The first duty, of the representatives of the people, being to defend the unity and the individuality of the Republic."

when the new *régime* was consolidated, and so-much-to-do had only ended, in giving some thousand of epaulettes to the young mulattoes of the Herard party, the " black people" understood that they had been, decidedly, forgotten ; and looked out to the four cardinal points to see if no one would offer themselves to give a *" revolution to he."* Candidates came forward, very soon, in crowds. The black Generals, Salomon and Dalzon revolted almost simultaneously, the one in the South, the other at Port-au-Prince. Some time afterwards, the black General Pierrot, having been defeated, by the Dominicans, went to the North to console himself, by proclaiming, there, his independence ; and the West, in its turn; pronounced in favor of the black General, Guerrier. But Guerrier, like Pierrot, like Dalzon, like Salomon, was only *black;* but, in the South there appeared a negro, the humanitarian negro, and eloquent speaker of the school of Jean-Francois. He was called Acaau, " General in chief of the demands of his fellow-citizens ;" had gigantic spurs on his naked heels ; and, followed by a troop of bandit, armed, for the most part, with *sharp stakes*, in place of guns, who overran the villages, which were depopulated by terror, at their approach, in the interest of " unfortunate innocence," and of " the *eventuality* of national education."

Acaau spoke especially " in the name of the country people, which were roused from the slumber, into which, they had been plunged." "What says the cultivator"—he would exclaim in one of his interminable harangues, in which the relentless obstinacy of the peasant was doubled in the negro, and refused to thank the Herard party for a single one of his promises—"What says the cultivator, to whom has been promised, by the revolution, a diminution of the price of his foreign provisions, and the augmentation of the value of his productions? He says, *he has been deceived!*"

The mulattoes, likewise, of Cayes, the chief centre of the last revolution, received the first visit of this formidable messenger of violence. The *bourgeoise* opposition, which had so long desired the political awakening of the people, had no longer any complaints to make. It was, nevertheless, gotten rid of, this time, through fear. A common interest of preservation, grouped the majority of the two colors, around the presidency of Guerrier; who, thanks to his black skin, could trample down, without trouble, the ultra-African element. But Guerrier died a few days afterwards, a voluntary victim to the duties, his new position imposed upon him. Although till then, always dead-drunk at eight o'clock in the morning, he had, though eighty-four years of age, the resolution to renounce rum; which, in fact, sometimes, had transformed him into a wild beast. This is what killed him.

Pierrot, the brother-in-law of King Christophe,

and the friend of Acaau—and who, after Guerrier, was most conspicuous—reached power in his turn; intermeddled with the foreigners; had all sorts of difficulties with our consul, M. Lavasseur; was again beaten by the Dominicans; and produced, anew, terror among the mulattoes. He was at bottom, only, a ridiculous, good natured sort of a man, yielding much less through passion, than stupidity, to the pressure of the ultra-African element; but good natured, after the fashion of negro tyrants. Some one, he had accused, was condemned to three months imprisonment. Pierrot, being very much dissatisfied with the sentence, remembered, after mature reflection, that the law granted the Executive, the right to commute punishments; and, all radiant, at this discovery, he *commuted*, the three months imprisonment, into the punishment of death; such was Pierrot!

His favorite dream was to advance in rank, if not in power and to exchange the Presidency of the North, West, and South, for a small royalty in the North. But one fine morning it happened, that, without saying a word, or firing a gun, the blacks and mulattoes gave him his discharge, which he accepted, without a murmur; only entreating the nation to leave him, at least, his old appointment of General.

The scrambles and disorders, which led to the fall of Boyer, were not, as is seen, without compensation. From this triple simultaneousness of opinions, and interests, which had, successively, reünited the great majority of the blacks, and the minority of the mulattoes, in a common thought of national unity around Guerrier—in a common desire of defense against Acaau—and in a common necessity of harmony and legality against Pierrot—there resulted this fact, as new as it was cheering, to wit: That the moral fusion, economical and political, of the two colors, was, already, nearly accomplished. It was only now necessary, to find a man capable of developing the consequences of this new situation; a man who could couple together, the best features of Christophe's system, and that of Pétion and Boyer; and could be as energetic, as the first, while continuing as humane, liberal, and civilizing as the second. Whether from reason or instinct, the national sentiment was not mistaken, in calling to the succession of Pierrot, the black General, Riché. Uniting to the influence, his color gave him, a certain sympathetic deference for the mulattoes and the whites, Riché realized, for a time, the ideal of the Haytien Government. He knew how to subdue the barbarous element, without crushing out, under the same pressure, the enlightened element; and he wished, and was able (without fear of exciting the susceptibilities before which Boyer recoiled) on the one hand, to open the country to foreign capital—and on the other, to reörganize domestic labor.

4

But, a sudden death* carried him off, two days, before the first anniversary of his elevation to power.

The Senate, to whom belonged the election of Chief Magistrate, was at that time presided over by M. Beaubrun Ardouin ; this body during eight ballotings was equally divided, between two black candidates—Generals, Souffran and Paul. The first had the army in his favor ; but he had served, and betrayed, all parties. The second was worthy of continuing the political task of Riché ; but, being an *improvised* General, and of recent date, the army did not know him. From the very equality of their chances of success, sprung, moreover, either a danger of national schism, or a cause of weakness to the successful candidate. M. Beaubrun Ardouin, cut short the difficulty, by proposing, suddenly, a third candidate, to whom no one objected, for the simple reason, that no one had dreamed of him ; and to the great surprise of the new President, and his superiors, the Senate elected *General Faustin Soulouque*, the 1st of March, 1847.

He was a good, fat, and peaceable negro. Since 1804, at which time he was a domestic to General Lamarre, he had passed through all the events of

---

* He died of a strong dose of cantharides—or "of Love"—to employ the delicate language of a Haytien, who related to me an account of his last moments.

his country's history, without leaving any trace, of himself, either good or bad. In 1810, General Lamarre was killed, in defending the Môle against Christophe ; and Soulouque, who had already become something, as aid-de-camp of his master, was charged, they say, with carrying his heart to Pétion. Pétion appointed him lieutenant of his mounted guard ; and left him afterwards as a legacy to Boyer, like a piece of furniture of the presidential palace. Boyer, in his turn, appointed him captain, and attached him to the special service of Mademoiselle Jute, a *Diane de Poitiers*, of the color of gold, who had been, successively, lady to two presidents. Soulouque remained, after this, completely forgotten, until 1843. But since that year, every revolution helped him with a push to climb that *mât de cocagne*, from which, he did not expect to disengage a crown. Under Herard he became chief of a squadron ; under Guerrier, a colonel ; under Riché, General, and chief commander of the palace guard.

The new President was from sixty, to sixty-two years of age ; but the clear tone of his eyes—the smooth and brilliant jet of his skin—the dark tint of his hair—at first sight, would not have allowed any one to accord him more than forty years. It is the privilege of negroes of good stock, not to begin to grow old, but at an age when decrepitude overtakes the whites ; and often, on an octogenarian head to preserve hair unmixed with any shade of silver. The regular and symetrical baldness, which marks the top of his head, only, displays to better advantage the fine Senegal type, which may be said to be almost Caucasian ;—a type, which is completed, by a nearly straight nose, lips moderately thick, and cheek-bones of not exaggerated prominence. From his eyes, which are of extreme softness, and slightly closed, there issue rather uncertain flashes, which recall, by turns, the limpid and wondering expression of a child six years old, and the intelligent and drowsy *finesse* of a tom-cat going to sleep. The double smile which passes from his nostrils and joins the two extremities of his mouth, contrasts, only by its deeply graven lines, with the youth and placidity of the whole physiognomy; but, in brief, his face attracts, if it does not awe.

The insurmountable timidity of the new President—a timidity which made him, sometimes, stammer in a most unintelligent manner, alone inspired his friends with serious inquietudes. But the next day, on the occasion of the *Te Deum*, which, according to usage, consecrated his elevation to the Presidency, they discovered that this was not his only moral infirmity. Soulouque having arrived at the Church, obstinately rejected the seat of honor, which had been intended for him, during this ceremony. They found out the same day, the reason of this singular repugnance: the seat in question was *conjured*.

We are going to relate how, and why, this *fauteuil* was bewitched; and by what gradations, this inoffensive and pitiful man—who believed, and believes still, in sorceries ; who stammered in speaking through timidity ; who blushed before every stranger, so that it could be read under his black skin ;—has known how, to make, mulattoes and blacks, pass from smiles to terror— from commiserating raillery, to prostration—and to throw over his old, negro shoulders an imperial mantle, which, all grotesque as it may appear, is most certainly of purple, for he had it soaked a whole year, in human blood.

IV.

Negro illuminism—Devotions of Madame Soulouque—The hunt for *fétiches*.

   Eh ! eh ! Bomba, hen, hen !
    Canga bafio té
   Canga moune dé lé
    Canga do ki la
    . Canga li.

 I am ignorant whether I chance to speak, in these words, the language of Senegal or Yolof, of Fouli or Bambara, of Mandingo or Bouriquis, of Arada or Caplaou, of Ibos or Mokos, of Congo or Mousombé ; all that I can affirm is, that it is *negro*. When these incomprehensible words, alternately chanted by one, and many voices, issued *en crescendo* from the midst of the night, the colonists of Saint-Domingo had their slaves counted, and the criminal police was put on foot. These words were known in the army of Hyacinthe ; they were howled, at midnight, around the great fires, lit in the camp of Biassou.

 Pétion and Boyer, had nearly succeeded in preventing their utterance ; but the bands of Acaau restored them to honor. Silent under Guerrier—

bold under Pierrot—dissimulating under Riché—the African chanters, who perpetuate thus their traditions, sing them at their pleasure, since the accession of Soulouque; for Soulouque belongs to the *vaudoux*, and these words are the sacramental hymn of the god, *Vaudoux*.

The *vaudoux* is an African worship, in great honor throughout the kingdom of Juida, but which originally appears to have come from the kingdom of Arada; for, according to the statement of Moreau de Saint-Méry, it was the negroes of this last country who, in old Saint-Domingo, preserved the principles and rules of this religion. They call, also, the supernatural being, *Vaudoux*, to whom they address this worship. The god, *Vaudoux*, knows all, sees all, can do all; and consents to manifest himself to his good friends, the negroes, under the form of a species of snake, not poisonous; and which is enclosed in a small box, one side of which is latticed, so as to permit a view of the interior. But he only receives their vows and offerings—and only transmits his virtue—through the intervention of a high-priest, chosen by the votaries themselves, and a high-priestess, designated by the latter. These two ministers are called, indifferently, king and queen—or master and mistress—or *papa-loi* and *mamman-loi*.

Like all primitive rites, the *vaudoux* numbers, among its cremonies, a particular dance, which the old slaves affected, sometimes to execute in public.

It was succeeded with a repast at which they only eat poultry, in order to induce the police to believe, that the mysterious reünions, about which they disturbed themselves, so much, were the most inoffensive pastimes in the world. As to the real *vaudoux*, the secret is rigorously observed; and this secret is guarantied by an oath, conceived in terms, and surrounded with circumstances, which are best calculated to give it the sanction of terror.

"Sometimes" — said Moreau de Saint-Méry, whose description seems written but yesterday— "sometimes, a vase, filled with the still warm blood of a she-goat, seals, on the lips of the attendants, the covenant to suffer death rather than reveal anything; and even to inflict it, upon whosoever shall forget that he is solemnly bound." We have heard a vaudoux-celebration spoken of, which was held a little before, or just after, the transformation of Soulouque into an Emperor, when, instead of the blood of a she-goat, they drank, with the addition of rum, the blood of a beef, killed during the meeting, to give greater effect to the ceremony.

The initiated assemble in an out-of-the way place, and carefully closed, which was designated at their previous reünion. On entering it, they put off their sandals, and encircle their bodies with handkerchiefs, the prevailing color of which must be red, and their number seem to be proportioned to the rank of each attendant. Another handkerchief, entirely red, encircles the forehead of the king, like a diadem; and a scarf of the same color would, generally, distinguish the queen. Both place themselves, at one end of the room, near a sort of altar, on which is placed the box enclosing the sacred snake. After adoring the snake, and renewing their oath, the king and queen, speaking by turns, extol the benefits, with which the god *Vaudoux* loads his believers; and invite the attendants to come forward and consult, or implore him. These present themselves, by seniority of rank, and utter their desires, in which morality would find much to condemn. At each invocation, the vaudoux-king collects himself, and awaits the coming of the spirit; then, putting, hastily, the box containing the snake, on the ground, he makes the queen get on it, who, by the contact, is seized with a convulsive trembling, and renders his oracles—lavishing, according to occasion, promises or threats. The consultation being finished, each one of the disciples deposits, in a covered hat, his tribute, and the proceeds of these collections constitute the public and secret budget of the association. The king and queen transmit, immediately, the general orders of the god *Vaudoux*, and a new oath of obedience is taken.

It is at this stage of their ceremonies that they proceed, if necessary, to admit new members; on which admission, the god *Vaudoux* has been previously consulted. The applicant is placed in a great circle, traced with charcoal. The king puts, in his hand, a package of herbs, horse-hair, and fragments of horns or bones, and, tapping him lightly on the head, with a staff of wood, intones the African song which begins this chapter. The assembly, repeat it, in chorus, and the novice, who begins to tremble and dance (what is called *monter vaudoux*) soon reaches, with the help of rum, such a paroxism of nervous exultation, that, occasionally, he only recovers his senses, and ceases to dance, under the impression of vigorous blows of a cow-hide.* If, in the wanderings of this epileptic dance, the novice crosses the circle, the chanters are silent in an instant, and the king and queen turn their backs, to disperse the evil presage.

The ordeal having terminated, the recipiendiary is admitted to take the oath before the altar of the snake; and the dance of the vaudoux is commenced. The king touches with his feet or his hands the sanctuary of the snake, and gradually

---

*Sometimes, indeed, the physical insensibility is absolute. A person, worthy of belief, told me that he saw a young girl, while *manifesting Vandoux*, leap with a single nervous bound, four or five feet high, make a half turn in the air, and fall vertically on her head, without the shock, which would have broken a buffalo's skull, causing her the least injury. In a nocturnal promenade through the environs of Port-au-Prince, I happened to surprise some details of a Vandoux initiation; and I saw the *papa-loi* execute before the recipiendiary gestures, like the *passes*, by which our magnetizers pretend to remove analagous effects of insensibility.

all the upper parts of his body tremble and work the wrong way, as if they were dislocated. Then a sympathetic effect is produced, which physiology can scarcely call in question, after what we know of the convulsionary sects of Europe; and which even those whites, who have been surprised prying into the mysteries of the *vaudoux*, have not always escaped. The excessive commotion, which agitates the head and shoulders of the vaudoux-king, is transmitted, by degrees, to all the attendants. Each one of them is soon the victim of a dizziness, which the queen, partaking of also, keeps up, by agitating the little bells, which ornament the box of the snake. Laughter, sobs, shrieks, faintings, bitings, add their delirium to the increasing madness of the fever, caused by rum. The more feeble end, by falling down, as dead, on the spot; and the hoarse bacchanals, bear them away, all the time dancing, and turn into a neighboring place; where, sometimes, under the triple excitement of promiscuousness, drunkenness, and darkness, scenes are enacted, to make the teeth gnash with horror, at all the insensible gods of Africa.

This is the classic vaudoux. This is the secret of that mysterious power which, in 1791–'92, transformed, in a single night, the indifferent, and scattered slaves, into furious masses; and drove them, almost unarmed, into those incredible combats, where the stupidity of courage disconcerted tactics, and where naked flesh ended by using iron.

The influence which the vaudoux chiefs exercise over the other members of the sect, is, in fact, without bounds. "There was not one of these," says the writer above quoted, "who would not have preferred anything to the evils, with which he was menaced, if he did not go assiduously to the assemblies, and if he did not blindly obey what *Vaudoux* required of him. We have seen that fear had operated sufficiently to deprive them of the use of reason; and in their fits of frenzy, they uttered howls, and fled from the presence of men, so as to excite pity." Belief in the vaudoux worship is so much the more readily preserved, as, in the religious opinions of the black masses, and even of a portion of the mulattoes, it does not exclude Catholic orthodoxy, for which the Haytien people profess a very sincere fervor, if it is not very enlightened. We will speak, presently, upon what a deplorable clergy, or rather *soi-disant* clergy, is devolved the mission of clearing up this chaos, engendered in African imaginations.

In the meantime, this thirst for the marvelous, which we find at the beginning and termination of every civilization is derived, in Hayti, from both religions. In the country, especially, we often see in the same house Christian baptisms, alternating with Mandingo funerals. On more than one breast, the Catholic scapulary hangs, by the same cord, with the *maman-bila* (an amulet of small limestones, in a bag) of the national sorceries; and

the old negress who dreads the visits of a *zombi* *
(ghost) goes, indifferently, to ask masses of the
curé, or conjurations of the *papas-vaudoux*. Either
they subject themselves to the influences, in the
midst of which, they live—or they find, (which
is most probable,) the *papas* fall, more readily,
into the pleonasms of negro devotion, holding at
the choice of their credulous flock, *wangas, neuvaines*, fetiche-lifeguards, and hallowed wax-tapers.

It was in this fantastic world, all peopled with
zombis and presages, things marvelous and frightful, that they went to find Soulouque. Is it at all
wonderful that he issued from it a little bewildered and amazed; and that at the moment of seat-
ing himself, on the chair of Boyer, he looked well,
lest he might sit down on a conjuration? Not one
of the four Presidents, who had succeeded each
other on this seat, since the year 1844, attained the
end of a year; two of them, had been smitten,
with forfeiture—two others, with death, before the
end of this term; and the death of Riché, especially, happening just on the eve of the anniversary
of his accession, confirmed the people, as well as
the most competent members of Haytien sorcery,
in the opinion, that he had been necessarily *conjured*
there. I know whites, who have been, some little

---

* Not long ago, some say, a *zombi* appeared on a palm-tree in the vicinity of Soulouque's palace; others say it was a virgin, dressed in white.

affected by this remark. In escaping this first danger, Soulouque was not yet at the end of his inquietude. Was it, indeed, to the chair? Was it not rather, to the national palace, itself—that this nameless influence was attached, which was so fatal to the four last Presidents? Opinion was very much divided, in this respect; but the time had come, when the newly chosen Executive was about to refuse, plainly, to inhabit the palace, whose tenants only left it by expulsion, or without life. A precious revelation occurred, however, to calm this uncertainty, and these apprehensions.

In the first rank of the sorcerers of Port-au-Prince, there figured a colored woman, who drew the cards, made stones and snakes speak, preserved children from lock-jaw, and assured for life, or a limited time, against the infidelity of husbands and lovers. She burned, also, before a statuette of the Virgin, a given number of small wax-candles; and, if one of them had a coal on it, or was prematurely extinguished, she conscientiously warned the consultants, who paid her to recommence the incantation. Madame Souloque, who was one of her most assiduous clients, sent for her. She shut herself up, burnt wax-tapers, exhausted all the resources of the vaudoux liturgy, and the sorceress, finally, predicted, that Boyer had concealed, on his departure, in the palace gardens, *a doll*, of which she gave the minutest description ; and, by virtue of which, every successor of the latter, was condemned, never to reach his thirteenth month of power. Soulouque had trembled before this unknown evil; now that it was defined, he attacked it bravely in front; and, by order of His Excellency . . . . . they began to dig up the ground, to discover the *féliche* buried by the Machiavellian Boyer.*

Let us speak seriously; for this matter is about to become the key of the most grave and lamentable events; and, it is of consequence to determine well, the proportion of responsibility which accrues to each one. The ill-suppressed laughter, with which the enlightened part of the mulattoes and the blacks, welcomed these anecdotes of the palace, were at the same time, an injustice and a fault. Of what consequence was it, after all, that a poor unlettered negro, preserved, in his family privacy, the worship of his paternal creed. The Haytien midst being given, should it not congratulate itself, even, on the community of superstitions, which morally attaches, to the governor, four-fifths of his subjects, and rallies to official action those influences, which, since the time of Acaau, had become a dangerous lever of sedition and brigandage? The essential matter is, that Soulouque

---

* About the same period a priest was accused of having, one day, while officiating before Soulouque, presented the Holy Sacrament, reversed, in order to cause Soulouque's death at the end of the year. The priest was banished.

understood how to strenghthen himself, by these influences, without fortifying them; and, from this point of view, he offered every desirable guarantee.

Under Pierrot himself—Pierrot, the friend of Acaau—Soulouque went to Cayes to arrest, in person, the principal lieutenants of the latter, without excepting the vaudoux prophet of the band, brother Joseph. From thence, he repaired to the seat of Acaau's military authority; had the principal mulattoes brought before him; and told them, in the very presence of the wordy bandit: "The mulattoes have as much right in this country, as the blacks. If General Acaau oppresses you take a gun and protect yourselves!"

The *debuts* of Soulouque, as president, proved more peremptorily still, that he designed to have nothing in common, politically, with this ultra-African party, with which his superstitions reconciled him. I have said that the fundamental idea of this party was hatred of France—a hatred, by which, it sought to maintain the only obstacle, which, since 1825, could oppose white immigration; and, as a consequence of it, an increase of the colored class. This was the great point with it. But the first message of Soulouque, asserted clearly, with a real effusion of gratitude, the good conduct of the French government.

This desire of happy relations with us, we will see, became one of Soulouque's fixed ideas, and continued with him, even till the awakening of those ultra-African passions, of which he would soon become the bloody personification. Such a desire, we say, was on his part, so much the more meritorious, as, the only political idea which, until then, had lodged in his head responded to diametrically opposite tendencies. The good, peaceable, discreet Captain Soulouque had, in fact, for once, in his life, emancipated himself, even to entering into a conspiracy; and, what is stranger, a conspiracy against Boyer, whom some ardent patriots wished to punish, for permitting the independence of Hayti to be granted by Charles X., in place of wresting it from us. Soon after his message, the project of a law, the idea of which ran back to Riché, developed this tacit conclusion, by proposing to legalize marriages between the Haytiens and foreigners. The explosion of regrets, which the death of the latter had excited, made a profound impression on the mind of Soulouque. To imitate the last president in everything was his great care; a care, which, displayed itself at times, in acts of naïve and touching good-nature. One day, for example, Soulouque rose up, saying: "When General Riché became President, he decreed a funeral service, in honor of General Borgella, who was his benefactor; and, it was a praiseworthy affair. Me also—I wish to do a good act, by ordering a service for General Lamarre, who was my benefactor."

And, in fact, this service had the proportions of of a national solemnity. After the ceremony, he had a reception at the palace ; and, the President, attended by the parents of General Lamarre, presented them, successively, to all the authorities of the city, saying : "This is the family of my benefactor, and it is my family."

Put this immense necessity for approbation, in conflict with raillery, and a terrible shock is foreseen. The negro fears ridicule, precisely because he loves to administer it ; and Soulouque must have been so much the more sensible of it, that the sneers came, in this case, from the enlightened class, the representative of which, like Riché, he aspired to become. He made marked efforts, by dint of attention and good will, to disarm the pleasantries, provoked by his superstitious terrors ; but, knowing, neither how to write, nor read—ignorant of all the details of administration—examining, without ever finding bottom, into an ocean of affairs, the least one of which was an unknown world to him—he grew more amazed than ever, from these useless excursions into practical life ; and a profound feeling of his incapacity which became even exaggerated, added to the sufferings of his African vanity. The ministers, fortunately, exercised an absolute discretion over the official ingeniousness of his Excellency ; it happened that something of it always got to the public, and their sneers were redoubled. Soulouque then changed his tactics; to the timid and humble questioner, who spelled, letter by letter, the why and wherefore of the most trifling passing matter, there succeeded the conceited man. If a minister, or the chief of a division, came to read him a dispatch: "Let us see!" said the President, in creole; and taking proudly the manuscript, he ran over, for some moments, with an expression at once reflecting and disdainful, the mysterious black lines of the *papier pâlé* (a speaking paper); then he refolded it carefully, adding, with a majestic assurance: "Well! I will think of it."

Indeed, the unhappy man thought of it so much, that the *papier pâlé*, finally, burned his hands. Then, to escape the tortures of a curiosity, with which, the fear of sorcery was always mingled, he ordered some employee—whose discretion had been previously proved, by means of an innocent espoinage, of which every one was aware—and made him read the dispatch. If a vascillating hesitation manifested itself in the voice of the reader: "Well, dear!" said Soulouque, softly: and, after having noted, in his inflexible memory, both the name of the latter and the suspected passage, he appealed to another employee, so as to compare the first reading.

A dangerous climax began: to the fear of spirits was evidently added, with Soulouque, the mistrust of men; and it was necessary, after all, to stop there. In this unequal conflict, which he sustained against unknown powers, could he regard as friendly that portion of the spectators, who laughed, instead of coming to his aid? A significant thing, and with which he ought to have been struck at first—the sorcery of the garden was the work of a *mulatto*. Hence this conclusion was inevitable: that the mulattoes were half accountable, with the undiscoverable doll. On the contrary, if an expression, of encouragement and sympathy, was manifested to sustain Soulouque, it came especially from the black portion of the spectators. So many affinities must necessarily end in contact; and the lowest depth of vaudoux, rising by degrees to the surface, finally overflowed the presidential palace. I leave it to be imagined, whether the antipathies of caste—the principle refuge of which was this association—profited by these circumstances. Soulouque was so much the more accessible to the new influences, which surrounded him, because he found there persons to talk with, unreservedly, and in pure creole, whose superiority of intellect did not humiliate his incurable vanity. The first revelation they had of these influences, was the sudden renewal of the project relative to legalizing marriages between Haytiens and foreigners. Already there had escaped, from Soulouque, some words like these: "I did not ask to be President; I did not dream of it; and I know that I was not prepared for it; but since the constitution has called me, why do they wish to rid themselves of me?"

It is in the nature of gratuitous prejudice, sooner or later, to cease to be gratuitous; and the cultivated class, from which he had isolated himself, by his perpetual suspicions, finally, took him at his word. This class restrained themselves so much the less in the expression of their fears, because the increasing ascendancy of the ultra-African cotérie, was much more attributed to the incurable feebleness of Soulouque, than to any menacing disposition on its part. In short, the frogs asked for a king. In truth, this opposition presented nothing serious; for the political necessities, which caused the election of Soulouque, still remained. But, as they did not conspire, and their dissatisfaction interpreted itself into street gossip—the echo only came the oftener, and sooner, to the ears of the "black people;" who, being already incensed, by the incredulity of the well-dressed people, at the places of sorcery, went every day to carry to the "President" this new proof of the complicity of the mulattoes, with the yet undiscovered doll of the garden. Soulouque became more and more gloomy from it. "I know," said he, "that they conspire against me; but, when I think of all it costs a family, *to make a man of twenty-five years of age*, I have not the courage to act." . . . Sublime words these, in that mouth!—but responding to a thought, in which strange struggles were betrayed. At such times, Soulouque recommenced with new ardor the excavations of the garden; and the sceptics laughed more heartily than ever, without thinking, that by dint of digging up the ground, he could the more easily open their graves in it.

V.

Similien.

It was in the midst of these inexpressible sufferings, his ears intent upon every noise, and every conceit—and trembling, at every step, lest he might walk over a conspiracy, or two cross lines—that the President passed the first five months of power. Towards the end of July, 1847—whether he wished to escape, by absence, from the invisible look of the *féliche*, or that, diverted from this besetment by some alarming rumors, which came from the Northern part of the republic, he seized anxiously the hope of finding himself face to face with enemies of flesh and bone—Soulouque resolved to make a voyage to the Cap. He expected to leave the 27th, but here on the 26th, at the end of the session of the Senate, he received the visit of his ministers, who froze him with terror, by handing him their collective resignations.

Was this the signal of a conspiracy?—or rather, did MM. Paul, Céligny, Ardouin, Dupuy, and Larochel, believe the moment had arrived, for them to separate their fate from that of an unfortunate man, who contended with supernatural powers? Such was, no doubt, the double suspicion which assailed his mind ; and Soulouque asked, with a troubled air, if it was a question of a new revolution ?—adding, that he was ready, if they wished it, to resign his power. These gentlemen endeavored to reässure him, by explaining that, their withdrawal was only occasioned, by the enormous reductions, which the Senate had made in the budget ; and, anticipating, themselves, his suspicions, they offered to accompany him, on his journey, although they had resigned ; a proposition, which His Excellency, accepted literally, with marked readiness.

Soulouque, therefore, left in the night of the 27th July, very happy to lead in leash his four hostages ; but as he could not assure himself, by the same proceeding, of the twenty and some thousand accomplices of the doll, which he left behind him, he, confidentially, charged Similien, the general of the black brigade, which kept guard over the palace, to hold these enemies in check until his return.

Similien executed, so conscientiously his instructions, that in less than two weeks, after the departure of the President, the colored inhabitants of Port-au-Prince crowded into the consulates to implore the protection of their flags. The same day, and even hour, at Jacmel, Cayes, Jérémie, Léogane—from one end to the other of the whole Southern peninsula—the stores were closed, and a violent panic was exhibted, among all the people of color.

To comprehend this occurrence, it will be necessary to describe Similien.

I have spoken of the conspiracy which was formed, on the subject of the ordinance of 1825, against Boyer. The future President, only adhered to it from necessity, and without knowing what he did; for which, he was held to account. Mademoiselle Jute answered in person for the fidelity of Captain Soulouque; and it was on this very occasion that she attached him to her, by giving him the superintendence of a sugar-mill she owned.

The negro Similien, who held in the corps, a grade superior to that of Soulouque, was also of that conspiracy; and his complicity was sufficiently evident and conclusive, to merit his losing his head; but the good-natured Boyer contented himself, with removing him from his corps, and putting him, with the same rank, into another regiment. He even preserved to Similien, the contract to furnish the army-clothes, because Similien was a tailor. At the fall of the *tyrant*, Similien nevertheless passed, as a victim, into the Herard party, and with all the profits belonging to his employment. Among the four or five negro generals who rose, successively, against Herard-Riviere, there was, as we will remember, a General Dalzon. He was killed in the affair; and the negro Colonel, Mercure, being implicated in the conspiracy, was condemned to death, with his own son, whom he had drawn into it. The latter was the godson of Similien, who thus found himself the *compere* of Colonel Mercure, a title more sacred in the colonies, and, especially, among the old slave population, than those created by ties of blood.

Similien declared, with tears in his eyes, that Herard was justified in shooting "*compere* Mercure, *but to put the son to death because he had obeyed his father!*"—this upset all his notions of justice and injustice; for, in the opinion of the negroes, there is no limit known to paternal authority. Mercure's son was shot, in spite of the supplications, and menaces, of Similien. He became furious against Herard; joined the schism of Guerrier; and began, from that time, to drink frightful quantities of rum, to console himself because of the injustice of men.

Guerrier having become President, had Acaau arrested, and put on trial. "It is just!" Similien said sententiously; "Acaau had no right to kill the mulattoes." But on learning that they pursued Acaau, even on the subject of the brigandages, he had committed under Herard-Riviere, and against the mulatto partizans of the latter, Similien became terribly angry. In his opinion a government, which owed its existence to the downfall of the *Riviériste* party, ought rather to thank the accused for what he had done against it; and following the thread of this idea, with the relentless persistence of a drunken man, he ended, after eight days, in publicly eulogizing Acaau. This fraction of the colored class, which Similien, had thus, given cause to exclaim, accused him of adopting the hatreds of caste, entertained by the dreadful bandit.

The accusation went straight to the impressionable heart of Similien. Exasperated, that the mulattoes did not, readily, apprehend the distinction made by him, between their color, which ought to respect Acaau, and their *Riviériste* opinions, which pointed them out to his justice, he concluded not to compromise his dignity with so much ingratitude. Excited by daily altercations, Similien, finally, vowed a furious hatred to all the men of color—to some because they were *Riviéristes*, to others because their complexion reminded him of that of the *Riviéristes*. This hatred embalmed in a constantly renewed bath of alcohol, was preserved pure, until the accession of Soulouque.

At that time, Similien was second in command of the guard; of which, as I have mentioned, Soulouque was chief commander. Judging by his own example, and by that of Riché and Boyer, that, from this last grade, there was but another step to the Presidency, Soulouque found it prudent to pull up the ladder after himself. He did not reëstablish this grade; and Similien continuing only second in command, found himself, thus, placed under the immediate orders of the new President. Hence there were daily and hourly relations between them, to which old souvenirs of companionship gave a new character of intimacy. Similien did not neglect, as was thought, this opportunity of revenging himself, on the ingratitude of the mulattoes; and the superstitious prejudices of Soulouque, only, disposed him to receive, too readily, the impressions of his confidant. In truth, the latter entertained, a rebellious incredulity, with respect to card-cutters, and *fétiches;* and this very thing must have, finally, ruined him. But Soulouque was, only, the more willing to participate in his suspicions. The sceptical Similien was almost an ally in the enemies camp. This is the reason, why Soulouque left him during his absence, besides the command of the guard, that of the fort which commanded the city; and further, (as they afterwards knew), certain secret instructions, which authorized him to act according to his pleasure, in case of eventualities, the urgency of which was left entirely to his own discretion.

But from the first day of his confidential dictatorship, Similien discovered two things: first, that the guard was almost the only regular force in the city; second, that the batteries of the fort could, if necessary, burn and batter down the city; hence he concluded, with the last evidence, that the man, who united the command of the guard with that of the fort, was master of the city, people and property.

I hasten to say, that if the first impression of Similien, at this discovery, was but little encouraging to the mulattoes, the second was a thought of clemency. Seized with admiration, at the spectacle of his own magnanimity, he, unfortunately, did not resist the desire of sharing this admiration with others. And in order, that the whole merit, he deserved for pardoning, should be better understood, he concluded that his full authority for threatening should be, previously, well established. Therefore, addressing, by turns, the soldiers of the guard, who were consigned to the national palace, and the bands of wretches who beseiged the iron-gratings, and watched, perhaps, for some sinister signal in the flood of incoherent words, which escaped the drunkenness of the orator—Similien boasted loudly of the discretionary powers he had received. The well known character of this personage, did not permit the least misapprehension, as to the nature of these powers, real or pretended; nor as to the use he would make of them, upon occasion. The wealthy class uttered loud complaints.

Thus the mulattoes persisted, in only divining half of Similien's intentions; and he got nothing for the display of his magnanimity. This new proof of "the ingratitude" of the mulattoes, appeared to him, to exceed all bounds; and, two cannon, with lighted matches, prevented, thereafter, all access to the national palace, except to the proved enemies of the class of color. These afterwards carried mysterious orders, some into the poor quarters of the city, and others into the country. Was it designed, at a given time, to masacre all the mulattoes, and pillage and burn their stores? This was the report which was suddenly circulated; and the simultaneousness of this panic, in all the populous parts of the whole Island, left no doubt that it was well founded. The blacks of the country, fortunately, refused to rush upon Port-au-Prince, which was to have been, they say, the signal of the massacre; and the measures taken, in the event of an attack by the troops of the palace, by generals Therlonge (mulatto), and Paul Decayet (black), the one commander of the subdivision, the other of the post, resulted in overawing Similien.

Only the minister of foreign relations, M. Élie, was at Port-au-Prince. On learning these events, of which he had, naturally, only received the most contradictory reports, Soulouque detached from his cortége, the minister of the interior, M. David Troy; who, after an investigation, signified to Similien, to go and render an account of his conduct to the President. As his only reply, Similien forbid the two ministers the *entrée* of the government palace; and wrote to the Cap, that M. Troy was the agent of a mulatto conspiracy, having for its object, a change of the Presidency, to the profit of General Paul, or General Souffran. Indeed, whether this was a manœuvre of Similien, or that the menaced class had really had some intention, of escaping from the permanent danger imposed upon it, by the *entourage* of Soulouque, these two names had been put forward at the height of the crisis, they did not well know on which side. To Soulouque, this was the most clear fact of the whole affair; and, very tranquil on the subject of General Paul, who attended him, as we have said, as a resigned minister, he ordered, by express, General Souffran, who remained at the head of the division of Port-au-Prince, to go immediately to the Dominican frontier. He did not appear to take any notice, at first, of the rest of them; then, two days afterwards, they could hear Similien boasting, of having received dispatches, which approved completely of his zeal; and the ministers, felicitated themselves upon receiving other dispatches, which approved entirely of their prudence. In the meantime, the President himself disclosed the secret of the enigma, and a kind of regularity was, finally, established amidst this disorder.

The stores were reöpened; the administration of the different departments were partially restored to their functions; MM. Élie and David Troy issued circulars; and the majestic Similien, still master of the fort, and the palace, drank rum, under the protection of his two cannon, with a crowd of hideous scoundrels in rags, to whom he constantly related some new act of "mulatto ingratitude." Notwithstanding the tacit truce of the two parties, three attempts to burn the houses of the mulattoes, testified to the eloquence of Similien, and the sensibility of his hearers.

Soulouque having decided on returning to Port-au-Prince, was preceded by a proclamation, not less ambitious, than his conduct. He deplored, in this proclamation, the *conflict* which had sprung up, during his absence, between the authorities; and threatened with the " sword of the Law the wicked persons" who had profited, by his absence, to *try* and produce discord and trouble, in the country. Who were those wicked persons? In this position, and in this language, must we not see fear, stupidity, or complicity? A piece of news, which arrived some hours before the return of the President, began to enlighten these doubts. In an address delivered to the troops, at Saint-Marc, and Gonaives, Soulouque had decidedly revealed his hatred of the colored class; and uttered sinister language, concerning an article in the *Feuille du Commerce*, in which, the abominable designs of Similien, had been very plainly exposed. On that occasion, His Excellency had dropped many phrases in succession, in pure French, which was an indication, with him, of great mental excitement. A decisive experience remained still to be made; and, at the noise of the salvos of artillery, which announced the return of Soulouque, almost the whole population gathered, at the entrances to the presidential palace, to be present, at the first interview of the latter with Similien.

Similien awaited him, in the principal door of the palace, at the head of his staff. They were able to foresee strange events, when they saw the

President draw, close to his breast, the author of such sudden alarms—thank him with effusion—and enter, arm in arm, into his apartments. Generals Therlonge and Paul Decayet, and Col. Dessalines, chief of police (the natural son of the famous Emperor,) all three of whom, had taken divers measures, to protect the inhabitants, against the fury of Similien, were severely reprimanded by Soulouque. M. David Troy, on his part, having, vainly, exacted from the President a formal disavowal of the conduct of Similien, for the two last months, resigned, which brought about an entire reconstruction of the cabinet.

V.

A Haytien trial of the press.

The complicity of the President, in the recent attempts of Similien, appeared from that moment evident; and, notwithstanding, there was nothing of it. The tergiversations of Soulouque, with Similien on the one hand, and MM. Élie and David Troy, on the other, were very sincere, even to the last day. It was General Souffran, himself, who sought to gain favor with the ultra-African party. Of the two candidates for the presidency, whose names had been put forward, Souffran was the only one who was found, at the time of the late troubles, at Port-au-Prince; and, feeling, that this circumstance designated him, very pointedly, to the mistrust of Soulouque, they say, he got out of the scrape, by affecting to undertake the defence of Similien. "It was the *little mulattoes*—it was this Courtois," he would say, "who got up this whole affair, in order to create an occasion for regaining power."

M. Courtois, a mulatto, and member of the Senate, was the author of that article, in the *Feuille du Commerce*, of which, we have spoken. The President readily believed this testimony, apparently so disinterested, from a man, whom a notable portion of the enlightened class had adopted, and who could not, especially, be suspected of belonging to the school of Similien. Hence, the reaction, which operated in favor of the latter, in the mind of Soulouque. There was, moreover, in that unsettled mind, so little aptitude, for a violent and premeditated resolution, that on learning the unfavorable effect, produced by these new tendencies, he immediately made a step backward. The chief of police, Dessalines, returned to favor. A foreign mission was, at the same time, offered to M. David Troy, who contented himself with responding:

"I have given no one the right, to suppose, that I would ever consent to represent abroad, a government so disgraced."

We could so much the more readily believe, that Soulouque was returning to moderate views, because a circular of the 18th October was issued, enjoining, in severe terms, upon the agents of authority, to maintain the prohibition, imposed on the vaudoux, and the Don Pedro;* but on the 6th of November following, another circular prohibited, in terms not less severe, the same agents from mo-

---

* *The dance of Don Pedro*, invented in 1768, by a black magician of Petit-Goave, Spanish in origin, is the *vaudoux* of the fifth power. Its movements are more jerking, and its effect on the spectators more contagious. They, many times, die in it. In order to make it produce the greater effect, the negroes put in the rum they drink, while dancing, fine gunpowder.

lesting the good people, who wished to amuse themselves by dancing the *arada*—the official euphemism of the vaudoux. Indeed, the *canaille* vaudoux had, in the interval, completely, returned to favor at the palace ; and frequented it, as in the happy days of the intermediary dictatorship of Similien. A manuscript article, written by M. David Troy, copies of which were carried away with eagerness throughout the republic, produced this new change.

In this writing, which the author did not hesitate to acknowledge from the first charge, M. David Troy, developed, and justified the measures proposed, by him, for preventing the recurrence of the terrible scenes, excited by Similien. He asserted the desperate resistance of the President, to every kind of repression ; and the protection, with which he had covered the authors of so many scandals, and inquietudes. The impossibility of maintaining the President, resulted clearly from these revelations of M. Troy. The mulattoes, who feeling themselves sustained, by the black *bourgeoisie*, as well as menaced by the Similien party, passed from fright to boasting, and loudly and freely expressed the convictions produced by this article. But, as M. Troy had not failed to cite, textually, certain replies of the future Emperor, the readers did not always preserve their gravity. Soulouque was attacked on his two weak sides :—

his anxiety about mulatto conspiracies, and his terror of mulatto pleasantries.

At this double shock, all the dangerous ferments, Similien had accumulated, in this poor machine, exploded. The session had scarcely opened (November, 1847,) when the President enjoined the Senate, to organize itself into a high court of justice, for impeachment ; and cause Senator Courtois to be arrested, immediately, who was guilty of exciting the citizens to arm themselves against each other ; and of defaming, calumniating, and injuring these same citizens. The citizens, whose susceptibilities Soulouque had espoused, so warmly, were, as I have said, Similien and the odious scoundrels, who, for a month, had imposed upon the city, a public menace of massacre, robbery and arson.

The denounced Senator was, only, an intermeddler of small consideration ; but, his personality disappeared, before the important and vital interests, raised by the proposed question. The two injunctions of the protector of Similien, betrayed the adoption of a resolution, so much the more menacing, because it had not even the excuse of an appearance of legality. The constitution only permitted the arrest of a Senator, in case of his *being taken in the act of committing a criminal offence;* and, by the terms of another article, *the form of proceeding, before the Senate,* must be *determined by a law;* which law had never yet been passed. Also, the presidential message was met in the Senate, by a very active opposition; but this opposition soon yielded, before a formidable military display, which was made, not far from the palace of the Assembly; whilst the whole town was overrun, in every sense, by numerous troops, and a multitude of officers, and Generals, on horseback. The report which suddenly spread, of the approach of the blacks, from the plains; and more still, the second command of the President to the Senate, to order instantly the required arrest—unless they wished to see himself, at the head of his guard, go and apprehend M. Courtois—finally, overcame all resistance offered by the Assembly, which was growing more feeble; and, at length it decreed the double illegality imposed upon it.

A commission of five Senators, at eight o'clock in the evening, waited on the accused, to inform him of the decree, and to make him a prisoner. They found him in his gallery, before the front door of his house, surrounded by his family, and his sash furnished with pistols. His reply was a distinct refusal to obey, and the threat, if force was employed, to put fire to a barrel of powder, placed behind him. His house remained surrounded, at a distance, the whole night, whilst terror reigned in the entire neighborhood; and the whole town was on foot. It was the next day morning only, that Courtois yielded, to the urgent solicitations of his friends, and a party of Senators, who assured him, (without probably believing it), that the President, disarmed by his obedience, would not push the matter any further; he consented to go to prison, provided, no agent of the public force accompanied him. On his entering the goal, reserved for ordinary criminals, they loaded him with chains. The stores remained shut, the whole day ; and the next day, Sunday, the public criers, preceded with music and tambours, interrupted the silence of terror, which hovered over the city, by proclaiming the *crimes* of Courtois, and his trial.

This proceeding, out of which there was about to spring a frightful struggle, was begun two days afterwards. It is to be observed, that among the number of complaints, preferred against the accused, by the government commissioner, there figured this one : of having often risked irritating France, by odious diatribes against its government, and King ; and by infamous accusations against our former consul-general, M. Levasseur. At a time, when hatred of France was still the favorite theme of the men of color, M. Courtois, raised in France, an old officer in the service of France, and married to a French woman, found indeed nothing better, to make himself popular, than to be extreme in opinions contrary to those, which this triple bond imposed upon him. The task of the defence was easy, for besides the two causes of error, and incompetency, mentioned above, the constitution sanctioned a liberty of the press almost without limit. But Soulouque opposed a powerful influence to the argumentation of the public minister. In the daily speeches, addressed, at parade hours, to his guard, during the continuance of the debate, Soulouque repeated, with an implacable persistence, that, if the death of Courtois was denied him, he would nevertheless have him shot.

This morning *speech* of his Excellency was applauded furiously every time, by the scoundrels, who had chosen their domicile at the gates, and even in the court of the palace, always on the watch for a sign to interpret against the mulattoes. Similien was radiant with satisfaction and serenity at this. Fear reached, by degrees, such a pitch, in the city, that no one dared to express a wish for the accused, under the persuasion, that this victim was necessary to satisfy instincts of cruelty, which had not been before suspected. Finally, on the evening of the fourth day, after eight hours deliberation, during which the most menacing injunctions were not spared, the sentence was rendered. The Senate, as they were supposed to have made a complete self-denial, had the courage, only, to condemn M. Courtois to one month's imprisonment, reserving to him his seat as a Senator. We can imagine the fury of the President, and the Similien party, at this news.

The guard, and the troops, remained under arms the whole night, whilst the most violent resolutions were agitated at the palace. The more moderate proposed, to order the chamber of Representatives to annul the sentence of the Senate ; and, in case of their refusal to obey an exigency so monstrously illegal, to crush out entirely the legislative power. I must say that Soulouque recoiled, at first, from such an eventuality. In his opinion, the legislative power constituted an integrant part of the governmental furniture, and he did not intend, to be more poorly furnished than his predecessors. At length, day having dawned, his Excellency resolved upon an expedient, which in his opinion, should reconcile all parties. He no longer proposed to annul the sentence of the Senate, which was free to render what judgment might seem best, but, simply, to have Courtois *rejudged* by a council of war ; to which the innumerable Generals, residing, or employed, in the capital, were immediately convoked.

The ceremonious Soulouque received them, in the midst of a formidable military display, having near him, the inevitable Similien—a certain General Bellegarde, (a man of frightful antecedents, who, as his first essay, formerly wished to assassinate President Boyer)—and another wretch named Belanton, who, in his moments of rage, boasted of his power, by a word, to hurl on the city the blacks of the plains. There was only wanting to this reünion, the brave General Therlonge, commandant of the arrondissement of Port-au-Prince, who had refused to obey three consecutive summons; and was, for this reason, replaced soon afterwards, by the abominable Bellegarde.

After violent recriminations, the President, summoning, one by one, the assembled Generals, proposed to each of them this question: "Is Courtois guilty in your eyes?" Some of them wished to prevaricate, and explain an opinion. "Answer, *yes or no!*" said Soulouque, instantly, in a coldly imperative tone, which had not before been known of him. No one dared to respond, *no!* The more fearless only added to their affirmation these words: "*Since the Senate has condemned him.*" The Generals were dismissed, at ten o'clock, with orders to return at two o'clock, in the afternoon, to sign *their decision;* and, whilst this decision was being committed to writing, Soulouque, who thought of every thing, gave orders to *have the grave of Courtois dug.*

The exasperated mulattoes passed the night, in preparing their arms, and making balls, resolved to rush upon the prison, and rescue Courtois, at the first attempt made on his life. But, the next day, a consideration of prudence was mingled with these belligerent preparations. The stores were closed. Some articles of value were carried from every part of the city, to the French consulate. Demands of protection and asylum were constantly made there, by those colored families, which were more noted, either by fortune, or the political position of their heads. They learned, in fact, that the blacks of the vast plain, which stretched to the East and North of Port-au-Prince, and those inhabiting the neighboring hills, had each received ten cartridges, with orders to rush on the city at the first cannon-shot, which should be fired from the national fort. Towards three o'clock, the members of the two chambers were convened, by their presidents, to an extraordinary sitting, which seemed to presage a decisive resolution. But, in the interval, all the Generals had returned to the palace, in obedience to the order received in the morning, and signed, in gloomy silence, their unanimous affirmation of the guilt of Courtois. At this moment, the tambours beat to the field, in the great court of the palace, which was filled with troops in order of battle, and cannon with lighted matches,—when the crowd of Generals, which thronged the grand hall of reception, separated in two lines, to salute the Consul of France, M. Maxime Raybaud, and accord him a passage.

Recently arrived in the country, representing a power which was reduced to play, near the Haytien government, the ungracious part of a creditor, and against which, so many inveterate prejudices had arisen,—exposed to the intrigues of the English and German merchants, seven of whom were provided with consulates, and, who, masters of three-fourths of the business negotiated with Hayti, professed themselves ruined by our last convention (the dispositions of which tended, in fact, to limit the regular benefits previously levied by them on certain official wastes)—M. Maxime Raybaud had already acquired, without seeking it, that immense personal consideration, of which we will see him, soon, make such a magnificent use. They were especially pleased with him, for his attitude during the events of the month of August.

After Similien had driven from the government palace MM. Elie and David Troy—and the silence of the President—and the absence of all armed force subject to their orders, had condemned them to an absolute impotence—the English consul, Mr. Ussher, (a proceeding very familiar to the British chancery,) sought out bravely these gentlemen, in order to hold them responsible, with threats, for the damage which might result, not only to his own countrymen, but those Haytiens, bound up in their affairs.

M. Raybaud acted very differently; far from wishing to add, by unseasonable reclamations, to an impotence that the two ministers were the first to deplore, he silently seconded the system of reserve, and temporising, which their situation imposed upon them; taking, in concert with M. Jannin, commander of our stationary corvette, the *Danaide*, all proper measures to protect the Europeans and Haytiens,—who, if occasion required it, would have to shelter themselves under our flag; but, avoiding, also, every demonstration, of a kind that could be interpreted, by the threatened class, as a sign of offensive alliance, and to plunge it into a struggle, the consequences of which might have been incalculable.

At the commencement of the trial—and whilst a regular jurisdiction remained in possession of it, M. Raybaud refused to mix himself up with an affair, altogether domestic. Before the urgency and gravity of the circumstances, he forgot his scruples. Implored, by a touching petition of Madame Courtois; solicited, even pressed by a number of gentlemen, who prayed him to prevent an immense effusion of blood; knowing, on the other hand, that orders had been issued for the arrest of M. David Troy,—of deputy Preston, (the richest merchant of Port-au-Prince)—of the three defenders of Courtois, one of whom was also a deputy—and of Senator Latortue, who had insisted most upon his acquittal; learning, besides, that *the grave was already dug;* he signified, to the minister of foreign relations, that he wished to be received by the President. It was only three hours afterwards that an aide-de-camp of the latter, informed the consul, that he was expected.

M. Raybaud, had previously, proposed to the English consul to unite with him in making a common effort; but, on that day, Mr. Ussher was not in the spirit of the matter, and resigned himself, to leave to M. Raybaud all the honor of a proceeding, the success of which was much more doubtful than the danger.

The distinguished marks of consideration which welcomed M. Raybaud, on his entrance, were of good omen; but the contraction of the features of the President, which appeared five minutes afterwards, when he sat down near him, informed the spectators, who were full of anxiety at this scene, that our consul had accepted a very difficult task.

M. Raybaud spoke to the President of the collision which would necessarily occur, if he persisted in executing Senator Courtois, in spite of the sentence rendered by the first body of the State; of the burning and pillage of the city; and, finally, of the enormous losses, for which, foreign commerce would have to demand an account of the Republic. " The Senate has outraged me. . . *If the man does not die, what will become of my honor ?"* Such was the invariable response of Soulouque; and the alteration of his voice, interrupted by painful silences, bore witness to the violent state of his soul. The conversation continued a moment, in a low voice; they could nevertheless understand, that M. Raybaud insisted on the danger of his not being able to stop himself, in the bloody career, into which the President was going to plunge, and on the mortal enmities, he was about to accumulate against himself. This consideration—to judge by the increasing contraction of Soulouque's features—appeared to make an impression upon him, different from what M. Raybaud wished to produce; then returning, with that obstinacy peculiar to children and blacks, to his first reply, he persisted, in expressing himself outraged by the indulgent vote of the Senate.

His eyes, which were injected with blood, (it is the blush of negroes) were filled with tears ready to fall—"No. . . . All will be finished this evening. . . . See! *every body is here for that!*" said he, finally, showing him the group of Generals, who, standing some steps distant, regarded the two interlocutors, with profound attention. These last words taught the consul much of his character—a diseased terror of opinion; such was evidently the fixed and dominant idea of this uncultivated pride, to which clemency was an avowal of feebleness.

M. Raybaud caused this cord to vibrate violently: "Very well"—said he, deliberately enough to be well understood, "if this honor, of which you speak, is so dear to you, it is proper that you should know that your reputation abroad will be forever disgraced, by the blow you are about to give it yourself. The more your resentments against this man appear to you legitimate, the more the sacrifice of them will be found glorious; and I dare assure you that *our king, so clement himself, will learn it with real satisfaction.*" The consul, not receiving any reply, thought himself, definitely discomfited, when Soulouque said to him:

"If the man is not put to death, I wish him to leave the country. . . . . and forever—*forever!*"—

he repeated with energy; "*it is in consideration of the King!*" It was useless to insist on obtaining something better than this banishment, which was always illegal.

After the tragedy—the comedy! At the moment M. Raybaud thanked the President, for having granted him Courtois' life, and for the calm which his promise would restore to the city, the English consul, attended by his vice-consul, entered the hall, precipitately. At the request of M. Raybaud, Soulouque repeated his promise before the new comer; and this brave Mr. Ussher, left not less hurriedly to go on horseback, at full gallop, for the purpose of announcing to Courtois' family, that he was about to save its head. They knew soon afterwards the cause of this sudden devotion of Mr. Ussher. His friend, M. Dupuy, who, standing at a distance, had been present at the interview, believing that the matter was taking a favorable turn, sent to urge him to come, and participate in a measure which would reflect some honor on the representative of France.

The ministers, who, in this whole affair had exhibited a pitiable weakness, wished also like Mr. Ussher, to have a word in the matter. In order to color with a semblance of legality this clemency, *à la Pierrot,* which consisted in *commuting,* a month's imprisonment into *perpetual banishment,* they distributed in profusion through the stupefied city, a proclamation, in which they made the President say, among other things:

"M. Joseph Courtois, having been pronounced guilty of an *unseasonable* article, had been delivered up to the sword of the law. The country awaited justice for this blamable and imprudent conduct; but yielding to my principles of humanity, and also to the generous solicitations of the Consuls of France and England, made in the name of their respective Governments, I have exercised the right of pardon, reposed in me by the 129th article of the Constitution. Since this act of clemency, Sieur Courtois has requested permission to quit the soil of the Republic; I have thought it best, for the interest of order, to *profit* by this disposition, to remove from our hearths such a subject of discord."

A monumental proclamation!—and which denotes an immense progress in the constitutional prudery of the blacks!

VII.

A negro Solution.

Happy in getting rid of this affair, upon such good terms, the yellow and black *bourgeoisie* passed, from rage, to an excess of condescension. The Senate, the very first, reviewing the reductions, it had made in the budget, voted, without calculation, all the money Soulouque asked for. They desired—but without daring to desire it too much—that the President would understand, in time, the wrong, his ultra-black *entourage* had done him. The opposers of public opinion were reduced, to the timid expression of this wish. Thus the poor black, so easy to confound, had already reached such a degree of power, that the enlightened class, whose nerves he formerly irritated, by his pusillanimity and ridiculousness, was ready to thank him for even letting it live.

These sudden changes of opinion, the manifest proof of his own force, appeared, on the other hand, to calm the superstitious presentiments of Soulouque. The policy of denial lost ground, decidedly, before the policy of perseverance; and through the large rent, he had made in the constitution, the President already embraced, with a look of visible satisfaction, perspectives much more extended than those bounded by his quadrennial power. At all events, he wished to put himself, *en règle*, with the future; and one morning, the 31st of December, 1847, Soulouque espoused without noise Madame Soulouque; who, not less provident, had already given an indirect pledge of the perpetuity of the future dynasty.*

All this is a curious side of Haytien manners, and we will again return to it. It is sufficient to say, that, under the circumstances, the marriage of Soulouque was equivalent to a political manifesto, and, created a sensation, in this view. This will be understood, if we remember that the two mulatto founders of the Republic, Pétion and Boyer, had successively espoused Mademoiselle Jute, only in the presence of the Supreme Being; whilst the black autocrats—Toussaint, Dessalines, and Christophe—were well and duly married in the church. The approach of the fatal month— the twelfth month—remitted Soulouque to all his terrors; and the 17th of February especially was passed, by him, in inexpressible pangs. I do not know whether the *doll* was finally discovered; but, at a small meeting of his friends, they made so many conjurations, that on the 1st day of March,

---

* Soulouque had, already, by her, a daughter—afterwards the Princess Olive. No male child followed her; so that, by the terms of the Constitution, the Emperor will be compelled to designate his successor by a sealed submission sent to the Senate.

Soulouque was found radiant with health, joy, and pride, in the same presidential palace, where Herard and Pierrot had fallen, and where Guerrier and Riché had died. The negro gods had triumphed.

Tranquil on the score of the spirits ; knowing, by recent experience, that he could dare to oppose men ; and persuaded, in short, on the faith of his *vaudoux* confidants, (certain remarks of whom, on the anniversary had been complacently echoed,) that he had passed this formidable danger of the twelfth month, only, by favor of an evident predestination, Soulouque, openly resumed, the favorite idea of the black chiefs, and of the black party— an idea, that President Guerrier had before, put forth, on his own account—that President Pierrot had, in his turn, followed—and that Riché was about to realize, himself, when he was surprised by death—to wit: Should he be an absolute king, like Christophe ; or a constitutional Emperor like Dessalines ? Soulouque did not comprehend much difference between them, which was, in fact, a great proof of his good sense. In the meantime, this innocent fantasy was complicated with many disquieting anticipations. News had arrived, from Santo-Domingo, that President Santana had had his principal minister shot, as being implicated in a Haytien conspiracy. But, did they know what struck Soulouque in this news? It was not the failure of a conspiracy, which he had bought up ;

it was the vigor displayed by that cow-herd (*hattier*)—a term of contempt, which he used to designate the Spanish chief.

This idea followed him, everywhere; even, into the council of his ministers; where it often happened, that, he interrupted the reading of a report, by some such disturbing question as this: "Do you know that that *hattier* has some character! He has had his prime minister shot! . . . Yes, that *hattier* has some character!" These presidential parentheses ought, frequently, to have made the new ministers quake; but Soulouque applied it, at the time, to the old ones. Apropos of the troubles provoked at Cayes, by the ultra-black party—M. David Troy was arrested at Port-au-Prince, and cast into prison with all his family. As to Gen. Céligny Ardouin, one of the most distinguished members of the colored class, he had been, while hoping something better, expelled from the Chamber of Representatives, under pretext of antipathies, which did not exist. Soulouque persisted, in a word, in the idea, that they conspired against him; and the certainty that the *fetiches* were now no longer in league with this party, gave an entirely new character, to the expression of his perpetual suspicions, which heretofore had been uttered in a tone of complaint.

"I do not desire to exhibit the foolish figure of President Pierrot"—he exclaimed in Creole. "Since I have reached power, without intrigues, I will burn all—I will kill all—rather than . . . . Apropos, do you know that that *hattier*, down there, has some courage?"

Never, certainly, had these suspicions been more gratuitous; for never had the depression of the class, against which they were directed been more profound, nor better justified. The men of color had, no longer, even the expedient of having themselves forgotten, by being lost in the ranks of the black *bourgeoisie*. The ultra-African party pointed them out there, with their fingers. Every Sunday after the parade, a band composed of blacks, the most noted for their hatred to the mulattoes, mingled with the *cortége*, which reättended Soulouque, and at the entrance to the palace, the following scene was regularly enacted, at every recurring presidential anniversary: "President!" said a compeer—"the *black people* ask such and such a thing;"—and one day—"the *black people* wish that all the men of color should be excluded from public employment;"—and another day—"that one of the two colors of the Haytien flag—the red—(emblem of the *sang-mêlés*) might be removed from it;"—and so on, one after another. And observe that this occurred in the month of March, 1848: "the black people" did not suspect, that, at the distance of two thousand leagues, "the white people" imitated them. On the 9th of April, it was feared the secret of this sinister comedy, would be explained.

The speaker of the band, added on that day, to

his previous demands: the reëstablishment of the Constitution of 1816, which changed the presidency to a dictatorship for life; the dismission of the cabinet; and the substitution, of simple secretaries, for the ministers. Soulouque adhered, graciously, to the two last parts of this request, and promised, as to the Constitution of 1816, to obey the "demands of the people, and the armed forces." From this connexity of unconstitutional demands, and cries of proscription against the class of color, was it necessary to conclude, that the policy of stability, and the existence of the class of color, had become inconsistent? Something unusual was announced, at the same time, for the Sunday following, the 16th of April. Was Soulouque about to proclaim the Empire or the Kingdom? This was almost the only question that was proposed; and, notwitstanding, an inexplicable impression of terror responded in more than one breast. On the day indicated, the parade passed off as usual; but, towards the middle of the afternoon, three cannon-shots were fired near the palace, and were immediately repeated by the fort.

At this signal of alarm, so rarely heard—and which announced, to the distance of fifteen leagues around, that the country was in danger—all the inhabitants, as it is prescribed in such case, precipitated themselves, armed, on the public roads. The Generals, Senators, Deputies, and superior functionaries, present in the capital, went, with the exception of the more prudent, to the palace to ascertain the cause of this signal, and to receive orders. They passed through the guard of the President, which occupied, with closed ranks, the interior court. The call to arms beat from every direction. Soon after, a general officer arrived, at the consulate of France, and returned with all the speed of his horse, after having dropped to the consul these words: "It is a scene, *entirely in the family*, which is transpiring. The President assures you that, *whatever may happen*, you need not be alarmed for your countrymen." This general officer was M. Delva; since, the Haytien Minister at Paris.

A few minutes had scarcely passed, when a repeated fire of musquetry was heard, from the quarter near the palace; to which, a great cry of anguish and despair responded from the whole city. Horses of the generals came from that direction, flying in fright, without riders, through a population, which hurried headlong, wild with terror, towards the consulates—and, even, into the houses of the foreigners. The iron-grating, which enclosed, in a great square, the whole precincts of of the palace and its appurtenances, was shut. Within, and near the entrance, Deputy Cérisier-Lauriston, chief of the department of foreign relations, and secretary of the last Haytien mission to Paris, lay gasping, in his blood; his head split open. In the open gallery, facing the court, the dying and the dead were stretched pell-mell; and among the last, two Generals, one of which was a black. A long line of fugitives, whom the balls thinned out every second, escaladed the iron-railing, on the side next the garden; but they were only feebly pursued. The body of the guard threw themselves, precipitately, into the very interior of the palace, massacring, on their way, the mulattoes wandering in the corridors; whilst Gen. Céligny Ardouin dragged himself, all covered with blood, to the bed-chamber of the President, who, hideous with rage, followed the tottering steps of the wounded man, and overwhelming him with menaces of death. The policy of stability had, at length, left Hayti; Soulouque was about to find a solution.

Here we are, and will be for a long time, in blood up to the neck. We are about to see Soulouque heap up, corpse upon corpse, to make a step to the throne; then, having discovered that the stride was too long, redescend quietly to the ground, in order to gather, and add to the pile of victims, a few corpses of the executioners. In the very midst of these saturnalias of negro barbarity, some relative guaranties of order, or, at least, of security, will finally be developed. We are saved from further surprises, in going along. Without knowing it, and as if by instinct, this delirious Caffraria proceeds to state, develope, and, what is more, resolve questions, which, about the same epoch, remained, fortunately, for us, undetermined; this seems to be the privilege of jaded and worn-out civilizations.

VIII.

Massacres—M. Maxime Raybaud—Negro communism.

At the time of the black reaction of 1844, the bandit Acaau, barefooted, and clothed in a sort of linen gown, and coiffed in a small straw hat, appeared at his parish-church, and there made a public vow, not to change his costume until the orders of "divine Providence" should be executed. Then, turning himself towards the negro peasants, assembled at the sound of the *lambis** (a conch-shell,) Acaau explained, that "divine Providence" commanded the poor people: in the first place, to hunt down the mulattoes; and, secondly, to divide, among themselves the property of the mulattoes. As indelicate as appeared this requirement to the higher class, the auditory could not call it in question, since it had the sanction of an *ex-garde champêtre*, strengthened by a lieutenant of the gendarmes; for such was Acaau's position when he announced himself, "General-in-chief of

---

* A large shell, having the inside shaped like an alembic, which the insurgent slaves used as a trumpet. It is nearly like the *caracol* of the half-African peasants of the *campagne de Valence*. But very recently, if the *caracol* resounded in the *huerta*, Valence expected to be pillaged.

the demands of his fellow-citizens." A murmur of disapprobation, nevertheless, ran through the assembly, whilst its attention wandered from some well-clad blacks to a few ragged mulattoes, who were lost in the crowd. Acaau understood it:— " Oh ! those are *negroes !*" he replied, pointing out the mulattoes, in question.

A black, thirty years of age, employed as a laborer at a *guildive* (rum factory) in the neighborhood, then issued from the ranks, and said to the crowd:

"Acaau is right, for the Virgin has said : '*The rich negro, who knows how to read and write, is a mulatto; the poor mulatto, who neither knows how to read, nor write, is a negro!*'" He, then, added earnestly his appeals to those of Acaau. This black was called Joseph ; and, from that day, he was called *brother* Joseph. Having his head bound up, in a white handkerchief, and being clothed in a white gown that confined his pantaloons, which were also of white, he marched along, holding a wax-taper in his hand,* through the bands of Acaau. He edified these bands by his *neuvaines* to the Virgin, and subdued them by

---

* The day, Toussaint Louverture entered on his campaign, with Rigaud, he, also, bound up his head, in a white handkerchief, and, holding a wax-candle in each hand, he prostrated himself at the door of the Church of Léogane—then ascended the pulpit to preach the extermination of the mulattoes. White is the mourning of negroes.

his well-known favor with the god Vaudoux; and whose rare opportunities of conscience, he decided in the hour of pillage, by the binding *distinction:* "*The rich negro, who knows how to read and write is a mulatto,—&c.*"

Negro communism was established, as we see, and nothing was wanting; neither that impartiality of proscription, which understood how to hold the balance even, between the aristocrats of blood, and those of fortune or of education; nor the mystical religiousness of the grandsons of Babeuf; nor even their pacific and brotherly hypocrisy, as witness the bulletin of Acaau, in which, he relates his expedition against the shop-keeping reformists of Cayes. "It was far from our thoughts to give battle," said the paternal brigand; "but we only desired to present our demands, in an *attitude*, which would prove that we held to them." . . . What more natural! As elsewhere, on the 16th of April, on the 15th of May, on the 23d of June, it had been well understood, that, if there was a conflict, it was the reaction alone which would seek it. In fact, at Cayes, as at Paris, the incorrigible *bourgeoisie*, whom they only prayed to be pleased to leave the key under the door, received this request very badly. Let Acaau speak: "I have made known, by a letter, to the municipal council, the cause of our taking up arms. A verbal response, relying upon the Holy-Week, when no serious matter is allowed, was the *only honor* done us; and the same day, at eleven o'clock, in the morning, behold three columns marched upon us. . . . After an hour's combat, victory smiled upon us. We have had to *deplore in the enemy's ranks, the death of many of our brothers.* God willed, that we should have only, one killed, and three wounded. I could have pursued, with advantage, the vanquished army, and entered the city pell-mell with it; but the *sentiment of fraternity restrained our steps."*

Before so much moderation, it would be certainly unjust to deny that: Acaau only desired the good of the mulattoes. But then, fraternity restrained his steps—just long enough, to allow the frightened mulattoes to escape, from their stores and houses, and seek refuge on board the vessels in the roadstead. This done—he decided to direct two columns on Cayes. "They were in the city, by ten o'clock; all having fled before us," added the bulletin, with modest simplicity. *"The justice of our demands are recognized, and property is respected."* What unction! what self-complacency! and above all, what scruples! The justice of his demands once recognized, Acaau had but one care: the respect of property. There was only a change of proprietors.* If, by chance, I am accused of break-

---

* Acaau did not boast. Once installed in the city, he had one or two of his own followers shot, who were detected stealing. In his respect for the rights of property, he had, at the same time, an officer shot, who was suspected of sympathizing with the ex-proprietors, who had taken refuge in Jamaica; and who, in Acaau's opinion, were, apparently, no better than robbers.

ing these reconciliations, I will establish for them many others. Unfortunate innocence plays, for example, in the proclamation of Acaau, the same part that the working of man by man does in certain other proclamations. "The eventuality of national education," that other chord of Acaau's humanitarian lyre corresponded manifestly to gratuitous and obligatory instruction; and he demanded again, in the name of the cultivators, who are the laborers of the lower grades of society, the reduction of the price of exotic commodities, and the increase of the value of their products. The negro socialist had certainly found the clearest and most evident formula of this famous problem of the white Acaaus: reduction of labor and augmentation of wages. We have hit, ourselves, in going along, upon some analogies much more conclusive; but, after these, we can no longer cry out against the counterfeit—if, indeed, the counterfeiters are not on this side of the Atlantic. Let us not forget, that the publication, and the first working of Acaau's programme, dates back to the spring of 1844.

Negro communism failed, like white communism, because of the extreme division of property. The first surprise having passed away, Acaau's army was reduced to a handful of vagabonds, which Guerrier easily brought to reason; which the feebleness, or complicity, of Piérrot recalled on the scene; and which Riché finished by dispersing. Hunted without cessation,—profoundly discouraged by the reception, his fellow-citizens gave the new science—Acaau resolved to abandon, to itself, that society which did not understand him; and, one fine day, he departed, by a pistol-shot in his mouth, for that Icaria, whence he will never return.

Brother Joseph, on his part, renounced casuistry, and opened, as I have said, a shop of sorcery. A little after the Courtois affair, Soulouque, who had so ill-used him, three years before, had him secretly recalled; and the vaudoux priest displayed such skill, in the conjurations, preceding the so much dreaded anniversary of the 1st of March, 1848, that his favor was soon, a secret to no one. The scenes of murder and confusion, in the midst of which, we stopped the reader, were only the reaction of this sudden popularity of brother Joseph.

On seeing their prophet in favor at court, the *piquets* (thus were designated the old soldiers of Acaau, in memory of the *sharp stakes*, with which, they were originally armed)—the *piquets* believed the time had come, to revenge themselves for the wrongs of the police. Having assembled, in the vicinity of Cayes, the theatre of their old exploits, they declared, they would only lay down their arms, when General Dugué Zamor, commanding the southern department—and who, in that capacity, had before hunted them—should be dismissed, as guilty of treason to the government. An officer of the palace was sent to the spot.

Hearing the cry: "Vive Soulouque!" in the two camps, he found the case very delicate, and employed the General, to go and bring verbal instructions from the President. These instructions were confined, to an order, to commit him to prison, without other form of process. The arrest of M. David Troy was connected, with the same incident. Reconciled to the sinister news, which grew out of the Courtois affair, the haste, with which, Soulouque yielded to the caprices of the *piquets*, carried terror into the Southern department, which was the principal seat of the mulatto population. The 9th of April, 1848, three communes of the arrondissement d'Aquin rose, declaring in their turn, through the organ of their military authority, that they would not yield, until General Dugué Zamor was set at liberty. It, by no means, operated to overthrow Soulouque—but to obtain from him, an indirect disclaimer of the threats of pillage and death of the men of color, which the bandits, encouraged by their former success, had already proposed.

I do not know what transpired in the President's mind; but—although he might have been informed of the movement, from the 11th to the 12th—it was not till the 15th, that he issued his first proclamation, against the petitioners (it would be too much to say rebels); and it was not till after a new delay of twenty-four hours, that he decided to have the alarm-cannon fired. On reaching the palace court, the functionaries received the news, that the insurgents were marching upon Port-au-Prince. This information had not the least foundation; was it a pretext prepared by Soulouque? Was it not rather a movement of Similien, and his confederates, to overcome the last hesitation of the latter?

The former Minister of the Interior, M. Céligny Ardouin, reached the President among the first. The latter received him with overwhelming abuse; accused him of being the soul of the "mulatto" conspiracy, and ordered him under arrest. In the state of fury, in which Soulouque was, all explanation was impossible, and the General, silently, gave up his sword to Bellegarde, whom he followed. In leaving the apartments of Soulouque, he was assailed by some subaltern officers, who attempted to tear off his epaulettes. In this brief struggle, two shots were fired almost in succession, at the General, but without hurting him, and he succeeded in reaching, under a shower of sabre-blows, the bed room of the President, where we left him, covered with frightful wounds, and exposed to the fury of Soulouque.

This was only the prelude. At the sound of this double report from the interior of the palace, the troops drawn up near the entrance, quickly faced about, and fired upon the crowd of Generals, officers, and civil functionaries, who occupied the peristyle. The soldiers thought, as they afterwards said, that an attempt was being made on the life of the President. But how happened it that, on that day, contrary to custom, their arms were found loaded? The probability of an ambush is more clearly developed still, by the strange concurrence with this fact of the mysterious orders to close the iron railing, so as to cut off the retreat of the fugitives. If, among the dead and wounded, which strewed the peristyle, there had been found blacks and mulattoes, it would have proved conclusively one thing: that Similien had adopted, with regard to the word *mulatto*, the definition of brother Joseph.

The body of the guard, as I have said, made an irruption into the palace. After only a few moments, either that he thought the massacre was over, or from the tumult, drawing nearer and nearer, of the steps and cries of that human pack of hounds, he feared to see the door of his chamber forced,—the President decided to show himself to the soldiers, whom he was able to restrain, only, by unheard-of efforts, and with the aid of some black Generals. M. Céligny Ardouin owed his life, for the time, to this abrupt diversion. Soulouque was content to have him thrown into a dungeon. Those of the colored Generals, who had been able to conceal themselves, in the apartments, were consigned to the palace, where they were obliged to wait many days, in gloomy fear; and without any information from outside, but the noise of the regular firing, which announced the continuation of the massacres, until their fate was decided upon.

Of the number of persons who had succeeded in escaping through the garden, there were General Dupuy, former minister of foreign relations, and General Paul Decayet, the last commander of the place, who passed, though black, for being devoted to the colored class. This group of fugitives left behind it a train of eight dead bodies, which were interred, be it observed, on the spot where they fell; that is to say, in the earth freshly turned up, by the superstitious excavations of Soulouque. Soulouque took very little care, as we are convinced, in concealing the marks of his vengeance; why, then, this unusual burial? Was it the mysterious complement of some vaudoux conjuration? And did this human oblation go to appease the wrath of the vanquished *fétiche?*

Let us now see what occurred in the city. At the signal of alarm, the national guards, which, at the time, had no colonel, repaired to the army staff of the place, to receive orders, and ask for cartridges. The mulattoes, who, because they were suspected, were more interested than the blacks in manifesting zeal, arrived first; and the vague presentiment of a common danger insensibly reconciled their groups. They were by this very circumstance, pointed out to the suspicions they feared; and the commander of the place, Vil Lubin, said very bluntly to them: "You have nothing to do here—you scoundrels ; go away." Under the circumstances, this exception had nothing encouraging in it. The mulattoes might have believed they were ordered to disperse, the better to arrest them, or perhaps to massacre them singly ; and the scene of terror, which began at that moment, near the palace, corroborated these apprehensions. Without its being concerted therefore, all the armed colored men found themselves reünited on the *Place-Valliere*. They directed their course, from there, to the quay, whence they might hope to escape, if necessary to the vessels, in the roadstead ; and arranged themselves, very confusedly, along the stores. Most of them wanted ammunition. Dessalines, the chief of police, soon came up, and examined them, in detail, and in silence. They cried : "*Vive le President!—Vive la Constitution de* 1846 *!*"

The second cry destroyed the effect of the first ; and some moments afterwards a detachment of the guard, infantry, cavalry, and artillery, under the orders of Generals Souffran, Bellegarde, and Similien, issued by two parallel streets upon the quay. The commander of the *Danaide*, M. Jannin, (whom information, hastily despatched by M. Raybaud, found *en route*) arrived, with four launches armed with mortars, and swivel guns, and manned with all the disposable force of the Corvette. At the time M. Raybaud concerted with him, to take measures for the protection, not only of the fugitives at the French consulate, but also those at the

English consulate, (Mr. Ussher had asked this,) the port-commander presented himself, with a request, on the part of the President, not to disembark the French forces; giving the most positive assurance, that energetic measures would be taken, at once, to protect the consulates, as well as the foreigners.

Similien summoned the men of color to lay down their arms, and disperse. A gun was fired from the ranks of the latter, we are assured, by a young mulatto of the Herard party. The fire soon became general. But, at the first discharge of artillery, the mulattoes disbanded, leaving fifteen dead on the ground; and of this number, was M. Laudun, a former minister. Night, which comes almost instantly in that latitude, permitted most of the wounded to escape, and regain their houses—the remainder were despatched on the spot. Most of the fugitives cast themselves into the sea; a great number of these were killed by the black fishermen, with their oars, or drowned; others, found among the ropes of vessels attached to the shore, were delivered up to the soldiers, and massacred on touching the shore. Gen. Souffran did not neglect this opportunity of clearing himself, in Soulouque's eyes, from all suspicion of connivance with these *"small mulattoes."* He displayed more fury than Similien, and Bellegarde, in this butchery of the prisoners, and the wounded. The launches of the *Danaide,* and those of the merchantmen, in the roadstead, succeeded, in gathering out of the water, some fifty fugitives. Among these, were MM. Féry and Detré, (former ministers,) and Senator Auguste Élie.

The French consulate, where most of the fugitives had gathered, was filled with groans the whole night; every moment new fugitives fled there, and their wives, mothers and sisters, learned from them, what they had suffered. The incumbrance became so great, that M. Raybaud was obliged to make an opening in the wall, which gave an outlet into the adjoining house. The two houses, fortunately, formed outside, but one edifice, and was thus equally protected by the consular flag.

The 17th, at day-break, feeble and intermitting reports of musquetry were heard, terrifying the people much more, than the copious fusilade and cannonade, of the previous evening. The executions began; they were ordered by Bellegarde.— The victims were professors of the Lyceum, merchants, doctors, &c., arrested during the previous night; some because their wounds would not allow them to fly; others, because they thought they might dispense with flight, not having taken any part in the events of the day before. All died with courage. These executions took place, at the end of the street, upon which the English consulate was situated, some seven or eight steps from its flag, and under the very eyes of the consul, and the fugitives gathered there.

The most regretted of those who perished there, was Doctor Merlet, one of the most honorable, and best informed men of the Republic. He fled wounded to the door of the Swedish consulate, which unfortunately was closed, and was there massacred, on the door-sill, with circumstances of great atrocity. This door was riddled with balls; a domestic of the consul, who happened to be behind it, was traversed with several shots. Another young man, happened to rush into the English consulate, and the soldiers dared to enter there, violently, for the purpose of seizing him. The consul then, in full uniform, went to Gen. Bellegarde to invoke the right of asylum for his flag. Bellegarde replied that it was gone. Mr. Ussher, being very much troubled, went to ask counsel of M. Raybaud; and together they went to see the President.

At the entrance to the palace, unhappy females, of the most wealthy families in the city, begged with tears in their eyes, permission to carry away the remains of their fathers, husbands, and sons. They were cruelly refused; and all these bodies were hauled away the next day in carts, and cast, pell-mell, into a trench, near the entrance to, but without, the Cemetery. Yet odious as this useless refinement of cruelty appears to us, it was much heightened in the estimation of local customs, and in the opinion Haytiens attach to the decorum of burial. Whilst nine-tenths of the people live in miserable huts,—whilst the edifices left by our colonists have fallen to ruin, and their negligent inheritors, philosophically, plant bananas in the vestibules of the old seigniorial hotels,—the cemeteries are covered with monuments, which more than one European city might envy. Black and yellow families, even the richest among them, are sometimes, literally, ruined by death. There are many negresses who spend their whole lives, in preparing, and enriching their funeral toilettes; and some poor devils, who dwell under two branches of a tree, live on unwholesome food, and clothe themselves with rags or a sunbeam, are able, by clubbing together, to furnish homeric funeral ceremonies to him among them, who precedes the others to the country of their ancestors.

The guard crowded the court of the palace, resting on their arms, with their feet in blood. They had lost seventeen of their number in the shock of the previous evening; and the funeral orations, uttered in their honor, were as disquieting, in their style, as their sentiments. The two consuls were received with an outburst of disapprobation. At the instant they crossed the steps, a captain, stepped out from his company, and addressing M. Raybaud, wished to know if he came again to "ask pardons." M. Raybaud, of course, did not deign to reply. On their arrival in the hall of reception, the President sent to them the provisional secretary of state, excusing his not being able receive them himself, and enquiring the motive of their visit. A laborious conversation was engaged in, from a distance, thanks to the coming and going of four ministers, between Soulouque and the consuls.

M. Raybaud demanded, energetically, the right of asylum for the consular flags. The President only wished to admit it, in favor of women and children ; requiring imperatively the return of the young man, who had sought refuge in the British consulate. He concluded by insisting on it only, in case it should be Professor Normil Brouard. This last point, on which the President consented, finally, to yield, was that, which gave place to the most lively discussion. But Bellegarde had anticipated all this ; and, without the knowledge of the two agreeing parties, the suspected person, in question, had been already shot.

Before leaving the ministers, the consul told them, it was high time that this horrible tragedy had ceased ; and after having, again, recommended the respect due, not only to the consulates, but also to the dwellings and property of the Europeans, he forewarned them that, for fear of some mistake, the French residents were about to be authorized, by him, to hang at one of their windows a tri-color streamer ; the President consented to this, without much difficulty. The houses inhabited by Frenchmen, became thus, in fact, so many new places of refuge. The consul, besides, reminded them, that a great many of the stores belonging to the natives, contained French merchandise unpaid for, and that in case of loss, demands of indemnity would necessarily result. The word indemnity produced its usual effect, and the ministers pledged themselves, with the most sincere *empressement,* to watch over this matter. This last guarantee was so much the more important, because, every house in Port-au-Prince was either a shop or warehouse; that there is scarcely one of these shops or warehouses where some of our manufactured products are not sold; and that, for want of advances, and especially of individual credit,* almost all the merchants are only, in some sort, depositories of foreign merchandise, upon which they speculate. In a word, without departing, in a single instance, from his consular attributes, M. Raybaud had found the means of covering, with our flag, the whole threatened portion of the city.

Mr. Ussher, who scarcely spoke a word during their interview, retired after this step, and shut himself up in his consular ark, not to appear again for a week, when this deluge of blood, began to recede. Mr. Ussher is a very honest man, who, in private life, enjoys merited consideration, and in a regular situation would hold his rank with much distinction; but in this human hell, in this

---

* Specie is so rare in Hayti, that they borrow it there, at a rate, which varies from 20 per cent. per annum, to one per cent. *a day.* As to credit, it does not exist even by name. Bills of exchange and notes are unknown in commercial transactions.

chaos of unlikely atrocities, where his British rectitude was found wandering astray for two days, Mr. Ussher, we must say, completely lost his mind.

This first measure of our consul was insufficient, nevertheless, to reässure the *bourgeoisie*. The warehouses and shops, even those of the blacks, remained closed. The deserted streets were, only, traversed by patrols and isolated soldiers, with pistols or sabres in their hands, and a few Europeans, whose white skin was their badge of security. Proclamation, after proclamation, was heard, beginning with these words: "*Whosoever &c.*"—and concluding, invariably, thus: "*Shall be shot!*" The usual supply of provisions were not brought in from the country; and, notwithstanding the prospect of famine, the citizens feared, much more than they desired, the arrival of the country-people. The *lambis* had resounded during the day, from many points of the plain, and some colored proprietors had been murdered on their plantations. Towards four o'clock, in the evening, the panic appeared so well founded, that our consul had the cash deposits of the chancellor's house removed to the corvette. The blacks of the vicinity began to flow into the city, and a general conflagration could be foreseen for that night;—but a flooding rain, which continued, from sunset to sunrise, happened to adjourn these terrors.

The 18th, at day-break, the report of a *fusillade*

announced that Bellegarde continued his work of death. One of these new executions took place, near the flag of the English consul, under his eyes, and in spite of his remonstrances. A mulatto, colonel of the staff, was massacred in the court of the palace itself. The last bonds of discipline were visibly relaxed; and we expected, hourly, to see the soldiery, deaf to the voice of their chiefs, rush on the city. An unclean crowd, the habitual auditory of Similien, provoked them, by cries and gestures, through the railing of the palace court. "It is the good God who gives us this!" cried these strange interpreters of Providence, with their frightful *naïveté*, as at the pillage of the Cap. The great apprehension of the moment, on the part of the families decimated by Soulouque, was, that overcome by the savage passions he had let loose, he would, finally, be sacrificed himself. Blood for blood; they considered themselves very happy still, to be sheltered under the axe of the executioner from the poignards of assassins. They soon learned, that the President rewarded, very badly, so much solicitude.

At the news of the dismal evenings of the capital, the pretended insurrection of the South became real, and gained ground. A courier brought the news; and Soulouque, taking, according to his logical habit, the effect for the cause, only saw in it another proof of the "mulatto conspiracy of Port-au-Prince," without being able to comprehend—the wretch!—that if the mulattoes cried out, it was because he bled them. He resolved to go himself, with the greater part of the forces, to the scene of revolt; and declared that he would leave behind him "neither enemy, nor subject of anxiety." The extermination of the yellow *bourgeoisie*, and pillage for the black *bourgeoisie*—these were therefore the double perspectives, for the morrow. M. Raybaud, in his numerous, wanderings about the city, was stopped, before every door, by the black friends of order, who entreated him to interpose. A few distinguished personages of the country gave him secret meetings, in some third house, in order to make the same entreaty. Indeed, he alone was able to attempt a supreme effort. Terror had stifled the voice of the few honest persons, who were yet found among the attendants of Soulouque. The smell of blood, as we have seen, made M. Ussher sick; and as to the consuls of other countries, situated as they were, in their position of merchants, depending continually upon the local administration, they did not enjoy the least influence.

But how could he reach the President? A happy chance—for the Haytiens—served M. Raybaud, at this conjuncture. News of the French revolution of February had reached Port-au-Prince, five or six days before, and the consul wrote, that he desired, as soon as possible, an audience with the President, to give him *official* notification of it.

The pretext was decisive; for Soulouque, being a very scrupulous observer of propriety with respect to foreigners, and especially so, as to us, replied to the consul, that he would receive him, the next day, the 19th, at eight o'clock in the morning. They scarcely doubted at that time, in France, but the revolution of February was beneficial for some purposes. M. Raybaud was received, with a grand display of military honors. The troops, in battle array, presented arms to him, and the President, in full uniform, surrounded by his ministers, and the black Generals of his staff, advanced to meet him, almost to the principal entrance of the palace.

Natually taciturn, especially with strangers, Soulouque hesitated always in introducing conversation. This day, on the contrary, His Excellency took the initiative, by a rolling fire of questions, on the events at Paris—falling, sometimes, into strange enough blunders; but, nevertheless, without going so far as a dignitary of the country, who, the very next day, persisted in taking M. de Lamartine for the *femme à Martin*. Soulouque, evidently, sought to mislead the conversation; and a very marked constraint was depicted on his countenance, when M. Raybaud introduced the real object of his visit.

The struggle was violent; full of irritation at certain moments; and, for a long time, indecisive. Soulouque enumerated, with volubility, his real or pretended griefs against the men of color, and with many repetitions, as he did in the Courtois affair, and his eyes filled with tears of anger. He also often stopped, his voice failing him. Then, he repeated after every pause, with the relentless persistence, with which, he pursued an idea, when he was convinced: "These gentlemen have proposed to me a game—their head against mine; they have lost! It is very mean in them to disturb you, and to take so many ways of paying me. Is it not so consul—that this is very mean?" But M. Raybaud stood firm on his side; and asked, with an equal obstinacy, not only the immediate cessation of the executions, but also a complete amnesty, in consideration of the blood already shed. Soulouque, finally, yielded the first point; but he only allowed, the promise of an amnesty, to be extorted from him, on condition of excepting a dozen names, which he reserved the right to designate.

When the consul was about to leave, General Souffran rushed into the hall, out of breath, telling the President that the French *were taking part with the rebels;* that a launch from the corvette had roamed about the whole night in the *lagunes,* in order to gather up those rebels, who succeeded in hiding in the mangroves; that we held, besides, the collector and the custom-house under the fire of the mortars on our launches; and that *all the Haytiens were indignant at it!*" The Secretary of State, for the interior, Vaval, a man of dirt and blood—who, whilst the consul pleaded the cause of so much misery, manifested, frequently, his impatience—excelled in this feigned anger. Soulouque's face was horribly contracted; all was lost! The consul replied, with mingled surprise and anger, that he promised himself the pleasure of congratulating our sailors, if they had had, in fact, the happiness to save a few more unfortunate persons; that, in politics, the victor of to-day is, often, the proscribed of to-morrow; and that Souffran, himself, *"might be soon in a position to beg that a hand be extended to him."* Vaval and Souffran remained very subdued at this remark; particularly, as these concluding words of M. Raybaud, did not seem very displeasing to Soulouque.

"President!" added M. Raybaud, "of all the persons here present, I am the only one, who is not dependent on you; and my opinion ought therefore to appear, at least, the most disinterested. Most of these gentlemen, in order to give you, in their way, pledges of devotion, flatter, more and more, your resentments, and urge you to the most sanguinary measures, without caring the least in the world, *for the judgment which will be passed on your conduct out of this Island.* I take with me the assurance you have given, and go to disseminate the news of it through the city."

The countenance of Soulouque, finally, relaxed; this appeal to European opinion had produced its usual effect. Moreover, because an incurable mistrust is the basis of his character, all counsel, even the most importunate, the sincerity of which he could not suspect, is calculated to impress him strongly. The President, pressed cordially the hand of M. Raybaud, and concluded, by requesting him to withdraw our launches. The latter promised that their withdrawal would take place immediately after the publication of the amnesty.

The next morning, the amnesty was proclaimed in the streets, to the sound of military music. The consulates were emptied almost completely; but none of the refugees, on board the vessels, dared to land, before three or four days; and then, only, after a scrupulous examination of their consciences, to ascertain if in the last ten months, they had not offended against Soulouque, either by thought, word, deed or omission. The latter intended, in fact, to limit the amnesty to Port-au-Prince, and to the events alone of Sunday. In order the better to assert his rights, in this respect, immediately after his interview with M. Raybaud, he gave orders for the trial—that is, *the condemnation to death*—of the former minister and senator, David Troy, and of many other notabilities, arrested, at the same time, with him.

The family and friends of M. David Troy, implored M. Raybaud to solicit his pardon. But the feeble spring of clemency, which the French consul had twice already succeeded in putting in play, would be so violently strained, by suddenly making a new effort, that it might break. To gain time, was, the only chance, which offered. M. Raybaud, therefore, called on the ecclesiastical superior, and engaged him to explain to the President, to whom he had easy access, that among christian and civilized nations, it is not customary to execute condemned persons during Holy Week; and, especially, on Good Friday, the day appointed for the execution. This touched again the tender cord. His Excellency promised, "in order that it might appear, said he, that Hayti is a *civilized nation*, David Troy will not be put to death until after Easter."

One of the proscribed persons on the excepted list, the former minister, M. Féry, had been rescued by our sailors. Seven others succeeded in reaching the corvette from time to time. The four remaining persons,—MM. Preston, a former president of the Chamber of Representatives—Banse, Senator, and one of the most honorable characters in the country—the merchant Margron, well known for the blind hatred, he had manifested until then against the French name—and finally, Blackhurst, founder and director of the posts, in the Republic—all succeeded, under different disguises, in reaching the French consulate. One of them was pursued; and the consulate, by order of Bellegarde, was surrounded, at a respectable distance, however; but, at the first request of the consul, the President, relieved him of this, at least, importunate attendance. Although the hotel continued to be watched, at night, by a considerable force, the four *proscrits*, (thanks to the devotion of Captain Galland, of the ship *Triton*, from Nantes, who waited for them one night in the midst of the *lagunes*,) were also able, at length, to reach the *Danaide*.

The share of our marines had been as large as it was distinguished, in this mission of humanity, which thus inaugurated, in the midst of the Antilles, our republican flag. The excellent disposition of Commander Jaunin,—the zeal of his officers,—the admirable discipline of his crew, the devotion with which he remained, himself, for seventy-five hours, exposed, on an infected shore, to the ardors of a devouring sun, and to tropical night-storms—in a word, this attitude constantly imposing, without being hostile,—all had given to the measures of M. Raybaud an authority, which it seems could not have been obtained, but in the presence of a station of many ships of war.

Nevertheless, all was near being put again in question. During the day, of the 21st, a real military *émeute* broke out, in the palace court. The troops of the guard, silently worked on, they say, by Similien, vociferated against the amnesty, and demanded pillage as a compensation. The President was no longer master of them; and the report, that Similien was about to be proclaimed, in his place, as the price of this so much coveted pillage, and the appearance of some men of frightful mien, who began to circulate through the streets, with torches of resinous wood in their hands, soon carried the panic to its height. The Corvette was anchored in nearer shore, and our consul had his archives, and flag, carried to an isolated house, sheltered from conflagration, and near the sea. On learning this, Soulouque, in great haste, sent the commander of the place, to inform M. Raybaud, that some measure would be taken to reässure the public mind; and a few moments afterwards, a proclamation was published, which authorized any one to kill, on the spot, whomsoever might be taken stealing, or seeking to burn, any property.

The President departed three days afterwards, for the South, leaving the city under the guardianship (little encouraging) of Bellegarde and Similien. The first few days passed, in mortal fear; then, astonishment succeeded fear; then, finally, thankfulness was added to astonishment. A whole week had passed away, without massacres, pillage, or conflagration! Either Similien, deprived of a great part of the guard, which Soulouque had taken with him, did not dare to risk the attempt,—or, by a reaction of secret rivalry, which already existed between the old and the new favorite, Port-au-Prince experienced, just as Paris did at the same period, the benefits of order, by disorder; and the infamous reaction began to restore what was left of good sense. Bellegarde, who, eight days before, was the terror of the *bourgeoisie*, became its favorite. They were greatly pleased with him, for not doing, or permitting to be done, infinite mischief; and on the 3d of May, a warm address from persons of note thanked him for it. France and Europe, alas! were they not also reduced to fondle some Bellegardes? News from the South was received, and mingled much shadow with all this rose.

Not content with being the heir of the prophet, Acaau,—Soulouque wished to inherit his army. Before leaving Port-au-Prince, and although he had taken away, with him, three or four times more force, than was necessary to reduce the rebels, he thought of appealing to the *piquets*. Their ostensible chiefs were, an old recluse, named *Jean Denis*, one of the most ferocious robbers that the country of Jeannot and Beassou had produced—and a certain *Pierre Noir*, a brigand philosopher, who, after having conquered cities and laid them under tribute, scorned to exchange, for the highest grades of the army, the modest title of *Captain*, which he held from himself alone. In 1847, the commander of an English frigate, threatened to bombard the city of Cayes if reparation was refused for an insult offered one of its officers, by the band of Pierre Noir. He was put directly *en rapport* with the latter, who said to him: "You wish to burn down the city?—On which side will you begin—so that I can go to work on the other? The business will be quicker done." A man, called Voltaire Castor, condemned to forced labor for theft, under Boyer, and who in the galley-prison passed as Colonel of Acaau's staff, was, after Pierre Noir and Jean Denis, the most important personage of the new allies of Soulouque. In order to reünite these, Pierre Noir and Jean Denis, made them rather inexplicit promises; but it was comprehended instantly. Soulouque himself feared to understand it, for his proclamation, on beginning the campaign, said: "The properties are respected—this is our motto!" A recommendation, which did more honor, to the perspicacity of His Excellency, than to the morality of his defenders.

Pierre Noir began by occupying the city of Cayes, which was very peaceable; let loose the malefactors detained in the prisons, and put, in their places, the principal mulattoes of the town.

As to Jean Denis, he threw himself on Aquin and Cavaillon, which were occupied by the body of the rebels, to the number of three or four hundred, and put these to flight, at the first encountre. The greater part of the vanquished, composed of mulattoes, who did not expect any quarter, took refuge in the hills, where many afterwards perished. A hundred and eighty-nine blacks of the wealthy class, who had taken sides with the mulattoes, and who laid down their arms, expecting at least, that their lives would be spared, in consideration of their color, were *garrotted,* and in this condition slain to the last man; so that the following speech of Acaau, and his prophet, was accomplished: *"Nigger rich, he mulatto, &c."* . . Voltaire Castor poignarded seventy of these wretches with his own hand.*

This precaution of the *piquets* was, at least, useless, for the Military Commission, instituted in the suspected communes, killed, according to regulation, almost as fast, and quite as certainly. At Miragoane, his first station, the President began by having his own aide-de-camp, Col. Desbrosses, who was mayor of that city, shot, with a few others. The same day, there were executed, at Aquin, Lelievre, General of Division, two Colonels and two Captains; and, at Cavaillon, deputy Lamarre and Col. Suire. Thirty others succeeded in escaping. General Lelievre, who was designated, in the sentence, as the head of the insurrection, was a paralytic old man; they had to prop him up as best they could, to shoot him. At the same time, there was condemned, at Cayes, another old man, almost an octogenarian, Col. Daublas, (former mayor, and chief of the first commercial house of that city,) Senator Edward Hall, and a dozen superior officers, only one of which, Col. Saint-Surin, had taken an

---

* A short time after, at Aquin, this same Voltaire Castor, armed with a *tromblon*, (a sort of swivel) entered a room where there were stowed away thirty *suspects*, and calmly began to fire upon them, not ceasing to reload and discharge his weapon, until the entire company was shot down. One of these unfortunate people, who was only wounded, succeeded in escaping. In another prison, Voltaire Castor, expedited his work by sabre cuts, not ceasing, as he afterwards boasted, to strike, until his arm fell from sheer fatigue.

active part in the movement. The President issued an order, to have the executions put off until his arrival, which would take place the 9th; but Daublas, and two of his companions, were slain, the day before, by the *piquets*. Souloque, on arriving, appeared very much mortified; not on account of this butchery, but at the disobedience of the *piquets;* and to punish them in his peculiar manner, he spared the lives of the other convicts. Their punishment was commuted to hard labor in public; and they were to be seen from the next day, with some forty others, of like rank, as companions, chained together two and two, traversing the streets of Cayes, from which they removed the filth under the whips of the blacks. The victims of this frightful oppression had never participated, either directly or indirectly, in the rebellion. It was on the simple denunciation of their personal enemies, or their debtors, that they were reduced to this condition.

Not content with exercising his authority, over the band of Pierre Noir, by refusing to grant it fifty heads—Souloque wished to disband it. He therefore, addressed the *National Guards* (the official euphemism of *piquets*,) a proclamation, in which he said: "You have shown yourselves worthy of the country! Peace being now established, return to your firesides, and give yourselves up to your *noble and useful labors*, and repose after your fatigues." To which the *piquets*, replied, that they asked nothing better, than to repose after their fatigues, but that they paid people when they were dismissed. Soulouque thought he would be able to get rid of them, by additional thanks, and a few *gourdes* (dollars.) The *piquets* after pocketing the *gourdes*, said it was not enough. Soulouque concluded, that honor was dearer to them than money, and, to the great discontent of the army, (which ought, besides, to sicken over this chapter) he let fall a real shower of grades upon the bandits.

The African vanity of the *piquets* was taken, at first, by this bait, notwithstanding the abuse Pierrot, and even Acaau, had made of it. During eight days, nothing could be seen in the streets of Cayes but plumes; after which, the bandits, feeling that immense void, left in the heart by human grandeurs, cried out, and, this time, in the tone of menace: "*N'a pas nous, non, ia prend dans piége cila encore!*" (They will not catch us again in this trap!). We must mention, that since their victory, at Cavaillon, their number had considerably increased; and, as usual, the *piquets* of yesterday exceeded, in their demands, those of the day before. As their last demand, they claimed, firstly, for each one of them five squares (carreaux) of land,—not wild, but in full production,—to be taken from the property of the mulattoes; secondly, a few houses in the city for their officers.

On learning, that Soulouque allowed these demands to be discussed in place of replying to them with cannon-ball, the ring-leaders of Port-au-

Prince, who were held in check a moment by Bellegarde, renewed their *ultimatum*, of the 9th of April; having however, added to it, from time to time, some articles, in comparison with which, the claims of the *piquets* were only moderate. By their new programme,—to the acceptance of which they made conditional the reëntrance of Soulouque into his capital,—the friends of Semilien besides the dictatorship,—a flag of a single color,—and the deposition of the last mulatto functionaries,—demanded: pillage of the warehouses of the mulattoes—the confiscation of all the houses belonging to them, except one a piece—thirty of their heads—banishment of a great number,—and (observe) of these, four black generals,—among which the name of their former friend, Bellegarde, figured, having become, decidedly, a reactionist. The friends of Similien claimed further, that the Government, (that is to say Soulouque,) should seize the *monopoly of products for exportation*, and that he should cancel the debt for French indemnities (this was, as we know, the equivalent of our millions to the emigrants) "considering," they said "that this indemnity had been agreed to by mulattoes, *since banished, or declared traitors to the country;* and, who had treated with the agents *of a king, who no longer existed.*"

Yet if what transpired, in the spring of 1848, is well remembered, and that the friends of Similien were unable to read, (which doubly removes the suspicion of imitation,) it will be difficult to deny the ubiquity of the social and democratic cholera.

IX.

The scruples of Soulouque—A negro *impromptu*.

We have to deal no longer with a poor irresolute negro, whom a feverish want of sympathy, from the enlightened class, kept, unconsciously, on the side of barbarism. The heap of corpses, which interposed between that class and himself, had broken the charm. Of the two men, which we have seen in Soulouque, henceforth there only remained the savage; a savage who had suddenly obtained a revelation of his strength; and who—proud of imposing the terror, which only seemed small in his estimation—drunk with joy in feeling himself free from the invisible bonds with which the intrigues of men and *fétiches* had fettered him—convinced of the legitimacy of his griefs, and the predestination of his vengeance—rushed, through the first opening which offered, to the gratification of his appetites for hatred and tyranny. Nevertheless, there is a kindness of government, which belongs to the *rôle* of power; and, if, as it is often seen, the most systematic and inveterate prejudices of opposition cannot resist this evidence of government responsibility, is it astonishing that this influence captivated an ignorant and brutish mind, which no preconceived opinion misled, simply because it had no opinions? The instincts of the savage would, even, in this case recoil before absurdity, almost as soon as the reason of the sophist. The only difference in favor of the second, is that the sophist being undeceived, would be able to generalize, for his own use, each of the revelations of experience, while the savage would see, nothing, beyond the present cause, and its immediate effect. It is unnecessary to seek, any further, for an explanation of the abrupt incoherencies—the alternations, from perfect good sense, to ferocious imbecility—which the character of Soulouque is now about to display.

The request of the *piquets* had, certainly, nothing in it, which could offend the notions of natural right, that might exist in the brain of a negro tyrant. To take a part of their property from the mulattoes, who, in his opinion, had endeavored to take power and property from him, was, in the eyes of Soulouque, almost an indulgence. He, nevertheless, received this request, very unfavorably. At the very time, that some civilized politicians, (who believed nothing could be done but by conciliation,) allowed themselves to compound with similar petitions, Soulouque, of himself alone, foresaw, that the property to be divided being limited, and the number of *piquets* threatening to become unlimited since being favored, their demands increased by reason of the difficulty of satisfying them. Hence, there was only one step, in order to conclude, that it was necessary to avoid all transactions with the *piquets;* and, although there was yet time enough, to disperse these national workshops of a new kind. But if, the instinct of the chief shrunk, from the country tastes of the bandits, the logic of the savage could not resign itself, to consider as dangerous—and to treat as rash— those, who manifested so much zeal against his pretended enemies.

In order to reconcile all, in his way, Soulouque struck, they say, the difference between them; while refusing to surrender the property of the mulattoes to the *piquets,* he abandoned their proprietors to them. Those pardoned on the 9th of May—Senator Edward Hall and his companions in misfortune—were the first installment of this tacit agreement. Soulouque consented that they might be massacred the 1st day of June. This done, the *piquets* began to hunt down the mulattoes, of the country; burned, killed, and robbed, under the very eyes of the black authorities, who kept silent, or approved of it.

From the mulattoes, the band of Pierre Noir passed to Europeans; and some Frenchmen, themselves were maltreated, and extorted—not excepting our own consular agent, at Cayes, whose residence the bandits devastated. At this news, Soulouque, whose letters to Bellegarde, invariably, terminated with this recommendation : *"Let us have no diffi-*

culty with the French!"—Soulouque was ready to sink, with anger and fright. This was the opportunity, if ever, to break with the *piquets*. At Torbeck, Port-Salut, Cavaillon, l'Aanse-d'Hainaut, Aquin, Saint-Louis, and other theatres of their exactions and atrocities, the people wanted but a mute sign, from the President, to get rid of this handful of wretches. At Jacmel the black garrison, and the mulatto *bourgeoisie*, had even taken the initiative of resistance. A band, which attempted to penetrate this city, by violence, was, vigorously, repelled, leaving behind some forty of their number prisoners; and there was no doubt, but that the President would permit an example to be made of them. But Soulouque reflected, in the meantime, that if the *piquets* happened to give him new embarrassments, with respect to foreigners, they had given new proofs of their zeal, with regard to the mulatto conspirators; and, seeing, that it would be inconsistent, to confound reward and punishment upon the same heads, His Excellency gave, simultaneously, the order to make reparation to the foreigners, by indemnifying their losses, and to give the piquets satisfaction, by throwing into prison the most respectable colored inhabitants of Jacmel, of whose services, the black authorities were, besides, deprived. We foresee the rest; the *piquets* continued to maltreat the foreigners, to the great anger of Soulouque, who was overwhelmed, anew, in reparations and excuses, but whom, they were sure of disarming, by fresh violence against the "*mulatto conspirators.*"

This negro version, of what is called, the see-saw policy, Soulouque applied to every thing. So far from opposing any obstacles, to the emigration of the yellow class, the authorities seemed, at first, to view it with a favorable eye. But the greater part of the emigrants, as I have said, being retailers, whose flight would prejudice the foreign consignees, these complained loudly of it.* Soulouque was so much the more affected, by this demand, because the most certain part of his revenues, (it will be henceforth folly to say the revenues of the government,) accrued, from duties on importations and exportations; that is to say, from bartering with foreign countries. Emigration was, therefore, rigorously prohibited; a decree denounced the emigrants, with civil death, and perpetual banishment. This very severity was of good omen; as it seemed to indicate, that the thought of reviving commerce, animated Soulouque; and, as a consequence, the termination of this system of terror, which depopulated the shops, and filled up the cemeteries and prisons.

Unfortunately, Soulouque reasoned thus—that emigration being prohibited, the mulattoes would

---

* We are ready to prove that none of our countrymen took part in this demand. Loss for loss—they preferred to see their debtors escape, than be killed.

remain in the country; that by remaining in the country, they would only be the more able to conspire; and this increase of danger could only be counterbalanced by additional precautions. As the first increase of precautions, he gave orders to have all the able-bodied mulattoes of Port-au-Prince enrolled, in order to watch over them more easily; and this press of mulattoes condemned, a great number of shops, to inactivity, which neither emigration, nor the executioner had yet made vacant.* As a second increase of precautions, (and it was well that the trifling insurrection of the South had ceased for want of insurgents,) Soulouque redoubled his fury against the mulattoes of that part of the Island. It is easy to understand, how it was that commerce was not benefitted by all this. A few men of color, who by this triple scourge, of forced enrollment, the *piquets*, and the military commissions, had not yet been driven from their warehouses, were compelled to seek, a last chance of safety, in clandestine emigration. And emigration was not limited to men; the vessels which coasted along this accursed country, already deserted by almost every flag, encountered every day at sea, miserable launches, filled with women and children, endeavoring to reach Jamaica. Incensed, at so much unwillingness, Sou-

---

* Many public administrations were even compelled, to suspend their functions, for the want of persons able to write.

louque was transported, with additional fury, against the mulattoes, who were so much the less excusable in his eyes, because he never ceased to proclaim, *his reliance upon them*, in the orders of the day—like the following:

"Haytiens! a new era has arisen for the Republic! The country having thrown off the shackles of all the *heterogeneous elements which obstructed its progressive march, has become prosperous*. The greater part of the traitors have sought refuge on foreign soil. . . . Citizens of Cayes! I will soon leave your city, to *explore* the rest of the Southern department. My stay here has restored *calm to the public mind;* and I am happy to say, that this calm and *security* have been noticed in, all parts of the Republic. . . . etc., etc."

In fact, he left Cayes the 2d of July for Jérémie, a city which had been very tranquil for many years, and vainly flattered itself to escape this terrible visitation. Besides a portion of his guards, and three or four regiments of the line, he carried with him a band of *piquets*, who scattered along the whole *route*, robbery and assassination;—some thirty Generals, that, through mistrust of their disposition towards him, he held under his hand;—a military commission to whom he delivered, from time to time, one of these Generals;—and a cloud of informers in rags, who, at every halt of the President, played the part of people in scenes like those, a recital of

8

which we have borrowed from an order of the day, of the 16th July:

"Haytiens! the population of Jérémie, which awaits the arrival of the Government chief, in order to make known to him their griefs and wishes, assembled in that city, the 13th of this month. *Orally and by petition* they have denounced as traitors to the country—" (Here follow the names of *fifty-seven* of the principal citizens; they were functionaries, whose places the staff of the *piquets* coveted, or merchants who, to their misfortune, had had dealings with the friends of the *piquets*. In his diseased predisposition to believe in the sincerity, and devotion, of all those who flattered his suspicions, Soulouque considered nothing further). "Haytiens"—added this head of the Government, in an impulse of paternal solicitude—"Haytiens, the citizens of Jérémie, who, like those of every other part of the Republic, *aspire to that peace which leads to happiness*, demand justice of these accused persons, whom they declare to be the only obstacles to public tranquility, in the *Grande-Anse*. You want peace—*you shall have it*. I promise it to you; I swear it by this sword, with which, you have armed me in defence of your honor, and the glory of Hayti. This sword shall never be returned to the scabbard, as long as there shall be left one of these perjurers to strike, who conspire the ruin of the country." In fact, they arrested the perjurers, in question, tried, and executed them.

One might be surprised, that having the *piquets* under his hand, Soulouque should have sacrificed, to prejudice, judicial proceedings. This is to be very ignorant of the individual. The law gave him military commissions, and he would have thought himself, deprived of one of his prerogatives, if they had demanded that he should yield them. It was, besides, a means of testing the suspected officers of his *suite*, to require them to sit, in these commissions, when, by chance, the accused person, might be one of their friends. The sentence was distinguished in such cases, by its sad brevity. The commissioners, being forced accomplices of assassination, wished, at least, to divide among themselves the sarcasm of a judicial parody. On the contrary, the military commissions, which were filled up from the ultra-black party, heightened by the luxury of forms their constitutional impudence. We have under our eyes many *proces-verbaux*, of these commissions. We read in them, almost constantly this phrase: "The informer has set forth the accusation, *but has produced no evidence.*" And this other: "The President has enjoined, upon the advocates, that they must say nothing against their consciences, nor contrary to the respect due to the laws, but they should express themselves, with *decency*, and moderation; and, that every offender shall be condemned *to a punishment, which will be defined by the law.*"

The advocates understood this, at a glance; and, in order not to be exposed to the retroactive effect of the *future* law, with which, they were threatened, they sang with stifled voices, and in guise of pleading, the praises of the Government chief. This formality through with, the *accuser persisted in supporting his accusation*, continuing, of course, not to produce any evidence of the charge. The vote was taken; and the council, *having seen the articles, &c.*, invariably condemned the *said accused to the punishment of death, inasmuch as the public order had been compromised*. It was in like manner, for example, that Senator Edward Hall was tried and condemned.

There was another feature, not less characteristic. The text, cited to sustain the conviction of this Senator—who was not a military officer, and had been put on his trial only under the pretext of conspiracy—was the 25th article of the military code, which applied, not to conspirators, but to *soldiers*, or persons attached to the army, who should have exposed any Haytiens to the effect of reprisals, either by committing acts not approved by the government, or in acting contrary to its instructions. Some text was necessary for these terrible boobies, and this had, at least, the merit of originality and surprise.

Again, among others, in the trial of the venerable Daublas, the President, in order to spare the scruples of his colleagues, altered, of his own authority, the decisive question—to wit: "*Is it certain that the accused, etc?*"—and said: "Is it certain, *or is it probable, etc?*" Then, in default of any evidence to the charge, the sentence was based on *some probabilities*, as thus: "seeing the *position of things*, and considering to what extremities men are carried, who are always seeking to annoy, and interrupt, the progress of government, by constantly intriguing to produce a *change* of the Executive *every year*, (an allusion to the *fétiche* hidden in the palace garden) which is very prejudicial to the country—and, finally, considering that these Messieurs, enemies of their country, have proved their designs, *by that pistol-shot which Céligny fired at the President personally*, (vaudoux version of the two pistol shots fired in the presidential palace at General Céligny Ardouin)—by these facts, the council. . . (*passing by the conclusions of the public minister* who had apparently abandoned the accusation)—condemn the aforesaid accused (Daublas) to the punishment of . . . death."

This frightful tribute of blood had been almost exclusively, at first, levied on the colored *bourgeoisie:* senators, deputies, generals, and superior officers, magistrates, merchants, and great proprietors, paid their contingent with resignation; when a black General of Division, named Télémaque, who commanded the arrondissement of Cayes was put, in his turn, upon trial in company with all the superior officers of his staff.

Not finding a shadow of guilt to their charge, and believing they could swerve in favor of the accused blacks, from the office of executioners, which was imposed upon them, in regard to the mulattoes, the military commission dared to acquit the prisoners. Soulouque instantly gave orders to have them *rejudged*, and to *make an end of it this time*—they obeyed; the General and his staff were massacred with great parade, on the principal square of the city. A short time afterwards, another black General, named Brice, was arrested on the Dominican frontier, and conducted, with a part of his staff, to the prison at Port-au-Prince, from which he was only released on becoming a maniac. The execution of David Troy, whom they thought had been forgotten in this prison until the return of the President, again sealed the bloody brotherhood which the latter renewed between the two colors.

Yet, though no suspected murmur arose from that vast solitude—half desert, half cemetery, which he had created in the peninsula (terror restricted itself to lamentations)—Soulouque suspected that order was scarcely reëstablished, and he returned to Port-au-Prince on the 15th of August. On entering the city, he and his troops passed through a succession of triumphal arches, ornamented with enthusiastic legends, upon which His Excellency deigned in passing, to cast the occasional look of a connoiseur, saying: "this is very pretty." The report spread, that the President had learned to read,* and the noisy delight of the "black people" was thereby increased. It was no longer the good will, which should exist between vaudoux coreligionists—it was a mixture of curious veneration, and pride, which urged that eagerly obedient crowd to welcome the transfigured Soulouque; respect for whom, was fear, and whose only sceptre was an axe.

Some scene of massacre was, at first, feared; and many colored families, solicited an asylum in the consulates; but yielding to the new impressions, which existed all about them, the two or three hundred scoundrels, who, for the last two months, had boasted, that Soulouque should not return to the city, but upon certain conditions, now dissimulated as much as possible. The city was illuminated for three evenings; and the houses of the mulattoes—houses which proscription or murder had visited—were distinguished above all the others, for the garlands of palms, and wreaths of leaves, which gave them an additional decoration.

From the marked coolness, which he exhibited to Similien, it was easy to believe that the President, himself, had returned to more peaceable

---

* Soulouque, in fact, exercised himself, secretly, in reading; and we are assured that printed letters were already without mystery to His Imperial Majesty. Soulouque did not make less progress in writing.

opinions; but this delusion did not long continue. Among the innumerable *suspects*, who, not being able to fly from this land of sorrow, filled the prison at Port-au-Prince, three were under sentence of death; these were Gen. Desmarêt, who had a command on the Dominican frontier—a colonel, and a magistrate. Some persons dared to hazard an application to the President, to spare their lives, at least; they only succeeded, in putting him in a state of frightful nervous excitement. M. Raybaud was entreated to attempt a last effort to save them.

Soulouque received the consul-general, with his usual warmth and courtesy; but, not without the constrained smile, he had prepared for the occasion, becoming fixed on his lips, which were agitated by an involuntary trembling. For the first time, in three months—during which, he mowed down yellow and black, without creating about him, any other murmurs than those of the falling bodies,—he found himself in the presence of a man, who dared to think and say, that Christian blood ought not to be shed like water. From the first moment of that long interview, Soulouque raved with anger.

M. Raybaud waited, until this torrent had passed by, when he set before him the numerous reasons, which the interests of the country, and those of the President himself, could suggest. Soulouque, apparently overcome by lassitude, renewed, with a sort of calm, his favorite argument: "that the mulattoes having proposed to him a game, and having lost, 'it was very mean in them to disturb the consul, instead of paying gracefully.'" But, by degrees, expression following, with difficulty, the swelling flood of thoughts, which pressed in tumult through his head, incoherent words succeeded to phrases, and monosyllables to words. At the end of an hour, the consul was less advanced than on entering. At length, Soulouque said: "*If my mother should issue from the grave, and fall at my feet, her prayers would not save them!*" After this oath "by my godmother"—(the most terrible oath that a Haytien negro can make)—M. Raybaud replied—"Grant me, at least, one of them." "The *half of one* if you wish," replied Soulouque; and, this time he managed to smile.

The savage had conquered; and he celebrated his triumph, in savage fashion—half laugh, half anger. Let us, however, remark that this formal revolt, persisted in by Soulouque, against the man who represented, in his eyes, French civilization, was only an indirect consequence, although a logical one, of the feeling which had induced him to yield, twice before. It was about the end of August; all the details of this European melo-drama were, therefore already known in the Antilles in one hundred and twenty days, on which the victory of June dropped the curtain. Soulouque who read, eagerly, the journals of France, and the United States, was delighted (as not long before he was on the subject of Santana) at the proofs of character given by the democrats from Madrid to Berlin; and it is, only, because the black chief piqued himself, upon borrowing from civilized Europe his opinions and clothes, that we can understand what new turn his dispositions had received from this influence. M. Raybaud in endeavoring to impose clemency on him, in the same way he had done the past year, was evidently rather suspected: '*the whites only ridicule the negroes,*' he would say.

However, the three condemned persons at Port-au-Prince had not yet perished; this is explained by negro physiology. During the first revolution, Commissioner Sonthonax, in order to perfect the new freed-men in republicanism, wished to introduce the guillotine at Port-au-Prince—then *Port-Republican.* A white man, named Pelou, a native of Rouen, suffered the costs of the first experiment. A compact mass of blacks, whom Jeannot, Biassou, Lapointe and Romaine-la-Propétesse, had surfeited, on every human atrocity, surrounded the place of execution. But, either the wind, that day, had a particular influence on the African nervous system, or, the terrible effect of the machine, bewildered the notions of these simple men, who had never put the whites to death except, inch by inch,—the head had scarcely fallen, when a prolonged howl of grief and fright, went up from the front rank of the spectators; and was, by degrees, communicated to that portion of the crowd, which had seen nothing, by means of that animal electricity, an example of which the *vaudoux* has already furnished. In a few seconds the guillotine was torn to pieces—and has never since been erected in Hayti.

More than fifty years afterwards, a similar scene transpired in Port-au-Prince. Soulouque ordered, that the executions should take place at Las-Cahobas, a village on the Dominican frontier. The three condemned men, in fetters, set out on the journey, under guard of a hundred and fifty policemen, and an entire regiment of infantry, towards this destination. But, whilst passing through the city, their sad and resigned bearing excited among the women, such an impulse of sympathy, such a tempest of cries and tears, that the effect became contagious and extended even to the blacks. In spite of the efforts of the soldiers, every body precipitated themselves towards the condemned men, embraced them, and squeezed their hands. The soldiers and officers, finally, could not restrain it; and soon afterwards, the most violent murmurs broke out, even in the ranks of the escort against so much cruelty. The dismal cortége departed, nevertheless, from the city, and marched for four hours, towards Las-Cahobas; but, either his own nerves had been shaken by this scene, or, because of the universal reprobation, which spontaneously assailed it, he wished to give himself time to reflect,—the President sent an order, to have the condemned men remanded to prison.

At night-fall, they, therefore, passed again

through the city, preceded, surrounded, and followed, by a compact mass of people of all colors, drunk with joy, who shouted, "*vive le President!*" It might have been remarked that the blacks of the quarters, Morne-á-Tuf and Bel-Air—those who were the most hostile, and excited, against the mulattoes,—shouted, laughed, and wept, more vehemently than any others; and the city being spontaneously illuminated, these quarters presented the most splendid illumination.

All was saved. Paper-money rose more than a quarter; the orators of Morné-á-Tuf proclaimed, that the mulattoes possessed some merit; and that, after all, they had suffered enough. Even Soulouque appeared to experience the contagion, decidedly; for, (what had not happened since the beginning of this reign of terror, even to the few *suspects* acquitted, here and there, by the councils of war) he, successively, caused fifteen, of those detained, to be freed; the most insignificant, it is true, of the five or six hundred persons who filled the dungeons at Port-au-Prince. But, three weeks afterwards, the enlargements ceased; the arrests begun; the President had eight of the principal colored inhabitants of Jacmel shot, of whom the *piquets*, as I have said, had complained. The populace of Port-au-Prince, insulted and menaced, not only, the mulattoes, but even the black *bourgeoisie;* and the country people, finally, spoke more than ever of coming to pillage the city. This was a financial experiment of Soulouque.

X.

The conspiracy of capital in Hayti.

Hayti presents this miracle of credit—a paper-money, not resting upon any metallic, or territorial pledge—a paper money, which the Government issues, at discretion, reserving the right, to redeem it when it pleases, and at such rate, as it pleases; and which, moreover, it declares spurious money, by refusing to receive it, in payment for importation duties. And notwithstanding all this, at the close of twenty years, on the accession of Soulouque, it still circulated, for about *one-fifth* of its nominal value. In other words, in 1847, about seventy-two *gourdes* of paper, (the real gourde is worth 5 francs and some centimes,) was necessary to represent one *doubloon*—that is, a Spanish gold-piece of 85 francs value.

The Haytien *gourde* has, as we see, a well determined character. The scenes of the month of April, and the terror following them, did not fail, nevertheless, to affect it. What has preserved its currency, until now, is the fact, that the importers of foreign merchandise, accepted it, from the retailers, thanks to the certainty of their being able to pass it, immediately, to the planters, in payment for their coffee. The planters receive it in preference to specie, which they mistrust much more. But the murders and imprisonments; the flight of the greater number of the retailers; and the serious fears, which such a condition of things caused the importers to feel, with regard to the solvency of others—arrested transactions; and as a consequence, the circulation of the *gourde*.

The little coin, which remained in the country, had also contributed, until then, to sustain the *gourde*—either by entering for a part stipulated beforehand, in the agreements—or, by supplying, as odd-money, the insufficiency of change, in the transactions of the retailers with consumers. But the *proscrits* and the fugitives, knowing very well that the Haytien paper-money, outside of Hayti, was worth only so much paper, had swept off, in leaving the Island almost all the metallic currency. This double support being wanting, the *gourde* suddenly lost more than a third of its current value.

The duties on importations are the principal resource of the Haytien treasury; in consequence of interrupting trade, the public revenue diminished, therefore, more than a half. This reduction of receipts, coinciding with the expedition to the South, and the levy *en masse*—that is, with an enormous increase of expenses—the ministers were soon compelled to announce, tremblingly to Soulouque, that funds were wanting. "We must make them," calmly replied the Executive. And the fabrication of paper-money—which was only done, occasionally, so as not to lose the art—was briskly carried on, to an issue, of from *fifteen, to twenty thousand gourdes* a day. But the notes, unfortunately, had this peculiarity—that the quantity, far from making up for the quality, injured it. The little foreign commerce which still supplied the daily consumption,* and, as a consequence, the Haytien retailers,† who were the intermediaries of this trade, at length refused, therefore, to accept the *paper-gourde* but at the rate of 185 to the doubloon, (nearly the *twelfth* of its nominal value.)

The "black people" have so entirely lost the use of money, properly so called—are so entirely accustomed to use notes as a normal money—that, taking (as the "white people" have done already, and with still less reason) the effect for the cause, they consider this depreciation of the representative value of the *gourde*, as a real rise in the price of products. Two facts have aided in producing this mistake. Firstly, the government, which cannot, honestly, encourage a depreciation, already so rapid, continues to pay off the civil and mili-

---

* This country, the richest in the world, is compelled to obtain from abroad, the fourth part of its articles of prime necessity—such as, meal, meats, salt-fish, soap and all articles of dress.

† By the terms of the law, all the retail-trade is the exclusive privilege of the citizens of Hayti.

tary functionaries, at the rate of the nominal valuation of the *gourde*. In the second place, as it is natural, that wages should fall in proportion to the diminution of transactions, and the emigration of the wealthy consumers, the day-laborer, because of this fall, continues, not only to receive the same number of notes for the same amount of labor, but, not being able to comprehend, that his work is valued less, he therefore concludes, from the acknowledgments even of capitalists, that the real value of the note has not varied. Therefore, there was a conspiracy, between the foreign merchants and the retailers, to starve the poor people, and to oblige them to pay, for products of first necessity, twice and a half dearer than in 1847; therefore, it was necessary to give a lesson to this infamous capital. The infamous capital, which they wished to oppose by mildness, only became the more ferocious by it, and the "black people" saw in this increased defiance, only a new proof of the conspiracy, in question. The financial programme of the friends of Similien—that is, pillage, combined with the industrial, and commercial monopoly of the government—responded (May and June, 1848) to this double prejudice.

The feeble hope of security, which, the pardon granted to General Desmarét and his companions, produced, reäcted on the *gourde*, which, from 185 to the doubloon fell, suddenly, to 150; but it was a depreciation, at least, of a hundred per cent., in comparison with the valuation of 1847 ; and the first outburst of African sensibility having passed by, the common people, recommenced their complaints, against the conspiracy of the merchants. Besides, when the French, English and American shippers had been informed, in the interval, of what occurred at Hayti, it happened that all arrivals from abroad ceased, (in September, the roadstead of Port-au-Prince had only a single foreign vessel in it,) just at the time, the small quantity of supplies, which remained in circulation, were consumed. Hence a rise in the price of products, (this time too real,) which was a new cause of popular effervescence, and commercial panic ; and the gourde was restored to 185.

The army, which, because of this depreciation, was compelled to feed and lodge itself, at the rate of *six centimes* a day to the man,—the subaltern officers, who, with their *hundred francs* a year, were reduced to ask alms, when they were not employed as laborers,—and the innumerable civil functionaries who made the counterpart of an effective military, proportionally seven-fold as great as our own, and who, seeing the hardness of the times, had not even the resource of pillage—all this world of gold-lace, and rags,—shouted famine, as loudly, as the common people. The Government was alarmed at it; and, in order to divert the storm, it became very necessary to encourage those prejudices, which it could only have dissipated, by avowing itself the author of all the evil. It proclaimed, therefore, on two occasions, that, it was about to put a stop, to the *outrageous rise in all the articles of consumption;* caused, it is said, by the enemies of the people,—only a part of which had succombed, to the sword of the law,—and by the bad faith of Haytiens, who *conspired* against the public good, *otherwise than by arms.*

On seeing the Government completely of their opinions, the black people understood at least, that they might leave the instrument itself of conspiracy, in the hands of the enemies of the public weal, and yet, the warehouses would not be pillaged. The panic reached its height. Fortunately, Soulouque and the Secretary of State for finances, M. Salomon, only intended to accept the second part of the financial programme of Similien ;—that is, monopoly complicated to the utmost—which was returning to the old idea of Acaau. M. Salomon, himself, for a long time, caressed this idea; and it was by this title, that the Similien faction, had given him, on the 9th of April, the portfolio of Finance.

The Government, however, at first, only monopolised two articles of export—cotton, and (the principal of all) coffee. It reserved the right, to monopolise these two articles, at fixed prices, and to distribute them among the merchants. The price of selling by wholesale, the greater part of foreign merchandise, was also fixed by the administration. The mere announcement of a system, which was about to give, in fact, a fixed and forced currency to the *gourde*, produced, let us acknowledge, one of the results M. Salomon expected; from 185 *gourdes* to the doubloon, paper fell again to 110. But this was, only, the consequence of a series of mistakes, more and more decisive, which we ask permission to enumerate briefly, and in order not to return again to it. The favorite excuse of white socialism is, that they have not been willing to put it to a trial. But the experiment has been made; it was a veritable socialistic experiment that Soulouque made.

First error: When the Government found itself, face to face, with the necessities of practice, it comprehended, willing or unwilling, that Hayti, not being the only country of America, which sold coffee, and bought meal, salt-provisions, soap, tissues, &c., all *tarification* of the one, or the other class of products, which would be onerous to foreign commerce, would only end in driving the latter from the national markets. Prices ought, therefore, to be so fixed, that the foreign merchants would not complain of it, and, really, there would be no demands; proof positive that these merchants could lose nothing, and, as a consequence, the producers and consumers gained nothing. Thus, the fundamental data of the system:—diminution of the price of foreign merchandise—and augmentation of the price of domestic products were abandoned, even before this system went into operation. Further, it was necessary to institute, in each of the eleven ports, open to importation, an *administration of monopoly;* that is, new machinery, and a new *intermediaire*, to use a technical term. The expenses, occasioned by this new *intermediaire*, would not fall, (for the reasons I have given,) on foreign commerce; and before however, burdening any one, they would fall, necessarily, either directly or indirectly, on the native sellers and buyers, whose situation, in consequence, was found aggravated.

Second error: The crop of coffee was, by chance, very poor that year; socialism did not insure against these kinds of accidents. Under the *règime* of free competition, high prices compensated the cultivators, for the scarcity of their products; but, as one of the objects of the law was, precisely, to give some fixity to the *gourde*, by making prices certain, —as, on the other hand, the government, after having taken away, from foreign commerce, the advantages of free competition, could not, at the risk of driving it away, impose on it charges, by a great increase of the fixed prices—the tariff was not altered. The deficit of the coffee crop was thus transfered to agricultural labor, (which they had pretended to benefit) by a clear loss.

Third error: Under the *règime* of free competition, certain ship-captains, by favor of older and more extended relations than those of their rivals, would succeed, in spite of the deficiency of the crop, in completing their cargoes. Many other vessels, it is true, would have to leave empty;—but their captains, or their agents, could only attribute it to the want of activity. From the time, on the contrary, that the Government monopolised the sale of coffee, at the risk of deserving the reproach of partiality, and driving away forever, from the Haytien market, the rejected importers, it could not exclude a single vessel from its share. The distribution was therefore made *pro-rata*, according to the value of the merchandise introduced. It resulted from this method of division, that a vessel such as had imported a cargo of the value of 50 or 60,000 francs, obtained, only, at great pains, and after long delays, a counter-value of from 5 to 6000 francs. Every body was constantly dissatisfied.

Those captains, who lost by this innovation, the benefit of a long acquaintance with the Haytien market—that is, those even whom it was most important not to discourage—returned from it, swearing that they would not be caught again, in that socialist nest. For similar reasons, the principal foreign consignees wrote, urgently, to their houses, to suspend all shipments. The receipts of the customs, which, by the cessation of emigration, had recovered somewhat, soon fell again. In order to arrest this commercial desertion, the Government authorised the foreign vessels to go, (by way of keeping them,) and complete their cargoes of coffee in all the open ports of the Island—even, in those, which had been, exclusively, reserved before this to the Haytien coasting-trade ; this ruined the latter. But here is the worst of it: the American vessels, loaded with meal, signified to the Government, that they would not unload their meal, but in exchange for *full* cargoes of coffee ; and it was necessary to take these from the quantity to be distributed, for scarcity was imminent. Those foreign importers, whose trade did not prevent Hayti from being taken by famine, reduced more and more their operations.

Fourth error: Some traders who were obliged, come what might, to dispatch their vessels, agreed to pay to contraband a premium, which rose sometimes to a hundred per cent. The speculators kept for themselves the half of this premium, and devoted the other half to buying . . . *the employees of the monopoly.* By the force of things alone, everything returned to the former condition, with this difference nearly—that the treasury was deprived of the duties on exports ; and the high prices benefited, not the producers, but extortioners, and stockjobbers.

Fifth error : Not being able to indemnify themselves, for the over-tax, with which contraband speculation oppressed the export of coffee, but by a corresponding rise in imported merchandise, the foreign merchants refused, suddenly, to deliver these goods, at the price, fixed by the monopoly law. The "black people," naturally, recommenced their threats against the *conspiracy of capital*. The retailers, especially, because of their being Haytiëns, were insulted every day, and struck by the populace. The *gourde* did not improve by all this; and M. Salomon accelerated the crisis, by endeavoring to stop it.

He began, by excluding from the division of the monopolised products, the trading consignees, who refused to sell at the tariff price; and, in order to prevent this interdict being eluded by fraud, he sought to compel the traders to deposit their merchandise, to be given out by the customs-officer, in a common locality, belonging to the Government, without guarantee against fire, robbery, or riots. Besides, he rendered the retailers liable to penalties and seizure, who refused, on their part, to submit to the tariff; and domiciliary visits, confiscation, and beatings, at length succeeded in bringing to reason this wicked capital. We foresee the rest. Scarcely a year had passed away, when M. Salomon was able to inscribe, on the door of his economical edifice; "Sold at *sixty-five per cent. discount* for the purpose of peremptory and general settlement." I do not exaggerate it: the monopoly prices were only bearable, at the valuation of one hundred and ten *gourdes* to the doubloon; but under the influence of these monstrosities, (which, moreover, were but the most practical, logical, and conclusive, consequence of the socialist principle, proposed by M. Salomon) the rate of the doubloon was, gradually, raised to *two hundred and eighty-two;* when, at the very height of emigration, arrests and executions, it had not exceeded one hundred and eighty-five. It is useless to add, that the cultivators, being obliged to deliver their coffee, at the rate of from nine to ten *centimes* the pound, ceased for the most part to gather it. It is unnecessary to speak further, of what became of the last receipts of the treasury, under the influence of a situation, where all things were, fatally, combined to exhaust the resources at once, without and within. At the present time, His Majesty, Faustin the 1st, (whose monarchical splendors we will soon have to relate,) would be, probably, reduced to clothe himself, with a banana leaf, and to dine with his Minister of Finance, if the latter, helped by a fortunate despair, had not brought his country, and his Emperor, back to the modest *régime* of the *bourgeoisie* political economy.*

At the time of decreeing this socialist experiment, Soulouque deigned to remember, that he had Chambers to enact laws; and the Chambers, recently so boastful, sanctioned by a vote, as mute as it was unanimous, the fantasies of M. Salomon.

---

* The monoply was abolished in the beginning of 1850. At the first departure from this system, the doubloon fell from two hundred and eighty-two *gourdes* to one hundred and forty-four; and coffee, which the cultivators were obliged to sell, at the rate of ten francs the quintal, rose to thirty-five, and even to forty francs.

Soulouque, as usual, opened the session in person; and, insensible as they were to this kind of emotion, an involuntary shudder ran along all the benches, when they noticed, in the presidential cortége, that very Voltaire Castor, who had poniarded, with his own hand, seventy of the prisoners garrotted at Cavaillon. His Excellency announced to the Parliament—'that the rebels being nearly *vanquished*, Hayti was about to reach, at *length, that degree of grandeur and prosperity, which divine Providence had reserved for it.*' The chorus of *vivats*, which welcomed this speech of the President, was less full than usual—and for a very simple reason: a third of the senators, and a portion of the representatives, were absent, because of proscription, or death.

In order to prove, certainly, that this was, neither discontent, nor coldness, on their part, the chamber of Representatives, two days afterwards, warmly thanked the President, for having saved the *country*, and the *Constitution*. There was not a single page of that Constitution, which had not furnished wads to the guns, before which, Deputies and Senators, had fallen, by the dozen. At one of the following sittings, a representative, 'considering, that the President of Hayti had merited well of the country, for his constant efforts, in maintaining order and the institutions, proposed to grant him, as a *title of national recompense, a house of his own choice, situated in the city;*' and the two

Chambers, moved as by a spring, rose, *en masse*, for its adoption.

Three months passed, afterwards, in silent votes; but soon this satisfied and decimated majority, trembled, when they found that their silence was taken, for an implied protest. And it hastened to burn, another grain of incense, at the feet of the negro tyrant. The orator of the Senate, said: "Already, Mr. President, we have shown the beneficent influence of your *sage* and *moderate* administration. . . . . At your voice, passions die, (he had cut their throats!), and the reign of established laws has become a *verity* to us all. . . . . *Circumstances* have, happily, conspired to put in relief your high character, exhibiting every thing noble and *generous*. Continue, Mr. President, do not pause. . . . . "

The orator of the Chamber of Representatives, in his turn, exclaimed: "How great is the love of the nation for your Excellency! How much is it honored by your *paternal* administration, by those noble sentiments of *fraternity*, by the *concord* and *clemency*, which animate you—and which have transported it, many times, with enthusiasm!" (*Moniteur Haytien*, the 6th of January, 1849.)

Toussaint, Dessalines, and Christophe, were able to exercise a tyranny quite as hard—but never, as well received, as that of this formidable poltroon, to whom, every shadow was a phantom, and every silence an ambuscade. And this was not the stupor of the first moment of surprise, which froze every will about him. From that parliament, bloody with the murderous blows struck at its inviolability, and which, wiped the blood from its own visage, to allow a hypocritical smile to be seen—from the remnant of that mulatto population, which was forbidden, even, the confederacy of sorrow,—from those prisons, whose limits, badly secured and guarded, enclosed enough *suspects* to form, at need, an avenging army—there has not even to this day, arisen, a single cry, which has not been one of servile devotion.

We ought not, after all, to complain of it; because the ultra-black faction, which remains, alone, standing in the midst of this universal prostration, must, sooner or later, attract and fix that suspicious look, which blights all that is not engulfed. And indeed, we are about to see, the three heads of this faction, suffer the consequences of those inexorable suspicions, which it excited. This second reaction will be, happily, let us remark, much less mournful than the first, although the victims of it are less worthy of pity. The one sprang out of a dream of extermination—the other is to issue out of a bottle of rum. Rum, naturally, leads us to General Similien.

XI.

A sun-set. The misfortunes of the *piquets*. A *voltairian papa-loi*.

I have drawn, at length, the portrait of Similien; and, if the moral conduct of this frightful personage, has not been too much lost to view, one will not be astonished, to see him fall a victim to his own sensibilities. Here is the new turn his feelings served him.

A few days after the massacres of April, 1848, Bellegarde, as we have seen, inspiring as much security, as he had previously caused fear, received a warm address of thanks from the *bourgeoisie* of Port-au-Prince. The only merit of the new favorite, and of his second, the commander of the place, was in having held Similien in check; but to make it plain, a dangerous challenge had been thrown down to the latter. After the example of that devotee, who, in order to avoid making enemies on any side, was careful not to forget the devil in his prayers, the *bourgeoisie* thought, therefore, it was prudent to include Similien in the official expression of its thanks, with the two men, who were the objects of it. This sudden stroke of flattery happened to surprise him, just at the time, he gave himself up, between two flasks of rum, to his daily meditations on the ingratitude of the mulattoes; and, being the more touched with such a return of sympathy because he felt he had done nothing to merit it, he was seized, while sitting, with the real tenderness of a drunkard, for that very colored population, which he was about to devote to massacre, pillage, and conflagration.

Similien was, fortunately, subject to seeing double, as well morally as physically. In returning his thanks to the mulattoes, he had no intention of embroiling himself with their enemies; the more so, that these, being deeply wounded by the obstacles, which Bellegarde opposed to their schemes of pillage, were the natural allies of the supplanted favorite. Accordingly, Similien divided his life into two parts, which he kept sacred—the one, to drink with the mulattoes, in order to discharge the debt of his heart—the other, to drink with the ultra-black leaders, to preserve their exasperation against the mulatto tendencies of his rival. This zigzag of drunkenness, had a two-fold success. Not content with bidding highest on the communist programme of the *piquets,* this coterie of plunderers, ultimately, demanded of it as I have said, the banishment of Bellegarde.

On their part, the men of color, measuring their urbanity by the increasing terror, with which, Similien inspired them, replied with an *empressement,* day after day, more flattering to the bacchanal politeness of this terrible associate. The latter concluded from this, that he was the idol of both the mulatto and ultra-black parties. His head was turned; and finding that the insignificant name, he had borne until then, was not in harmony with his high destinies, Similien desired to be called thenceforth, only, *Maximilien*.

Until the expiration, either by law or revolution, of the presidential powers, would allow him to add, to that sonorous name, the title which he already entertained in his mind, Similien thought he could not dispense with being, at least, the second personage of the State. Therefore, it was necessary to evict Bellegarde; and as the sudden favor of Bellegarde, formerly a simple colonel, could only be explained by the influence of the *vaudoux*, of which he was one of the wildest votaries, Similien conceived the bold project of sapping the edifice, at its base, by discrediting the *vaudoux*. Soulouque being still absent, the unbelieving tailor approached, Madame Soulouque, on this subject. He remonstrated, with her, in a paternal tone, that brother Joseph was not, what vain people thought; that he was, in a strict sense, permitted to render, to the Supreme Being, the homage of a pure heart; but he (Similien) blushed to see, the Chief of a free country, open his palace to drôles, and drôlesses, who burned wax-tapers, cut cards, or made serpents speak, for money.

The President's lady, who, during this tirade, had several times nearly fainted, could not restrain the indignation, which the monstrous scepticism of Similien produced. Hurt at the reception, his friendly counsels had received, the latter, in his turn, became incensed, and they came to angry words. "I will write to the President about it!" exclaimed Madame Soulouque. "Very well!" majestically replied the commander of the guard—"say for me, to the President, that he is *as foolish* as you are; that he will have a difference with me himself; and that to return to Port-au-Prince, he must submit to my conditions."

Similien, however, I am told, was unconscious at the moment, of all he said under the influence of anger; but believing it necessary to console himself for the ingratitude of women, as formerly he had done for that of men, by a double draught of rum, he was unable to recover a lucid quarter of an hour, before the return of the President, to afford him an opportunity of retracting his menaces. The ultra-black faction had even aggravated these threats by taking up the matter; and I leave the reader to imagine whether the President's lady, Bellegarde, and brother Joseph took part, from this circumstance, in the daily denunciations which they were careful should reach Soulouque. Hence the cold reception His Excellency gave Similien; and in order that he might be left, in no doubt, as to his disgrace, the next day, he rebuked him, with an evidently affected severity, in relation to some insignificant details of the service. The exfavorite believed he could reclaim Soulouque, by invoking the souvenirs of an old intimacy; he, therefore, replied as a companion—that is, with a familiarity, which made his despotic friend knit his brows.

Similien concluded from this, that the friendly expression, which he desired to give his words, was not sufficiently manifest; and he declared it to such a degree, that his familiarity degenerated into impertinence, which ended in injuring his prospects. It was, therefore, his fate to be always misunderstood. At the end of his expedients, the sentimental drunkard remembered, that, in a similar case, he had succeeded in conquering the hearts of the mulattoes, by showing them what it would cost to become embroiled with him; he imagined, by an analagous proceeding, to regain the heart of Soulouque. In other words, Similien undertook to conspire in earnest, which, with the help of rum, was very soon a secret to no one. The President dissimulated several months;—when, one morning, at the parade of the guards, he said in a brief tone to the old favorite: "General Similien, I deprive you of your command. Go; and remain under arrest, in your house, until further orders!"

On hearing himself thus addressed, in the midst of that very guard, whose fanatical devotion he had so often proved, Similien concluded, in good faith, that the President had become crazy; but he thought he dreamed himself, when the confident and sneering look, he cast rapidly about him, only met indifferent countenances and mute mouths. Not a man stirred. Similien had been, already, some days under arrest, when three or four officers, first dared to hazard an opinion on that measure. Removed during the night, these officers were taken, by sea, to the dungeons, at Môle Saint-Nicholas, and spoke no more.

After mature reflection, Similien discovered the secret of the enigma. The people and the army, evidently, expected to rise, in his favor, when Soulouque was engaged, in his next expedition, against Santo-Domingo; they had only affected indifference, in order to conceal more effectually their scheme. Indeed, Soulouque entered upon the campaign, the 5th of March, 1849, and from that day Similien, expecting hourly, that his friends, the mulattoes and ultra-black leaders, would come, arm in arm, to supplicate him to accept the Presidency, took no pains, afterwards, to conceal his legitimate hopes. Six weeks, however, had already passed away in this feverish expectation, and the future President began to be disturbed; when, finally, an unusual movement was made about the house.

Considering the heat, Similien was, properly, found in a condition of toilette, which recalled much more the formal sitting of a Mandingo chief, than that of a Haytien President. Fearing to compromise the dignity of his *début*, he, hastily, leaped into his pantaloons, crying to the numerous groups, which he heard already in the house, to be pleased to wait a little. But such was the impatience of the visitors, that they forced the door open, seized Similien, bore him, in the twinkling of an eye, into the street, and there drove him with blows, not towards the palace, but to prison. They cast him, half-naked into the same dungeon, from which David Troy, his first victim, had issued some time before, to proceed to execution; and, strange coincidence, this occurred the 16th of April, 1849, a year, to the day, after the scene of the massacre, which inaugurated the programme of Similien. By a coincidence, not less singular, Similien suffered in that dungeon the effects of the very suspicions, of which he had been the principal instigator. Believing himself, in fact, sure of the ultra-black element, he had turned exclusively, in the last few months, towards the class of color, upon which he relied to work out of the difficulty; so that Soulouque finally regarded him, as nothing more than a "mulatto conspirator." A few screams from the women, which seemed rather produced, by astonishment, than commiseration, were heard on the passage of the escort, which carried along the old favorite; but that was all. The male part of the population, which, formerly, would have burned the city to have pleased Similien, did not stir, any more than the guard had done previously. The "philosophers" (orators and good talkers) of the quarters of Bel-Air, and Morne-à-Tuf, were content, to point their fingers to the two opposite points of the horizon, and say: "*The sun rises there—and sets there*"—a negro sentence, which is intended to express the instability of human grandeurs.

The ascendancy of respect and terror, which Soulouque exercised, even at a distance, did not alone explain, however, this new attitude of Similien's friends. In thinking to sap the *vaudoux* creed, the latter had been unconsciously digging for the last ten months, the mine in which his popularity was swallowed up. Soulouque only delayed his action, until this silent work, whose progress his spies had followed day after day, produced its results. The counter-part, in a word, was complete: the *vaudoux*, which was the first cause of the ultra-black irruption, became the first instrument of reaction.

To finish with Similien, let us remark, that he was not shot; but some months afterwards, he wished for nothing better. A step was taken in his favor, on the occasion of proclaiming the Empire:—"*He get out of prison!*" exclaimed His Imperial Majesty—"*he will be covered with moss first!*" Similien sent word to Soulouque that his legs were so swelled by the pressure of his fetters, that they were about to mortify:—"I do not care for that; *when they fall off, he can be chained by the neck!*" said Faustin Ist, adroitly. The ex-favorite died, *very mysteriously*, in prison, about the end of 1853.

In the interval that elapsed, between placing Similien under arrest, and sending him to prison, the principal chief of the *piquets*, Pierre Noir himself, also, paid his tribute to that suspicious despotism, one of whose most frightful instruments, he had become. Faithful to his habits of modesty, Captain Pierre Noir had obstinately refused the grade of General, which fell to his lot in the shower of promotions, of which his band was the object in 1848. He only wanted the emoluments of it; and yet, feeling ashamed, to receive, what he could take, levied these emoluments himself on the public; attacking the foreigners by preference. Our consul-general was worn out, asking reparations,—always heard, but always to be renewed. At length, losing patience, M. Raybaud summoned the Government, once for all, to deprive Pierre Noir of the possibility of harm; adding that the deference it used, towards this abominable wretch, induced the belief, that the President was, really afraid of him; and therefore, he boasted of it. Soulouque, who, for six months, had shed human blood, in streams, to prove that he possessed character was, you may well imagine, very sensitive to this suspicion of cowardice. A courier immediately took the order to Pierre Noir, to report himself at Port-au-Prince.

Judging that this trip would be injurious to his health, Pierre Noir took care not to obey, and he called together the whole body of the *piquets;*—but measures had been so well taken, that before he could assemble his band, he was arrested, in the vicinity of Cayes. When he was led out to be shot, with two of his lieutenants, the bandit offered to make the officer, commanding the escort, his prime minister, if he would allow him to escape; and, what is rare in Hayti, the officer refused, although Pierre Noir was perfectly able to keep his word, if the case had happened. In demanding justice, only, of a simple cut-throat, M. Raybaud had, in fact, disembarrassed Soulouque of a conspirator, much more dangerous than Similien. It was proved, that the modest Pierre Noir, only awaited the time, when the President should be found fighting with the Dominicians, in order to organise a small African kingdom, in the South, to the exclusion of *every heterogeneous element;* that is, to the exclusion of the mulattoes, who would have been massacred, simultaneously, at all points on the peninsular; and to the exclusion of the whites, who would have been massacred, after the mulattoes, beginning with the two French and English consular agents. The execution of this bold rascal, who reached, after ten months of impunity, an ascendency almost without limits, diffused through the black populace of the South, an impression of superstitious respect, with which, Soulouque had already struck the robbers of Port-au-Prince. The *piquets* contented themselves, in manifesting their desolation, by an extravagance of sorrow, which ended in fatiguing the President. "This has become too silly," said His Excellency, one morning; and, three new executions took place, to impose silence on the sobs of the brigands.

Let us remark, in order not to recur to it again, that after Similien and the *piquets*—that is, after the military and the bandit elements of the ultra-black tragedies,—the vaudoux element also had its turn. Some months after his accession to the throne, Soulouque suffered from a swelling of the knee. The doctor prescribed some leeches; and brother Joseph having become Colonel, and Baron, concurred in the advice of the physician; but the distinguished patient indicated, his preference, for conjurations. Either *Voltairianism* suffered, or vexed at seeing, for the first time, his counsels disregarded, brother Joseph had the imprudence to say, that the Emperor would not recover from it. Soulouque, who paid his sorcerer, to dispel bad presages, and not, to make them, gave orders, immediately, to have brother Joseph conducted to the dungeons of the Môle-Saint-Nicholas. His Imperial Majesty got into difficulty then with a formible party, considering the power, the sorcerers had, of injuring even from a distance. But the vessel, which carried the disgraced *papa-loi* to the Môle, providentially, capsized, on the way; and, by a most remarkable chance, brother Joseph only perished of all the people on board of it.

In conclusion, a little good had already sprung out of the very causes of so much evil. The fear of being ridiculed about his vaudoux beliefs; the diseased anxiety of escaping the suspicion of feebleness;—and finally, the fear of witchcraft, which alone, had driven Soulouque back into the ultra-African party—had become, by turns, the cause of the reactions which had successively, carried off three scoundrels, who personified that party. Unfortunately, much was wanting, to make this reaction systematic. Soulouque, so ready to generalize his suspicions, and hatreds, with regard to the mulattoes,—Soulouque only appeared to see the danger here, in proportion, as he encountered it; imprisoning, or shooting without deliberation the ultra-black conspirators, whom he detected in the act of offence; but, without leaving his confidence with the rest of the party, which had become the nursery of the dukes, counts, and barons, who, now puffed up the powerful Empire of Faustin. It is true, there was about Soulouque an emulation of hatred or fear, to flatter his prejudices against the oppressed class, whilst the ultra-black party found itself protected, by him, because of the very excess of these prejudices.

How could he oppose hostilely the *piquets*, without declaring himself, more or less, the friend of their victims? Not one of the seven, or eight, honorable men, who remained in the *entourage* of Soulouque, dared to hazard such an interpretation.

In the meantime, the *piquets*, and their friends, continued, by force of the powers, with which, they were invested, the system of terror they had exercised, in 1848, on the great high-ways. Either, because of an enthusiasm of gratitude to the man, without whom, they would be, again, reduced to steal sugar-cane, or beg—or, because the greater part of them did not feel their consciences very clear, with respect to the conspiracy, which cost Pierre Noir his life—all these strange Generals, took pains, to prove devotion, after their fashion; that is, by discovering in every *bourgeois* a suspicious person. Under the influence of these besetments, which no one could resist, the impulses of savage distrust, which Soulouque, sometimes, revealed against the real *suspects*, resumed their first direction. The prisons, and dungeons, gave up none of their captives, except those that disease or starvation delivered; and, if the arrests and executions had become more rare, it was because the material began to be exhausted.

The influence of the consuls only could reach this matter; and occasions were not wanting for its exercise. Hatred of the mulattoes being in some sort, with the drunken rabble of the place, but a shadowing of its hatred for the whites, there was no kind of insults and exactions, which they spared the latter. One day, some Europeans, (and our consular agent of Cayes was of the number) were insulted, and struck, at the conclusion of a hearing, by a justice of the peace, before whom they had been summoned, as witnesses; and the local authorities brutally, refused them any protection. Another day, a trap was set, for some captains of vessels, ready to sail, in order to catch them in the very act of smuggling; and the snare not having succeeded, the authorities, notwithstanding, detained the vessels, offering, (verbally, to be sure,) to spare the captains, upon being paid, the ruinous delays which would follow a judicial enquiry. Upon the slightest pretext, the foreign merchants were arrested, and carried before the tribunals. Here is an example of these pretexts:

In 1850, a young black, fifteen years old, working on a plantation, took it into his head to poison a Frenchman for pastime, who superintended the estate. He introduced into the earthen bottle, from which he was accustomed to drink, some bamboo down and rose-apple roots. Scarcely had the Frenchman drank of this beverage, than he regarded, with suspicion, the young black who had presented it to him. The latter fled at full speed; was apprehended, and taken before the commander of the place, at Cayes. He confessed, that he really designed to poison the Frenchman; but he did so, because *this white man had made seditious motions against the government.* The startling political precocity of this young *drôle*, extorted a smile of approbation, from the representative of authority. He sent for the Frenchman, and after having grossly insulted him, had him cast into a dungeon, for trial. This commander is a drunkard, named Sanon, who, a short time ago, was a trumpeter; but now, is *Count de Port-à-Piment.*

The commander of the province, an old chief of *piquets,* Jean Claude, alias Duke des Cayes, had had incarcerated, some days before that, for reasons quite as curious, another Frenchman, who was a peaceable merchant, and had been established, for thirty years, in the country. A captain, out of service, who happened to be discharged by this merchant for whom he had worked, as a day laborer, had him accused of saying: " That there were too many Generals in the country, and not enough laborers on the coffee plantations." It was proved, by the declaration of the witnesses to the charge, themselves, that only half of this innocent speech had been given ; and, that the informer had made, on the contrary, the following proposition, which was much less innocent : " That unless things changed, they would kill all the whites." The Frenchman was nevertheless condemned ; for in such cases, Monseigneur, the Duke des Cayes had the hall of audience surrounded by an armed force ; and this means never failed, of its effect, on the tribunal. When a foreigner is rescued, from these trials, by the intervention of his consul, it is not without difficulties. The head of the first English house, at Cayes had a sad experience of it, one evening. The unhappy Englishman, reached his dwelling some minutes after the hour, which it pleased this terrible Duke, his persecutor, that every one should be at home; he was apprehended, bodily, by a patrol, who had waited for him, at the very door of the house, where he had spent the evening, and took him to the guard-house, kicking and beating him with a cane on the way. He passed the night, there, in company with thieves, and vagabonds, insulted and abused till morning.

The foreign military marine, itself, is not exempt from such insults. Near the end of 1849, some officers, of an English steamer which had anchored at Cayes, were making some hydrographic observations on the sea-beach. They were arrested, by the guard, and conducted with extreme brutality, in the midst of the hootings of the populace, to the inevitable Duke, Jean Claude, who received them with every possible obscenity. He, however, consented to release the captives;* but, not

---

* The commander of the English steamer, who had, himself, been treated with extreme insolence by General Jean-Claude, sailed after complaining of his consular agent, who was content with a hackneyed expression of regrets, without requiring the punishment of the guilty parties. The English consulate took an honorable revenge, a short time afterwards, by exacting from Soulouque the pardon of an architect condemned to death; *who was unfortunately, executed nevertheless.* The vice-consul bitterly complained of this to Soulouque; who ascribed it to some administrative mistake. And, for the purpose of quieting the consul, surrendered to him an old General, who was dying in prison—adding that, as a General was of much more consequence than an architect, the vice-consul should regard this last favor as so much the more precious than the first. It is scarcely necessary to say, that Soulouque demanded money of his General, in order to make the compensation exact.

without first having turned, over and over, in his hands, with suspicious attention, a barometer, which he had taken from them—adding, that they did not carry quick-silver in a glass tube for nothing; and, that this very quicksilver, was conclusive proof, that these *Messieurs* came to search for hidden treasures. I do not answer for it, that Monseigneur, the Duke des Cayes, did not operate, on his own account, by digging in the suspected place.

A short time afterwards, the commanders of two Spanish ships of war, which put into the bay of Flamands, were wandering ashore, when a certain General, who by a double antiphrase, was called, M. de Ladouceur, *Comte de l'Asile*, had them seized, bodily, and required that one of the commanders should remain as a hostage. Whilst M. Raybaud, and our consular agent at Cayes, negotiated the reparation due the Spanish flag, the crew, of a third ship of the same nation, went ashore to get some provisions, at l'Arcahaye, and were received, on landing, with such hostile demonstrations, that they were obliged to return to sea, leaving the ensign in command, a prisoner. The next day, the captain landed alone, and had himself conducted to the commanding General of the subdivision, before whom he demanded, energetically, the respect due to Spanish sailors. At this word, *Spanish*, the General, divided between anger and stupidity, spoke of nothing less, than having the audacious rebels shot, immediately. This *qui-pro-quo*, which would have gone beyond the bounds of comedy was, finally, cleared up. The captain proved, by all kinds of unquestionable evidence, that there were other Spaniards, in the world, besides those of the *Dominican* part of it. The General was shaken, but not convinced; and, in order to relieve his responsibility, he sent the ensign to Port-au-Prince, where he arrived on foot, escorted like a malefactor—and, after having been insulted, along the whole route, with the epithets of *pirate* and *spy*. At Port-au-Prince, the fact of Spain's existence was readily admitted; and a third reparation was added to the two already demanded.

At every difficulty of this kind, which the *expiquets* threw on his hands, Souloque exhibited according to circumstances, contrariness, irritability, or consternation. His grief being well established, he hastened to acknowledge it; if necessary, he had the subaltern agents of this system of exaction, and outrage arrested; he even compelled, in grave cases, the principal representatives of authority to frame public excuses, with accompaniments of salvos of artillery, and a general illumination; but this was all.

Jeane Claude and his associates were not sparing, either in excuses, powder, or lamps; but, some days afterwards, they recommenced their outrages, sure of the obstinate indulgence of Souloque, though it cost his vanity the most cruel discomforts, for all crimes which appeared to be an excess of devotion and zeal.

We regret to say, the British consulate as if it sought to create for itself a claim, by contrast, on the Haytien Government, did not always second, as much as was in its power, the energetic persistence that our agent put in operation, to obtain reparations which concerned it, against this weak side of the black chief. The English sailors, and residents, often complained of certain unseasonable conduct; and we are inclined to believe that the *Foreign Office*, itself, might, for once, regard favorably, the departure of its agents from this seesaw system, which is the classic proceeding of the English chancery in Hayti. As to the French Government, it expresses itself on the wrongs, occurring to our countrymen, without ceasing; and in terms, which shows its intention of stopping them, by putting an end to it, once for all." The most efficacious method of repression—that which has always succeeded with M. Raybaud, is to take the Haytien Government on its weak side, *money;* and to exact, for every wrong committed against European residents, not only, reparation for their material losses, but, also, costs and damages, as compensation for the impositions suffered by them. This is nothing but common right.

If these means are insufficient—if Faustin Ist prefers to pay, every day, compensation for injuries, rather than get rid of these strange favorites,—we do not see why, France and England should hesitate, to strike at the root of the evil, and exact, imperatively, the submission, *en masse*, of these official bandits, to whom Soulouque has surrendered the whole province of the South. This would still not be going beyond common right; because, all reparation implies, on the part of the person granting it, the undertaking to prevent, within the limit of his power, the repetition of the wrong repaired. But it is proved that the belaced *canaille*, which he has to deal with there, is incorrigible; and it is, equally, beyond doubt, that in order, to bring to reason, if necessary, those of the disgraced *piquets*, who would renew the undertakings of the late Pierre Noir, Soulouque would not have to expend a hundredth part of the brutal energy, which he has gratuitously displayed against their victims. Indeed, it is high, to estimate at a thousand scattered over the whole country, the entire body of these scoundrels; who pretend to isolate, from the white race, a country, whose only resource is its foreign commerce; who, retain, by their influence, in the prisons or in exile, the class which serves as intermediaries to this commerce; and who feed an increasing fire of hatred, savagery and disorder, in the bosom of a people, the most slothful, I am convinced, but the most inoffensive, hospitable and governable in the world.

XII.

Victories and conquests of Soulouque. A sorcery trial. The Empire and the Imperial Court.

Let us take up the order of events, by which, Hayti progressed to the era of the Faustins.

Soulouque, one day, asked how Napoleon had arrived at Empire. They replied, that it was by gaining the battle of Marengo; and the black chief, who prided himself, as we have seen, upon following our fashions, wished also to have his Marengo. The Dominicans—*those mulatto rebels*, as he styled them—must pay the expenses of the thing. It would be a double blow; for, on the same occasion, Soulouque would succeed, in getting rid of the mulattoes who were not rebels, the largest possible number of whom, he had had enrolled, with the intention, of exposing them to the first fire. For the six years that the Spanish portion of the Island had been declared independent, these expeditions had been the signals of conspiracies and Haytien revolutions; but Soulouque had taken good care of this, by always taking with him, as hostages, the innumerable Generals, whom he suspected of looking more or less to the succession. As to Similien and the *piquets*, as I have said, the first remained under arrest, subject to the surveillance of the new favorite Bellegarde—and the second, taken unawares by the violent death of their chief, only, dreamed of watering, the grave of the late Pierre Noir, with rum and silent tears.

This war was, profoundly, distasteful to nine-tenths of the Haytiens; and the possibility, of a Dominican ball cutting short the august days of Soulouque, was not of such a nature, as to bring desolation among the innumerable families, about to be decimated. Never, however,—never did more sincere and ardent hopes of success, accompany an enterprise. The idea, that Soulouque might return beaten, and a prey to exasperation, alone, caused the bourgeoisie, black and yellow, especially the last, a real agony of terror. The first news of the expedition, happily, somewhat calmed these apprehensions. The 19th of March, 1849, the Dominicans, having been driven out of Las-Matas, by a corps, which left the Cap, with the President at their head, lost their artillery: and the next day, Soulouque, proudly, encamped at Saint-Jean, an almost central point of the Island.

As it had not been ever before thought of, Soulouque, after reaching this point discovered, that he had set out on his expedition without provisions. He soon after found there were some at Azua, which had been evacuated without resistance, by four thousand Dominicans, commanded in person by President Jiménez; but, he committed the blunder, of consuming these supplies on the spot, awaiting, for an entire week, submissions which did not take place. Driven from Azua by famine, the black army, however, succeeded in reaching, after many other unexpected successes, the river Ocoa—distant, about twenty leagues, from the Dominican capital. This unhappy little people were lost, without help. The wealthy families of Saint-Domingo embarked, hastily; and congress, seeing the impossibility of any defence, were about to hoist over it the French flag.

All this was known, day after day, at Port-au-Prince; and the entire population were, literally, about to prepare the triumphal procession, which was due to the conqueror of Saint-Domingo, when suddenly, on the 30th of April, a sinister report circulated through the city. From the vicinity of Bani, the Haytien army, abruptly, fell back to Saint-Jean, passing over this distance of forty-five leagues, in less than four days. Whilst the Haytiens slept, in the pleasures of Azua, the Dominicans had had time to summon to their aid Santana, who had withdrawn, for a time, from state-affairs; and Santana gave a new proof of character to his admirer, Soulouque, by completely beating him in two engagements, which cost the Haytiens six pieces of cannon, two flags, three hundred horses, more than a thousand guns, a quantity of baggage, and hundreds of slain, several Generals among the number. Santana, then, drove back the Haytien army towards the sea-board, where it was, cruelly, cannonaded with grape shot, by the Dominican fleet, posted there to intercept it.

The causes of a defeat, so unexpected, remained to be explained. To attribute it to the improvidence of the President, was to sport with one's head; but the *bougeois*, remembering, opportunely, that France had served them for forty years, as a shield in every instance in which they had reason to fear, some out-burst of the fury of the ultra-black party —the *bourgeois* hastened to set down, this defeat, to our account. Although the consul-general of France had spared no means for a year past, of diverting Soulouque from his conquering fancies, they suddenly discovered that the counsels, prayers, and importunities of M. Raybaud had, only, pushed the President into an enterprise, for which he was not yet prepared. The perfidious M. Raybaud knew, in advance, that he sent him to a cut-throat place; because, the pretended Dominican fleet was neither more nor less than two—then seven—afterwards fourteen—and finally *nineteen* French ships of war. Messieurs, the mulattoes, who, with nearly five or six exceptions, thought themselves obliged to cry louder than any others, discovered this figure of *nineteen* ships; two of which, especially— the *Naïade* and *Tonnerre*—which had been absent from that station for many years, had powerfully contributed, in their opinion, to the success of the ambuscade. The mulattoes, also, discovered that

M. Raybaud, who was only the day before their idol, had added to his wrongs that of sending to the enemy, Soulouque's plan of campaign, which had been, apparently, confided to him. The black authorities concluded by accepting literally this romance, in which, alas! fear held the pen. Our countrymen were the subject of menaces. The city was over-run, in every sense, by orderlies on horseback; and the forts were armed, for the purpose of sinking our stationary Corvette, which they supposed was making preparations, on its part, to bombard the city.

M. Raybaud, whose nerves were tolerably well inured, seemed very little moved by all this bluster. However, he had, already, taken some proper measures to protect our countrymen, when two proclamations suddenly appeared, restoring to order the enthusiasm and joy of the day; and, by giving it another direction redoubled the inquietudes of the unfortunate *bourgeois*, who, by too great zeal in manifesting their *gallophobia* on this occasion, had made themselves the heralds of a defeat, which was henceforth to be disclaimed. In one of these proclamations, the President said:—

"Soldiers! from triumph to triumph, you reached even to the banks of the river Ocoa. You occupied, at that place, a position, whose advantages justified me in leading you further; *but I did not think proper to abuse your courage*. . . . Having reached your firesides, you will have much to tell those, who were not present on these battle-fields, which recalled the glories of our ancesters. . . Soldiers! I am content with you!"

In another proclamation, addressed to the people and the army, Soulouque, after having enumerated his triumphs, adds:—

"But entirely favorable as may have been these circumstances, wisdom recommended me to return to the capital. . . . . The Government *wishes, still, to allow its wandering sons time for reflection and repentance.*"

It remains to be said, that the garlands of palms and leaves, which were thrown aside for a short time, the next day decorated the houses along the *route* of the magnanimous "Conqueror of the East," who returned to the city, amid the noise of prolonged salvos of artillery; and this intrepid gasconnade was completed, by having a *Te Deum* chanted for his successes. Arrests and executions were then expected. In the interval, the parents and friends of the *suspects*, were very much embarrassed what kind of countenances to assume—fearing at the same time, if they appeared sad, to seem to insult the *official* joy—and if they affected joy, to seem to offend their actual griefs. Soulouque, moreover, neglected nothing, on his part, to give the *diapason* to public opinion. Every reception, at the palace, was marked by scenes like the following—only the substance of which can be reproduced—because, of the impossibility of exhibiting, on paper, the embellishments of Créole antics and rhetoric.

After having testified his displeasure at the ridiculous reports, which had been circulated, about the pretended interference of a French squadron, Soulouque repeated to the civil and military notabilities, who listened to him, with eager attention, trembling painfully to catch the minutest detail of the presidential version—Soulouque repeated, I say, that he had not, by any means, intended to engage in a final expedition. The occasion, the tender grass, and the surprising triumphs, which marked each of his steps, on the Dominican territory, had alone led him on, and in his own defence, up to the gates of Santo-Domingo. But, the rebels of the East finding themselves plunged into the most frightful wretchedness, since they had renounced the benefits of national unity, their own soldiers having nothing for several days, to subsist upon except an ear of corn, divided between four men— this had decided him to postpone a conquest, already, accomplished in fact.

"And who would believe"—exclaimed the President—"that this glorious expedition has only cost the Haytien army about *fifty slain!*"

An Interrupter.—"Forty-eight, M. President!"

Soulouque.—"Let it go for forty-eight. . . In retaliation, this magnificent campaign, which only cost us the death of forty braves, has left cruel souvenirs to the rebels. They lost so many of their people, that they were incommoded, *for many leagues, with the stench of their corpses.* Is it not a fact that they were incommoded by it?"

The Generals.—" Yes, President," (with a general contraction of their nostrils, as though they smelt something bad. A future duke, even, made a show of seeking for an absent pocket-handkerchief.)

Soulouque (smiling.)—"It was not their fault; for, these cowardly rascals little dreamed, of finding me in command. How they run, the poor devils! how they run! . . Apropos; have we not heard of a pretended cannonade that the fleet of the rebels would have given us on the way? . . . (Knitting his brows)—I will be curious to know, whether it is not the mulattoes here, who have put this report in circulation."

A General (of the last promotion.)—"Yes! President."

Soulouque.—"I think I will decide, after all, to give a lesson to these *Messieurs*, the mulattoes. They have spoken, also, of abandoned cannon. . . ."

Numerous voices.—"No, Mr. President, you did not abandon any cannon!"

Soulouque (dryly.)—"You are deceived about that; I did abandon a few of them; and I know why I did it. Since we are going to occupy, definitely, the insurgent territory, in six months—are we not certain of recovering them?"

At this announcement of a new campaign, which they were sick of at the bottom of their hearts, the

Generals, one after the other, came forward, and solicited the favor of the President, to be made part of it. "Yes," said the President, becoming excited, by degrees—" you, and all the others—old and young—all those in a condition to march. . . . . the *piquets* also ! I will put forth, if necessary, all my resources. Even my existence ; for I swear to subjugate the rebels. We must not leave among them, *either a chicken or a cat alive.* I will pursue them to the depths of their forests—and even to the top of the *Cibao*,* without pity, as though they were *wild hogs!*" A general chorus—"*Like wild hogs!*"

A violent hiccough of anger, habitually, interrupted these explosions of His Excellency, whose eyes became always blood-shot, and his lips ashy. The President only recovered a little serenity, by narrating the injuries, he had had time to inflict on the Dominicans, in his retreat—to wit : the burning of Azua,—of all the dwellings and distilleries within a radius of two leagues,—the wood-yards of mahogany, and the fields of sugar-cane ; the destruction of Saint-Jean, of Las-Matas, and, finally, of all the *bananaries.*

It remained to be seen, what victims would pay the expenses of this victory by the Dominicans ; for there was no doubt, but some blood was still necessary to appease this thirst of vengeance.

---

* The name of a chain of very high mountains.

Brother Joseph was charged to settle, in this respect the hesitations of the President; who, among the five or six hundred prisoners, confined in the prison and dungeons of Port-au-Prince, experienced some embarrassment of choice.

A friend of one of these prisoners fancied, that, in order to save him, he would employ the immense influence, which brother Joseph still enjoyed with the President. He therefore sought out the sorcerer, and, playing the part of believing, supplicated him to use, his well-known influence over the god, *Vaudoux*, in favor of the prisoner. Brother Joseph replied, that, in fact, the serpent had some favors for him; that he would promise to supplicate it, and what is more, gratuitously; but, for the purpose of helping the conjuration, some wax-tapers, *neuvaines*, and masses, were, indispensably necessary, and all these cost "*money—a great deal of money.*" This was the reply his questioner expected; and a sufficiently round sum was given to the sorcerer, who, being suddenly illumined by a magnificent idea, replied in that soft tone, habitual to him: "My God! it costs no more to pray for a hundred, or a thousand, than for one; and, if they will furnish me the means for it, I will deliver all the other prisoners, at the same time with *Masson*"—the name of the prisoner for whom he acted.

Masson, being informed of this offer, hastened to communicate it to his numerous companions in captivity, who, for the most part, eagerly accepted it. It was, indeed, holding out the hope, that, in order to sustain his reputation for witchcraft, brother Joseph would attempt a secret measure with Soulouque. These prisoners, having put together all their resources, in money or in kind, (General Desmarêt, among others, gave his epaulettes) succeeded, with the aid of their friends outside, in collecting a value of about two thousand *gourdes;* which brother Joseph pocketed, recommending it to be kept secret. Some few of the prisoners, on the contrary, had the imprudence, to refuse any encouragement to the mockeries of this scoundrel. The sorcerer proposed a discount to them ; and, in order not to be disappointed in it, even offered, finally, to be satisfied with a simple formality, which consisted in wearing, a collar of a certain form, upon their necks. They sent him to the devil; and brother Joseph swore to send them to the executioner.

The sorcerer, then, returned to the palace with the two-fold intention—of denouncing the few prisoners from whom he could not extort money, as having offered to pay him, to work witchcraft against the President,—and, of demanding, on the contrary, the liberty of those, who had allowed themselves to be extorted, with a good grace. But, on the way, brother Joseph reflected, that the first part of his request, only, had any chance of success ; and, calculating, that the cheated prisoners might ask him to return their money, after the failure of the second request—or, at least, treat him as a swindler, which might injure his consideration as a prophet—he said to himself, the shortest way, with them, was to shut their mouths. Therefore, he denounced, in the same charge, both, the prisoners who had disregarded his vaudoux influence, and some of those who happened to pay tribute to this influence; certain that the other subscribers to this salvage to crime, would see in him a counsel eloquent by discretion.* Let us say, however, that moved by a scruple of delicacy, he accused those prisoners, who had paid him,—and whom he only denounced because of the necessity of his position, —much less than those, of whom he had reason to complain.

Among these last—that is, among the incredulous,—was General Céligny Ardouin, who had lain in chains, for the past fifteen months, in the dungeon, where he had been cast, slashed all over with sabre-cuts. Soulouque had not yet had him condemned; and no one could say why not, for he was never heard to pronounce his name, without falling into one of those terrible fits of fury,† before which

---

* I am assured, that some hidden hatred had indicated, to brother Joseph, the prisoners he should denounce in preference; and that this was to the *papa-vaudoux* another opportunity of speculation, quite as lucrative as the two others.

† By a strange fatality, the unfortunate Céligny Ardouin had, two or three years before, through the influence of his position as minister, saved the life of his denouncer, brother Joseph, who was then

every counsel of clemency was silent. The denunciation of brother Joseph, therefore, flattered, doubly, the superstitious hatreds of Soulouque. The General was immediately put upon his trial, with nine of his companions, (July 1849). The only witness to the charge preferred against him refused downright to take the oath ; giving as his reason, that he was not satisfied to take this oath on the crucifix. The judges did not pause, at this circumstance ; but the statement of the grounds for the sentence announced, stoutly, the fact, to which this witness was about to testify—the fact of money having been given to procure conjurations, and *neuvaines,* designed to cause the President to perish, or to render him a fool. The compilers of our judicial formulas, in use in the Haytien tribunals, never suspected that one of them would serve, in the year 1849, as the frame of an accusation of sorcery. After having paid, this tribute, to the universal cowardice, the judges, however, had the courage (under the circumstances it was really courage) to pronounce sentence of death only against three of the accused. Three others were condemned to three years imprisonment ; and the remaining four acquitted, but left by a last agreement, *to the discre-*

---

under sentence of a capital condemnation. A more strange coincidence, still, is that the brother of the man, against whom, Soulouque seemed to have summed up his hatred for the colored class, was precisely the person, to whom, as we have seen, he owed his elevation to the presidency.

tion of the President. Among these *avant-derniers* was General Céligny Ardouin.

When he was apprised of this result, the President tore the minutes of the judgment to pieces, exclaiming furiously, that they had, precisely, condemned to capital punishment those, whose death was indifferent to him. The judges, wild with terror, excused themselves, because of the timidity of the witness, who had been thrown into a dungeon. The collective sentence was annulled; and the ten accused persons were remanded before a new council of war, sitting at Croix-des-Bouquets, about three leagues from Port-au-Prince.

But Soulouque had calculated, that day, on a large execution. He remembered, conveniently, that he had in confinement three unhappy persons, who had been condemned to death, for more than a year past; and, having been disappointed in a grand tragedy, this was a very fit substitute, for his eager impatience of slaughter. The unfortunate men were, General Desmarêt, and his two companions;—the same who, in 1848, immediately after the expedition to the South, had been spared by the request of the entire population. They were executed at once; but none of them were killed at the first fire. Here was again exhibited one of those proceedings of Soulouque's distributive justice. The *suspects*, having extenuating circumstances in their favor, were shot, as they shoot a soldier everywhere;—whilst the others, those who were specially recommended, were allowed to die by inches. Either because Soulouque was more terrible, vanquished than as victor—or, that the question of sorcery, which was mixed up with the affair, had enlisted, on this occasion, all the vaudoux sympathies of the city, on the side of the executioner—the people did not even murmur against this ferocious retraction of the three pardons they had obtained. The execution passed off, without any other incident, than the appearance of the Executive; who, surrounded by a numerous staff—whose presence did not even disturb a band of dogs occupied in licking up the blood—came to witness the executions, and count the red marks on this human target. As to General Céligny Ardouin, and his nine co-accused, they were conducted on foot, and in chains, to Croix-des-Bosquets. The road had been rendered so impracticable, by the rains of the season, that, they took seven hours, to pass over this distance of three leagues, although the escort drove them forward with blows. M'lle. Céligny Ardouin prefered to follow her father.

The consul-general of France, joined by the vice-consul (for the time, at the head of the British consulate) desired to make a supreme effort, in favor of the unfortunate General. The usual scene transpired; excessive exhaustion interrupted, only from time to time, by short silences, the furious incoherences of Soulouque—incoherences, which, on this occasion, had the invariable refrain: "*I must have his blood!*"

"But"—said M. Raybaud, "wait at least until he is positively condemned; and if he is, he will still have the right to sue for a review of his sentence."

"No! no!" replied Souloque, "it will not end there . . . since, I tell you, his blood is necessary to me. He will be shot immediately—*and like a dog!*"

"At least have pity on his wife, and his unhappy children!"

"I swear it! let them *all, all, perish!*"

The English vice-consul, in despair of the case, replied: "Put him in one of your terrible dungeons, at Môle-Saint-Nicholas; but, at least, spare him his life!"

"I will take good care of it! *He will enter that dungeon, whence no one returns!* . . ."

Having been condemned to death, at two o'clock in the morning, the unhappy General was executed, at nine o'clock, in spite of his right of appeal. He died like all the others, with an admirable coolness—and, notwithstanding he was also left to die by inches; he was particularly *recommended*. The arrest of some other persons of distinction, filled the void, immediately, that this triple speculation of brother Joseph had made in the dungeons.

Souloque intended to have had himself proclaimed Emperor, on his return from the *conquest of the*

East, in the church at Gonaïves, where Dessalines had been proclaimed; and, the East not wishing to allow itself to be conquered, this supremely ridiculous idea seemed indefinitely postponed. But the new, and brilliant victory, which, the President had obtained over the intrigues of sorcery, suddenly, restored him to the feeling of his predestination; and, he yielded himself to the soft violence of the half-a-dozen *droles*, who had beset him with this idea, since the close of 1847.

The 21st of August, 1849, he began to hawk about, at Port-au-Prince, from house to house, and from shop to shop, a petition to the two Chambers, by which, the "Haytien people, jealous of preserving intact the sacred principle of *liberty*, . . . appreciating the *inexpressible benefits* which His Excellency, President Faustin Soulouque, had conferred upon the country, . . . recognizing the incessant and heroic efforts he had manifested in *consolidating the institutions*, . . . do *bestow* upon him, without further ceremony, the title of Emperor of Hayti." No one, of course, carried his contempt of life, so far, as to refuse his signature to this document. On the 25th, the petition was taken to the Chamber of Representatives, who seconded, with double eagerness from enthusiasm and terror, the *wish of the people;* and the next day, the Senate sanctioned the decision of the Chamber of Representatives.

The same day, the Senators, on horseback, went

in a body to the palace. The president of the Senate carried, in his hand, a crown of *gilt pasteboard*, made during the night. He placed it, with formal precaution, on the august head of Soulouque, whose countenance became radiant at this desirable contact. The president of the Senate, then, attached to the breast of the Emperor, a large decoration of *unknown origin*,—passed a chain about the neck of the Empress,—and, pronounced his address; to which His Majesty Faustin replied with spirit:

"*Vive la liberté! vive l'égalité!*"

The Emperor and his cortége, then proceeded to the church, to the sound of the most terrible music possible to imagine, but which was lost, happily, in the frenzied *crescendo* of *vivats*, and the deafening noise of salvos of artillery, which continued, almost without interruption, the whole day. On leaving the church, His Majesty, marched through the city; and, I leave the reader to imagine, the profusion of garlands, triumphal-arches, suits of hangings, and inscriptions, that were displayed! At the end of eight days, the illuminations, by order, still continued; and the police watched, with a suspicious eye, the *freshness of the leaves*, with which each house—especially those of the mulattoes—continued, during the order, to be decorated.

In the meantime, Faustin Ist, shut up in his cabinet, passed his entire time, in contemplation, before a series of engravings, representing the ceremonies of Napoleon's coronation. Not being able to wait any longer, His Imperial Majesty had the principal merchant of Port-au-Prince called, one morning, and commanded him to order, immediately, from Paris, a costume, *in every particular like* that he admired in these engravings. Faustin Ist, besides, ordered, for himself, a crown—one for the Empress—a sceptre, globe, hand-of-justice, throne, and other accessories, *all to be like* those used in the coronation of Napoleon. The finances of the Empire did not recover from this expense for a long time; for all these objects were delivered, payed for, and what is more, used, as we will see further on.

Whilst His Majesty discussed the price of his throne, his sceptre, his royal mantle sown with golden bees, and all the *et cœteras*, the departments advertised by public rumor (for there had not even been a question of consulting them), that they had an Emperor—the departments, hastened to send in, adhesion upon adhesion. It is unnecessary to say, that the most flourishing signatures and the most eccentric paraphrases, belonged to the *suspects*, yellow as well as black. This graduation of universal enthusiasm, reproduced itself, under all possible forms: thus, the most noted localities were content to fire, in honor of Faustin Ist, twenty-one cannon—whilst the most *obscure* places, went up to two hundred and twenty-five. The ultra-black party, however, surpassed all others in the pomp of forms. The words *Sire*, or *Emperor*, in their opinion was too inexpressive, and they were substituted by—*magnanimous hero*, or, *illustrious sovereign*, or *illustrious grand sovereign!* In the sermons, preached for the occasion, by the adventurers, disguised as priests,—who compose the greater part of what is called the Haytien clergy,—Soulouque became the *very christian* Emperor, or *His very christian Majesty*.

The *Constitution of the Empire* dates from the 20th day of September. The imperial power is there declared hereditary, and transmissible from male to male, with the right of the Emperor in the event he should have no direct heirs (which is the case with Soulouque, having only a daughter) to adopt one of his nephews, or to designate his successor. The form of promulgating the laws, is as follows: "In the name of the *nation*, we . . . by the *grace of God* and the *Constitution of the Empire*," . . . which gave satisfaction at once to the partisans of republican right—to those of divine right—and to those of constitutional right. The person of the Emperor is *inviolable and sacred;* and the sovereignty resides in the *universality of the citizens*. The Emperor names the Senate, which does not prevent the Senate from uniting such attributes, as are much more sovereign than the national sovereignty, from which it does not emanate; and more powerful than the Emperor by divine right, whose creature it is: and so forth.

We see that the Haytien Constitution has no reason to envy, in point of absurdity, any other constitution. Practice, in this case corrected, at least, the contradictions of theory; for it is well understood that any Senator, or Deputy, who should think of differing with the Executive power, would be immediately shot; this diminishes the chances of conflict. As to the Haytiens, they would have nothing to desire, as regards political and civil rights, if the Constitution could guarantee them a last privilege: *that of dying a natural death.*

The compensation of the Senators and Deputies is fixed, at 200 *gourdes* a month—or, about eight hundred francs a year, at the actual currency of the *gourde*. One day, having the boldness to ask an increase of pay, His Imperial Majesty was very near having them shot.

The civil list is fixed at 150,000 *gourdes*, which, as to every other person, would signify sixty thousand francs, but, for Faustin Ist, means 150,000 *Spanish dollars;* or nearly eight hundred thousand francs. Here is a detail of interpretation, which has not even been raised. Every proportion of the population being considered, Louis Philippe would have to possess, a civil list of fifty-eight millions, in order to attain the splendor of Faustin Ist.

The Empress received an appanage of fifty thousand *gourdes*. An annual sum of thirty thousand *gourdes*, the distribution of which was left to the

Emperor, himself, was allowed to the nearest parents of His Majesty. Soulouque has not yet definitely stopped this list of his parents; because, the statute *concerning the Imperial family*, has these words, in the preamble: " We decree the following: Article 1st—The Imperial family is composed, *for the present*, &c.," which is a hook of consolation to the forgotten cousins. Such as it is, this list has, already, a reasonable length. Besides the brother of the Emperor and the father and mother of the Empress Adelina, we see figuring on it eleven nephews or nieces of the Emperor, and five brothers, three sisters and five aunts of the Empress—in all, twenty-seven princes and princesses *of the blood;* they are very glad to be on it, for they will have some shoes during their lives.

As to the Empress' aunts, one is a Duchess, and the four others are Countesses. Her brothers and sisters are, also, Counts and Countesses. *Serene Highness* is limited to Monseigneur, the Prince Derival Lévéque, and to Madame, the Princess Marie Michel, the father and mother of Her Majesty, Adelina. *Imperial Highness* begins with the brother and nephews, or nieces of the Emperor. The first, has the title of *Monseigneur*, whilst the nephews are simply called *Monsieur, the Haytien Prince.* The nieces are, only, *Madame* very short. The daughter of the Emperor (Madame Olive) is *Princess Imperial of Hayti.*

Will the new Court be exclusively military, like

that of Dessalines—or, feudal, like that of Christophe? All that we can conjecture, on this grave question, is that, it will be settled, in the most extravagant sense. The expectations, which the friends of mirth entertained on this subject, were even much exceeded by the reality.

Christophe, at the end of four years of his reign, had only named, three princes, eight dukes, nineteen counts, thirty-six barons, and eleven chevaliers—*seventy-seven* nobles, in all. Soulouque, himself, improvised at the first batch, four princes of the Empire, fifty-nine dukes, two marchionesses, ninety counts, two hundred and fifteen barons, and thirty chevaliers—*four hundred* nobles in all; more than quintuple the aristocracy of Christophe, and equivalent to what would be, in proportion to the population of France, a batch of nearly *twenty-nine thousand* nobles. The princes, and dukes, are chosen among the Generals of Division; the counts, among the Generals of brigade; the barons, among the Adjutant Generals, and Colonels; and the chevaliers, among the Lieutenant-Colonels. The civil functionaries have been the object, of another batch of nobles, who have, considerably, increased this figure. The Senators and Deputies, for example, are all barons—that is, assimilated in rank to Colonels. These titles are hereditary; but Soulouque, differing in this respect from Christophe, has not attached territorial privileges to them; although, a feudal name is joined to the titles, as far as the class of barons, exclusively. The *de*, as under Christophe, has been put before all the names—what do I say?—even before the first names; as for example, in place of writing, M. le Baron Louis *de* Léveillé, they write, le Baron *de* Louis *de* Léveillé. When they took this aristocratic particle, they did know how much of it to use.

The four princes of the Empire bear the title of *Serene Highness*. At the head, figures Monseigneur Louis Pierrot; in other words Ex-President Pierrot, who, having been banished, after his fall, into the interior, did not expect such good fortune. Monseigneur de Louis Pierrot bears, by exception, the title of *Prince Imperial*. His three colleagues were the Generals, Lazarre Tape-à-l'Œil, Souffran, and Monseigneur de Bobo. Bobo was the first who accorded Soulouque the title of *Illustrious Grand Sovereign*. Such a delicate attention merited, from him, another, and His Majesty named him Prince of Cap-Haïtien—a city, for which Monseigneur de Bobo had, in fact, an old passion. He loved this city so much, that he was near carrying it away, piece-meal, in his pockets. This miserable wretch was imprisoned, at the time of Boyer's fall, for robbery, and other atrocities, committed after the earthquake which overthrew the Cap.

Of the four Princes of the Empire, the eternal Pierrot is the only one now remaining. Lazarre Tape-á-l'Œil and Souffran survived only a short time, after this magnificent advancement. As to Bobo, it is reported, that at this time he is a runaway in the woods ; and the following is the reason of it:

The ex-bandit belonged to that ultra-black coterie, which, after peopling the prisons, and cemeteries, with mulattoes, in its turn, paid abundant tributes of blood to the ferocious suspicions which it had excited; and which, for its own benefit, it justified. In fact, we can affirm, that each of its members had, more or less, dreamed that, the marvelous destiny of Soulouque would be his. Faustin Ist was not ignorant of this ; reciprocal denunciations had apprised him of it, at need ; and, his silent police were the more watchful of Bobo, because he commanded, in chief, the province of the North, which was very jealous of the metropolitan preponderance of the West, and had often aimed at constituting itself a separate Government. In the month of April 1851, and after having tried his hand, by the execution of his minister of justice, Francisque, (another notability of the ultra-black party) Soulouque, therefore, deprived Bobo of his command, and ordered him to come to Port-au-Prince, and ask his august clemency. Monseigneur de Bobo knew, all the time, by experience, that, in refusing to obey this invitation, he would be condemned to death, but, that in obeying it, he would be shot; and he escaped this dilemma, by the least dangerous alternative—*by flight.*

Soulouque expected an attempt at revolt, and he had taken measures to repress it; but many months passed away, without Bobo giving any signs of life. The unknown, mystery, as we know, exercised a terrible influence on the suspicious mind of His Majesty; and, wishing to touch, with his finger, the invisible danger which covered, in his opinion, the inaction of the disgraced favorite, Faustin Ist marched to the North, at the head of a real army. Arriving at the Cap, he declared, that prince Bobo, having become "the rebel Bobo," had forfeited all his titles; and he put a price on his head, by declaring, every one an accomplice of said rebel, who, knowing his refuge, did not, immediately inform the authorities. But the religion of hospitality is, still, so perennial among the negroes, that the proscribed noble has, until this day, escaped the clemency of his august master.

With regard to the minister Francisque, death surprised him, in the class of dukes; and his history is sufficiently characteristic, to merit a second digression. On a certain night, the *entire post* of custom-house officers broke into the counting room of a foreign merchant, and stole, from it, a considerable sum of money. The investigation, ordered on this occasion, led to the discovery of a revolutionary manifesto, and, also, a list of the members of the provisional government, on which flourished the very flower of the Similien cotérie, or *Zinglins* party, (as they were called at Port-au-Prince); something like the party of the *razors*. In this list, figured the name of Francisque's own brother. The latter was, very soon, deposed by a decree, which, instead of giving him his title of Duke de Limbé, called him simply *citizen* Francisque; which was equivalent to a double disgrace; and, a short time afterwards, he was put under arrest. They only removed him from the dungeon, where he had lain, chained with *his feet in the air*, for several days, in order to conduct him, with nine co-accused, before a council of war, whose jurisdiction he, vainly denied, not being himself a military man. Francisque had not, really, taken any part in the conspiracy; but, to the challenge that the accused could furnish an easy proof of it, the imperial commissioners replied, at first, by jovial pleasantries, and, then, by asking, against him and the four other accused persons who had been specially recommended, the sentence of death;—a sentence, which was drawn up, midst laughter, and the noisy yawns, of the *Messieurs* of the council.

Although, he had appealed from it, the tribunal wished, on the spot, to furnish a spectacle of the degradation of a Duke, and they brutally tore off from Francisque his decorations. The council of revision had the courage to annul the sentence. The five condemned persons were, then, taken before a new council of war, sitting at Croix-des-Bouquets; and which was presided over by the same man, who, in this very place, had pronounced the condemnation of General Céligny Ardouin, one of the victims of Francisque. An hour, afterwards, the latter, who had, moreover, made an appeal, was executed with two others. He did not fall until the third discharge. Francisque was the third minister shot, in three years. On the evening of the execution, an expression of pure joy illuminated the face of Souloque—who exclaimed with the accent of a satisfied conscience:

"They will not say this time that he had no trial!"

But let us return to the new Court. Every duke was addressed as, *his grace Monseigneur de N.* . . *Excellence* belonged to counts; and barons, were designated, uniformly, by *monsieur*. It is not the first offence in creating dukes of *Marmelade* and *Lemonade*. The nomination of the latter relaxed the most gloomy foreheads; for, as to lemonade, it had never been known but as *tafia*. Monseigneur de Lemonade, having been, besides, appointed *grand pantler* (master of the pantry) wandered from door to door, like a troubled spirit, vainly, asking what was the nature of his functions. In despair of his case, his grace addressed the Emperor, who not knowing any better himself, was content to reply: "*It is something good.*" There is a duke *du Trou* (of the Hole), and a duke *du Trou-Bonbon* (of the sugar candy Hole); a count *de la Seringue* (of the Syringe), a count *de Grand-Gosier* (of the Great-Gullet), a count *de Coupe-Haleine* (of

Short-Wind), and a count *de Numero-Deux* (of the Number-Two). [See *Moniteur Haïtien.*]

As under Christophe, these kinds of designation have geography for their excuse. Some barons bear names to kill, such as the Baron *de Arlequin* (Harlequin,) the Baron *de Gilles-Azur* (of Blue-Clowns,) the Baron *de Poutoute* (of All-louse); or gallant names, such as the Baron *de Paul Cupidon* (of Paul Cupid,) the Baron *de Jolicœur* (of Goodheart,) the Baron *de Jean Lindor*, the Baron *de Mésamour Bobo* (Hurt-my-love-a-little,) and the Chevalier *de Pouponneau.*

Many of these dignitaries have been in the galley-slave prisons, and others, ought to have been there: they are not perfect. The *piquet*, Jean Denis, for example, had been named *Duke d'Aquin*, the principal theatre of his robberies ; the executor of the eminent works of the *piquets*, Voltaire Castor, has become his excellency M. de Voltaire Castor, Count de l'Ile-à-Vache. Here and there, on the contrary, a few dukes appear, some counts and barons, who, in such a midst, really merit to be distinguished ; and who feel themselves, very badly at ease, among their terrible peers.

Haytien *high life* is not allowed to be very accessible. The duchesses and countesses persist, for the most part, in selling—this one, some tobacco and candles—that one, some rum—and another, some fish or other eatables ; neither more nor less than Her Majesty did the same, before the elevation of her husband. Without these useful industries, the dukes, with their seventy francs a month, would scarcely sustain the grandeur of their rank. Many of them are, even, crushed out under the burden; and do not scorn, from time to time, visiting the simple *bourgeois* in order to borrow from them a few *gourdes*, destined to purchase, shoes, pantaloons, or, some other little accessories, of every aristocratic toilette. They ask, occasionally an increase of pay, but His Majesty is without bowels for these illustrious unfortunates.

Not satisfied with having a *noblesse*, Faustin Ist has created an Imperial and Military Order of Saint-Faustin, with chevaliers, commanders, and so forth; besides, an Imperial and Civil Order of the *Legion d'honneur*. The ribbon of the Legion d'honneur was originally purely red; but, since, he has modified the thing—which I regret to announce to certain French democrats, who, allured by the similarity of names, have solicited of Faustin Ist, under color of being negropolists, (and one of them with offers of money) this *vain bauble*, of which the red is decidedly bordered with blue. Here again I exaggerate nothing. The demands of this kind have been so numerous, that Soulouque, finally conceiving himself a high estimate of his two Orders of chivalry, expressed the regret of having been too prodigal with them, since their creation. Everybody, in fact, are members of these two Orders, to begin from the rank of captain inclusively.

The organization of the household of the Emperor, and of that of the Empress, is the same, as it was under Christophe; who had, himself, blended together the ceremonial of the Court of Louis XIV., and that of the Court of England. Only, Soulouque has infinitely more governors of chateaux, chamberlains, masters of ceremony, huntsmen, stewards, &c., than Christophe ever had, and even, I believe, than Louis XIV. The traditions of the *salons* of Toussaint and Christophe are nearly lost in Hayti, so that the solecisms of etiquette are very frequent, in the new Court; Soulouque is not exempt from them, himself, although he begins to improve. They do as well as they can.

XIII.

The Haytien Clergy—Ceremony of the Coronation.

At the same time that he ordered, from Paris, the ornaments of the coronation, Faustin Ist ordered a Bishop from Rome; and here we are led to speak, of one of the most characteristic eccentricities of this eccentric Empire—the Haytien clergy.

Although the Catholic religion has been, for a long time, the only one recognized in Hayti—and although, it embraces almost the whole population there,—no hierarchical tie binds the Haytiëns to the rest of the Church. Christophe, it is true, had *an archiepiscopal see erected in the Capital, and episcopal seats, in the chief cities,* of his kingdom of two hundred thousand inhabitants; but there is no need of bishoprics without bishops,—and his black majesty, who, in *notifying* his accession to the Pope, asked him to send him a few, had the affliction not even to receive a reply,

We can conjecture what must be the Haytien clergy, in the absence of every institution, and all control. As the first proof of its morality, we will state, that the greater number of the forty-eight, or fifty, individuals, French, Savoyards, or Spanish, who compose it, live in public concubinage, raising, at the parsonage, the children which result from this relation; and say, without ceremony, to the friends who visit them: "I present to you my governess and my *children*." Every year, until the present, the *Moniteur Haytiën* has published some terrible circulars against the *governesses* who are too young, but without success. The more scrupulous, among these foreign priests, confine themselves to preserving appearances, by taking *two* governesses, instead of one. Are they menaced with expulsion?—they hasten to the minister of justice, and there humbly represent that the goverment cannot, without cruelty, make their children orphans. One of these adventurers, Corsican in origin, who was finally expelled, for having *taken up arms* in favor of Herard, said to the minister: "The Government does wrong in suspecting me; how can it be that I am not a man of order? I have a numerous family to raise; I have so many children, by such a woman." But the woman, he designated, was lawfully married to an inhabitant of the country. The minister, really, not knowing whether to laugh, or be angry, at this candor of cynicism, replied: "But what you allege as an extenuating circumstance, is neither, more nor less, than the crime of adultery, which is prohibited by the penal code!" The unfortunate man seemed confounded by this remark; he had not before even dreamed of it.

To complete their disrepute, the *curés* are, continually, quarrelling with their flocks, before the justices of the peace; for, most of them are usurers, or keep a shop, at the parsonage, by their governess—combining thus, in a way, as unexpected as little edifying to religion, the property of the family. They live, besides, upon the best terms, with vaudoux sorcery; finding their profits, completely, in selling it consecrated wax-tapers, which are resold to its customers; and, in saying masses, which, in order to give them greater consequence, are sometimes made to intervene, in the conjurations. This smuggling trade, on the frontier of *fetichism* and christianity, is by no means the least productive of the perquisites of the Haytien *curés*.

After this, is it astonishing, if construing in their way the example of men, whom they respect, on the faith of custom, as the living types of duty, that the free negroes of Hayti are, morally, and socially likewise, behind—perhaps more behind than the slave population of Saint-Domingo was, formerly; and, because they see still, alternating in the same house, christian baptisms, philosophical marriages, and Mandingo funerals? I ought to speak severely of these things; now here is the explanation of it.

With four or five very honorable exceptions, the most worthy among the deserving Haytiens, these adventurers are priests expelled from their dioceses; and, who come to seek their fortunes in a country, where the absence of hierarchical bond screens their past conduct from all enquiry, and their present behavior, from all efficacious surveillance. Besides, they are only priests after their own fashion, by virtue of false certificates; and there are found, among them, those, who, not having had time, or the sagacity, to learn their new *rôle*, do not really know how to officiate.

In his double capacity of *very christian majesty*, and of grand vaudoux dignitary, Soulouque practices, in regard to funerals, both rites, at the same time. Sometime after his elevation, he celebrated at Petit-Goäve, the place of his birth, a funeral service to his mother. The day was consecrated to the ceremonies of the church; but, after nightfall, Faustin Ist, with some friends, went to the cemetery, secretly, and with his own hands sprinkled, the blood of an immolated goat, over the grave of the old slave, who had given Hayti an Emperor. According to negro usage, the *fête* continued a week; and Faustin Ist had a *hundred* beeves killed, for the fifteen or twenty thousand vaudoux guests, which had assembled, from every part of the country.

At the very time, Soulouque was applying to Rome for the conclusion of a *concordat*, the vaudoux worship which he had only practiced from the beginning secretly, tended visibly to become the semi-official religion. In travelling, for example, if His black majesty hears the tambour of a *papa* beating in the distance, he will instantly stop, and seem absorbed, for some seconds, in a kind of interior contemplation; then, followed by some friends, who were, ordinarily, Bellegarde, Souffran, and Alerte, he would hide himself, a moment, in the woods, to perform out of the way, some mysterious compliment of the ceremonies required, in such cases, by the *couleuvre*. After these African side-prayers, Faustin Ist renewing conversation, on his favorite subject—that is, as to the negotiations with the Holy See—asked for new details on the organic laws, whose spirit he had not well apprehended, and on the *concordat*, which he took to be a man.

Under Boyer, after the recognition of Haytien nationality, there were serious efforts made, to suppress these monstrosities. Some regular negotiations were opened, to this end, between the Government at Port-au-Prince and the Court of Rome, which sent an American Bishop to the spot, with full powers to conclude the basis of a *concordat*. Unfortunately, the Bishop was not sufficiently conciliatory. He required, among other things, the suppression of that article of the code, which subjects, to the common law, the ecclesiastics convicted of uttering seditious speeches. On their side, the mulatto party, who, with regard to religion, were still of the opinion of the Directory, showed themselves still less conciliatory, fixing, as the extreme limits of their concessions, the Napoleonic system, in which was contained the *recognition of the right of divorce.* Although the commissioners, delegated by Boyer, might have been personally more competent than the body of the party, and although there was among them a very able negotiator, M. B. Ardouin, the conference very soon became unpleasant. A well-known negropholist succeeded, in embroiling every thing, by writing letter after letter to the Haytien Government, in order to demonstrate, as clear as the day, that it was about to throw itself into the lions-mouth of Jesuitism. Briefly ; it did not understand the matter, and the young Republic, happy and proud in having escaped the yoke of Jesuitism, continued to sacrifice to snakes on the altar of philosophy.

If, by the elevation of Faustin Ist, snakes had become, more than even, in honor at Port-au-Prince, as much could not be said of philosophy ; and there is reason to believe, that the obstacles to a *concordat* did not proceed, this time, from the Haytien Government. Soulouque was, certainly, the man to have any defender of the rights of the Government shot during the session, who should be sufficiently imprudent to raise questions of such a nature as to cause his coronation to fail. There was in this matter to the black monarch, more than a question of principle—there was a question of *toilette ;* for the Imperial mantle, sown with golden bees, and its splendid accessories, could only serve for that occasion.

Dressing is, very certainly, one of the greatest cares of Soulouque. He has been seen, sometimes, to show himself, in the city during the same day, under three or four different costumes, each more dazzling than the other. He ordered, for example, in 1847, from Paris, a certain green dress, which did not cost less than thirty thousand francs; just the actual budget of public instruction. Faustin Ist, for a long time, had doated upon a certain gold and scarlet costume, ordered for Riché, the cut and color of which, has never been adopted but by Haytien Presidents and Swiss doctors. The first time Riché put it on his back, a flatterer exclaimed: "I have seen a similar dress on the Duke de Nemours." Riché, still a negro at heart, in spite of his energies and civilized instincts, became very pensive from that time; and, finally, said, in scratching his ear: *But Duke de Nemours, he not first chief."* This discovery disgusted him, immediately, with the said costume, which he hastened to put off, and never afterwards put it on. Soulouque had it enlarged, from head to foot, including the boots, for his own use. It is proper to add, that Soulouque, especially on horseback, has a very fine appearance, under all this fabulous luxury, which certainly makes him the most *stylish* Emperor of our era.

But a fatality was decidedly mixed up with this business. A certain Savoyard abbé, named Cessens,—the grand chaplain to the Emperor, and cure of Port-au-Prince, with the title of

Ecclesiastical Superior,—in the meanwhile, found the secret of supplanting the Haytien merchant, M. Villevaleix, and of having himself sent, in his place, to Rome, from whence he counted certainly upon bringing back a *mitre*. This is what precisely spoiled the whole affair.

This Abbé Cessens had the advantage, over many of his brothers, of being really a priest, and of not being an excommunicated priest. The information which reached Rome concerning him was, however, of such a scandalous nature, that, at the first audience, he was severely reprimanded, by the Holy Father, and, formally, rejected at the second interview. The Abbé Cessens was not pleased with this disappointment.

On returning from Rome, he related, what he wished to be thought the pretended success of his mission ; and managed the thing so well, that two French journals,—numerous copies of which were sent to Saint-Domingo—successively announced in good faith, the passage from Marseilles of Father Cessens, *Bishop of Hayti;* and, the departure from Havre of *Monseigneur* Cessens, clothed with full powers for the Coronation of the Emperor Soulouque. The latter, to whom it was very necessary to tell part of the truth, was not careful to test a fable, of which he had the profit, without the responsibility. And understanding that the Emperor did not wish to be undeceived, the few Haytiens who knew the foundation of the whole joke, prudently kept silent. Not a single member of the clergy dared, to protest, openly, against this sacrilegious hoax; the more courageous satisfied themselves, by informing our Consul-general, M. Maxime Raybaud, that they would not sanction it, by their presence.* M. Raybaud, charitably, remonstrated with one of the ministers, M. Dufrene, alias, *his grace*, the Duke de Tiburon, on the necessity of preventing the scandal, which would result from this forbearance, by making Soulouque forego his project of a coronation.

M. Dufrene promised to do it; but reflecting, afterwards—on one hand, that he was a mulatto, (that is, *a suspect*,) and on the other, that His Majesty had had one of his ministers shot, every year, and that the execution of the last was nearly a year since—Monseigneur, the Duke de Tiburon concluded to abstain from a communication so hazardous. The *Bishop* Cessèns concluded, besides, with being satisfied with the title of Vicar General—a title, equally, usurped, but which, by implying the idea of a delegation, permitted a certain degree of likelihood to the pretended powers, with which he claimed to be invested.

Soulouque, therefore, was about to be crowned at last!!

About the close of March, 1852, Port-au-Prince

---

* This threat was not carried out. According to the *Moniteur Haytien*, the clergy of the Empire were present in a body at the ceremony.

was, literally, crowded by a multitude of deputations called together by the occasion, from all parts of the Empire. Sunday, the 4th of April, new uniforms, were distributed, to the troops of the guard and the garrison. The Sunday following, there was a blessing, and distribution of Imperial eagles. Finally, on the 17th of April, at sundown, a hundred cannon, to which an immense clamor of public joy replied, in the popular quarters of Bel-Air and Morne-à-Tuf, announced that the festival of the coronation had begun ; that is, that it was necessary to illuminate for seven nights, and dance for seven days, continuously.

The next day, the 18th, at three o'clock in the morning, the Imperial guard, and the military deputations, occupied the *Champs de Mars*, where a church had been erected ; for the construction of which, all the carpenters of the Empire were required, to the last moment. The constituted corps, the consular body, the officers of the French steamer, the Crocodile, and the representatives of foreign trade, assembled in this church, and at nine o'clock, to the sound of bells, of drums, of the cannonade, and of the most terrible music possible to imagine, *Their Majesties* left the Imperial Palace.

The march was opened, by the Chevalier de Dufort, king-at-arms, whom twenty-seven heralds-at-arms and ushers of the palace followed, on foot, six abreast ; the first, were dressed in crimson velvet, and armed with a *caduceus*. Then came, in the same order, the chevaliers, the barons, and the counts; as to the dukes, they marched all abreast. If the *Moniteur Haytien* is to be believed, all these various dignitaries wore costumes appropriate to their rank—costumes of unequalled magnificence; as witness that of the princes and dukes, such as an Imperial ordinance of the 9th of November, 1849, had prescribed:

"A white tunic, which must descend below the knee; a royal blue mantle, the length of which must fall below the calf of the leg, broidered in gold three inches in breadth; a doublet of red taffetas, fastened at the neck with a tassel of gold; white silk stockings; square gold buckles; shoes of red morocco, covering the instep; a sword, with handle of gold, at the side; a round hat, turned up before, trimmed with gold lace, floating plumes of the national colors, for the princes and marshals of the Empire—and, with seven waving, red plumes, for the dukes."

Witness again the costume of the counts:

"A white tunic; a sky-blue mantle, broidered in gold, of the breadth of two inches; doublet in white, even longer than that of the princes and dukes; white silk stockings; square gold buckles; shoes of red morocco, &c. . . ."

By a singular omission, which, at first, seemed justified by custom and the heat of the climate, breeches were omitted, in the prescribed costume, of the first dignitaries of the Empire. It was however a pure over sight, for we see them appear in blue taffetas, in the uniform of the barons (red coats,) and in red taffetas, in that of the simple chevaliers (blue coats); but, alas! (and may it not displease the *Moniteur Haytien*) nearly all this magnificence, which, under Christophe, was literally realized, was in this instance, *entirely wanting except on paper*.

The photographic reproduction of the ceremony, which we had an opportunity of consulting, the following year, at Port-au-Prince, did not exhibit the prescribed costume, except in seven or eight dukes and counts. With these exceptions, the more rich or more formal among the grand dignitaries, had replaced the ceremonial costume, by the uniforms, appropriate to the grade they held in the army.

We could study, among forty others, the innumerable differences, which distinguished the city dress from the Court costume; the military uniforms, from the bourgeois clothes; and the rest were obliged to compensate, by dignity of attitude, for the excessive simplicity of their *tenue*.

In view of the enormous difference, which existed, between the nominal and real value of the *gourde*, those princes and dukes, whom the Emperor had not allowed a share in the acknowledged robberies, had only a provision, as we have seen, of a little more than forty cents a day, with which to support the splendors of their rank; which was evidently not enough for so much taffetas and laces. We can estimate from this, the share of proportional luxury, which accrued to the counts and barons. And what shall we say of the unhappy chevaliers! Among these, we could name more than one, who showed "the calves of his legs," notwithstanding the explicit prescriptions of the ordinance of the 9th November, 1849.

After the order of the *noblesse*, the three ministers of the Emperor, and his chancellor, marched abreast, to wit: Their Graces, Monseigneur de Louis Dufrene, Duke de Tiburon and Marshal of the Empire—Monseigneur de Louis Étienne, Duke de Saint-Louis du Sud—Monseigneur d'Hippolyte, Duke de la Bande-du-Nord, and His Excellency M. de D. Delva, Count de la Petite-Riviere-de-Dalmarie. The princes of the Imperial family followed, also abreast, with the exception of the Duke de Port-de-Paix, brother of the Emperor, who marched alone about four steps behind. Twelve platoons of the different corps of the Imperial guard, behind which, marched six *aides-de-camp* of the Emperor, preceded, immediately, the carriage which held *Their Majesties*, and the young Princesse Olive. Before and behind this carriage, drawn by eight horses—the magnificence of which would not be disowned by a more real monarch— were drawn up eighteen pages.

Two simple colonels,—the colonel of the light-horse, grand equery of the Emperor—and the first equery of the Empress, both on horseback, marched on each side of the Imperial carriage. The carriage of the Princesses Imperial, Célia and Olivette, which came next, was drawn by only six horses, and escorted by only two lieutenant colonels, six *aides-de-camp* of the Emperor, and two platoons of the guard, which separated it from those, which contained the other ladies of the Imperial family, to wit: the nieces of the Emperor, the princess Marie Michel, mother of the Empress; then, three sisters and two aunts of the latter, who were simple countesses. The programme placed, in succession, the carriages of the ladies of honor, ladies in waiting, princesses, duchesses, countesses, barons and chevaliers; but, with four or five exceptions, the programme on this point was not carried out. Most of these ladies, as I have said, exercised some useful calling, and would scarcely have been able to exhibit any carriages, except the small handcarts and wheel-barrows, upon which, they transported their goods. Many among them, more faithful to etiquette than their husbands, however, put on the court dress, the tails of which they made their *little negroes* carry.

Arriving at the Champ de Mars, *Their Majesties* entered a tent, to put on the costume of the coronation. Some minutes afterwards, the curtain of the tent was raised again, and the radiant face of Soulouque—that large, fat, infantine face, which the fear of spells, or the thirst for blood sometimes changed, in such a strange way—was detached, between a splendid diadem, and the blue mantle, spangled with gold; but the mantle was too small, and the diadem too large! His Majesty carried, besides, the sceptre, and the hand of justice. Through the influence of habit, and all engrossed as he was with his new *rôle*, Soulouque could not avoid, in the short passage from the tent to the church, casting some suspicious looks before him; it was useless trouble. The most minute examinations had been made, in time, and they could not discover, even with a microscope, on all the passage of the Emperor, either sprigs of grass, or grains of dust, shaping the form of a cross. The incredulous, as we know, were not less interested, than the believing, at these precautions; because, at every evil présage, which had struck Soulouque, for four years past, a human hecatomb had answered for it.

The Empress, covered with her mantle, but without ring or crown, and escorted, by her chevaliers of honor, opened this new march. The princesses, Olive, Olivette, and Célia, held up her mantle; theirs were supported, by the chevaliers, de Sampeur, Léandre de Denis, and Myrtil de Latortue; and that of the Emperor, by the princes, Jean-Joseph and Alexander de Jean-Joseph. Each of the *honors*—to wit: the sword, the collar, the rings, the globe, &c. &c., were carried on a cushion, by a high dignitary, escorted by two other dignitaries of equal rank. A magnificent *dais* had been raised, in the church, for Soulouque and Madame Soulouque; and a large and small throne served to receive, by turns, these two strange Majesties, according to the different phases of the ceremony. We must forego a detailed description of it.

The complicated evolutions, by which, the objects composing the toilette of the coronation passed, from the hands, the heads, and the shoulders, of the august couple, to the altar ; the benediction and *tradition* of each of these objects ; the triple unction, which Their Majesties, kneeling on a cushion at the foot of the altar, received on the forehead, and both hands ;—the Latin interrogations addressed sharply to the Emperor, at which, he opened his staring eyes, uncertain, in this rolling fire of new words, which confused his memory for an hour, whether it was proper for himself too to speak Latin on that occasion ; the vigorous effort, by which he recovered his presence of mind, and comprehended that it was proper; the rapid combat, which the promising words, indicated by the ritual—and the confessing words, more familiar to his christian souvenirs, displayed on his lips ;—finally, the respectful, but noisy kiss, which the abbé Cessens impressed on the cheeks of the Monarch ;—all these would much exceed the limits of this volume—and even then, we would not have reached the second part of the ceremony.

The programme alone, which was moreover limited to the most summary indications, was not included in less than eleven mortal pages in folio, of small print. A striking episode distinguished the close of the coronation. The Emperor, who was anxious to receive from the hands of the Church the sceptre and the sword,—by a noble movement of pride (which was, besides, anticipated by this programme) took the crown from the altar, himself, and placed it on his own head. As to the august Adelina, she was crowned by her husband.

This other provision of the programme: "prolonged cries of '*vive l'Emperor! vive l'Imperatrice!*' heard in all parts of the Church,"* was not less faithfully filled; and that, at two different times, before the *Te Deum*, and after the constitutional oath, taken on the Holy Evangel by the Emperor. The Abbé Cessens gave the signal for the first acclamations, by exclaiming on the march from the great throne: '*Vivat Imperator in œternum!*'; and the king-at-arms gave the signal to the others, by saying, in the same breath: "*The very glorious, and most august Emperor, Faustin Ist, Emperor of Hayti, is crowned and enthroned. Vive l'Empereur!*" The programme should have certainly dispensed with carrying anticipation so far. A very natural

---

* That nothing might be wanting to complete the imitation—the programme was textually copied, and without any other variation, than changing the past tense into the future, in the *proces-verbal* of the coronation of Napoleon and Josephine.

love of life with some, and a real fanatical devotion with a larger number, guaranteed, beforehand, the spontaneity and unanimity of these acclamations. Among the common people, especially, the enthusiasm, excited by the dances, the noise of the tamborines, cymbals, bells, and the cannonade, became delirious. Moreover, on this occasion, a profound sentiment of pride mingled with it; for Soulouque was, certainly, the first *papa-vaudoux*, who had had the honors of a coronation,—and, of a coronation exactly like that of Napoleon,—that demi-god of negroes.

The music of the grand mass was, by turns, executed on trumpets, clarinets, cymbals, and the tambours of the Imperial guard—a formidable orchestra, which would give the tooth-ache to a dead man—and, by the musicians of their majesty's chapel, which was composed, of a first and second master, of twenty-five chevaliers; together, presenting an effective of eleven violins, three violoncellos, a clarinet, seven flutes, two *cornet-à-pistons*, and *but a single* singer, the chevalier Théogéne de Poule —and, finally, twenty-four *knight's ladies*. Some of these performers had real merit; but, in the choice of others, there was much more regard paid to birth, than to talents; and harmony was, only, in the hearts of the latter. At the offertory, the Abbé Cessens received, from their Majesties' own hands, two wax-tapers, incrusted with thirteen pieces of gold; besides, a *loaf of silver*, and a *loaf of gold,* and a vase. These five offerings were borne, by a princess and four duchesses, escorted by an equal number of counts.

Let us pass over the ruinous magnificence, which for eight days, celebrated this coronation; but the bill of expenses did not even stop there. Some time afterwards, the Haytien Chambers voted, for the consecration of the Abbé Cessens, 250 thousand *gourdes,* (1,250,000 francs); appropriated, both to meet *unforseen* expenses, and because (said this model parliament) "it is becoming the dignity of the nation, to surround with *every kind of consideration,* the Sovereign who enjoys its love and sympathy."

XIV.

The principle of authority in Hayti—The Secret of Soulouque.

Every one has considered Soulouque's elevation to Empire, only from its comic side. Some American journals thought they discovered in it, nothing less than the first official manifestation, of the scheme of a black confederation, which would group, about the Haytien nucleus, the slave and enfranchised populations of the other Antilles. It is, indeed, possible, that the colored men of Gaudeloupe had dreamed of some such thing, before the scenes of April 1848, which edified them as to Soulouque's tenderness for the men of color. It was, moreover, possible, that this idea had originated at Paris, in the brains of certain mono-maniac negropholists; in whose opinion, emancipation would not be complete, until they should see, in our colonies,—widowed of every vestige of European civilization,—white or mulatto slaves expire under the lash of black planters. Finally, in proof of this it appears, that, in the Spring of 1849, the black insurgents of Sainte-Lucie assailed the Governor's palace, and burned some dwellings, to the cry of *"Vive Soulouque!"* But the man, who had lent his name to these vague designs, was certainly the last person who would have had a hand in them.

On learning the part, these stupid or culpable expectations had assigned him, Soulouque manifested as much irritation as fear, and exclaimed: "This is another turn of these *mulatto rascals*, in order to embroil me with France and England—indeed, with all the world!" As to Soulouque's subjects, the idea of demanding from abroad the benefits of a solidarity of their race, was, if possible, still more foreign than it was with him. To give only one proof of it; the news of emancipation decreed in 1848 in our colonies—news which it would seem ought to have afforded real joy to the future Emperor, was received by him with absolute indifference. He, only, concerned himself about the negroes.

Since we are tranquilised on this subject, we can speak in a friendly way of this Emperor, without parallel, and of this Empire without an equal.

The first question, which presents itself, is that of duration; and this, appears to us, settled in favor of Faustin Ist. The three preceding black despots had fallen, without doubt, by the coalition of like hatreds and terrors as those which Soulouque has accumulated about himself for the past seven years. But Toussaint, Dessalines and Christophe were surrounded, by the Generals of the war of Independence; that is, by so much of the influence of a rivalry, which the remembrance of a long continued equality, rendered impatient of the restraints imposed by the capricious tyrannies of the very one of them, they had made their master; and who, as each wielded an authority, without limit, over that portion of the army, they had organized, were perfectly prepared to manifest their rancor in rebellion. There was nothing like this about Soulouque. Perfectly unknown until the very day, that an electoral expedient raised him to supreme power, he exercised, over his trembling *entourage*, the ascendancy of surprise and mystery; and the illusion was so complete, as it descended from the beginning on his character, that it even impressed upon the general weakness, the exaggerated aspect of every reaction.

In the second place; the warlike and disciplined generation, of the three epochs, of which we are treating—that, which the old aggregation of the work-shops had grouped, in compact and distinct masses, about each chief—had completely disappeared. A long peace was sufficient, besides, to prevent the reconstruction of the great military influences of former times. The greater part of the actual Generals were only so, in name and by a fiction, which consisted in assimilating the principal civil functions, to corresponding military grades; and with regard to the real Generals, they shared the immense unpopularity, which now burthened the military service. The Haytien army has been increased to more than twenty-five thousand men, out of a population of a half million* of souls, in which the women figure at least for three-fifths; this is equivalent to an effective, quintuple that of our own. We can understand how intolerable such a military system is in a country, where thirty years of absolute unrestraint has rendered the masses unaccustomed to all dependence on each other—where, the absence of industry, and the systematic division of property, binds almost all the sturdy men, to the soil—and where the facilities of concubinage, now the recog-

---

* In his "Geography of the Island of Hayti," published in 1832, M. A. Ardouin inclines to the figure of 700,000 souls; of which, he assigns 125,000 to the Spanish part of the Island, which leaves 575,000 to the French part. But the author, at the same time, indicates the tendency of the country people to flow into the cities, where the hygiénic conditions are very inferior. But, it is not too much to estimate at 75,000 souls the deficit, which should result, as much from this increase of the causes of mortality, as from the civil troubles of 1842 and 1843; from eight years of war with the Dominicans; and, finally, from the conclusive facts of emigration, and executions, since the 16th of April, 1848. All exact, or even, approximative estimates of the population are, moreover, impossible. The country blacks, who attach a high importance to having their children baptized, bury the greater number of their dead, as a compensation, after the idolatrous rites; so that the civil list being in the hands of the clergy, is not registered with any accuracy, except the number of births, which renders all comparative estimate impossible. The number of births taken, separately, would be a basis of calculation quite as uncertain; for it is a notorious fact, that the mortality of infants is much greater, in Hayti, than any where else.

nized condition,* have imposed upon each of them family ties.

The enticement of a month's pay of four *gourdes* (at the rate per day of one franc fifty centimes) out of which, the Haytien soldier must lodge, feed, and, in part, equip, himself, is not of a nature to overcome this legitimate repugnance. Not being put in barracks, they can, in truth, dispose of their time, between the periods of service; and the greater number of them, take this service very much at their ease. Nothing is more common, for instance, than to see, in a vacant sentry-box, a peaceable gun watching, all alone, over the safety of the Empire. Do they project another expedition against the Dominicans?—the whole body of the black army gather with an enthusiasm, difficult to describe, at the distribution of provisions and cartridges; and the soldiers, are no sooner on the march, than they desert, right and left of the way, by bands; taking the air, in the woods, while the provisions last; and wasting, foolishly, their cartridges in petards. This relaxation of discipline exhibits the little moral authority, which the Generals now enjoy; and as, by some remaining scrupulousness, the deserters think they are bound to hide themselves, or, at least, to buy the indulgence of their chiefs, they experience towards

---

* Out of 2,015 births shown by the *Moniteur Haytien* of the 10th of August, 1850, in some localities taken at hazard, there were only eighty-four legitimate children; a little less than *four per cent*.

these, a sentiment, in which, the hatred of the offender, is augmented by the hatred of the debtor.*

Free from the influence of these rivalries, in which were personified, by turns, the complaints raised by Toussaint, Dessalines, and Christophe, Soulouque had, besides, a point of support which these had not. Toussaint and Christophe, with their party, being violently taken with civilization, repelled unmercifully the vaudoux; and Dessalines, in spite of his sincere, or affected, fondness for African savagery, was himself embroiled with the *papas*. Being then only General, he had himself "physiced," on the day of battle, by one of them;—that is, his body was covered with amulets, designed to render it invulnerable; but, all physiced as he was, he was, exactly, wounded at the first fire. Furious at this, Dessalines beat his sorcerer, with his own hands, and made him return the ten Portuguese dollars paid for the consultation; and declared, from that day, that the *papas* were only a set of odious intriguers.† Sou-

---

* About the end of December, 1847, the Dominicans having stopped on the Haytien territory, Soulouque sent against them three regiments, which, at the time they marched, presented together an effective strength of only 700 men, although each regiment is organized with about 600 men. After the first distribution of rations, five-sixths of the soldiers were absent at the call; one of the regiments was found reduced even to *fifteen* soldiers, and *forty-three* officers.

† On another occasion, Dessalines, then inspector general of worships, learned that a vaudoux council was held in the plain of *Cul-*

louque, whose tyranny was, on the contrary, only a vaudoux reaction, has, in the innumerable adherents of this negro free-masonry, as many spies as decoys, ready to apprise him of the least symptom of conspiracy, or to create, by a mute understanding, a void about the conspirators;—as witness the sudden and profound indifference, with which the fall of Similien was received. And yet, by reason of the boldness with which his old familiarity with the President inspired him, and by his rank in the presidential guard which had become the last centre of that *esprit-de-corps*, that formerly rendered military revolutions so easy,—Similien was the only person who filled the two conditions necessary to repeat, in opposition to Soulouque, the part which was, successively, played by Dessalines and Christophe against Toussaint; by Christophe against Dessalines; and by Richard against Christophe.

Soulouque, therefore, for the time, had no conspiracy to fear; for the instrument and the subject —the army and the masses—were wanting for such

---

de-Sac, under the presidency of an old black woman—and that a great number of farmers had left their work to be present. He surrounded the place of meeting with a battalion; dispersed the assembly by firing into it; and having taken fifty prisoners, had them bayonetted immediately. M. Thomas Madiou who relates this fact, adds: Toüssaint held in horror every thing pertaining to vaudoux; he often said that he spoke through his nose, only because the vaudoux had thrown some spells on him.

a conspiracy. Not being able to believe in treachery where treason was powerless, every *suspect*, finally, considered real the noisy evidences of devotion, which terror created about him ; and if some timid desire of deliverance sprang up, here and there, in their hearts, we can affirm, that there was not in all Hayti, two men, two friends, even two parents, sufficiently, sure of each other, to venture an interchange of their opinions. A double, a triple espionage, that often changed the informer into the accused, proved but too surely, moreover, the universal distrust, which was practiced at even the distance of two thousand leagues. The proscribed Haytiens, whom we questioned, invariably replied, by praising Soulouque ; as though, they feared that the reflux of the Alantic would bear back, to the illiterate old negro, who reigned over their vacant firesides, some involuntary sign of disapprobation, in order that the invisible vengeance of the master might be visited upon them here.

The very excess of this fear produced everywhere else, some outbursts of individual despair ; but, though the incentive of ambition was wanting, that of vengenance was not less to be dreaded by Soulouque. In the prostration of that yellow and black *bourgeoisie*, which seemed to have only the courage to die, all was not really compulsion and stupor. There was, also, much of that veneration, instinctive in the African, for the hand which strikes him, or the foot which tramples him under.

Despotism existed in their manners, before it was developed in state affairs; and I will give a single proof of it. During the butchery of the mulattoes, at Saint-Marc, by the orders of Christophe, a General, to exhibit his obedience, slew with his own hands his wife and children. But unreasonable as he was in this point, Christophe, himself, thought that it was an excess of obedience, and with a violent blow of his cane, some say,—and with a kick, say others,—he knocked out one of the murderer's eyes. The thought of this abominable devotion, which, everywhere else, would be but baseness approaching idiotism—this thought, found a place in a mind, if not the most cultivated, at least the most upright, the most firm, and the most eager for civilization, which had arisen for long years past, in the ranks of the black caste. This General was, neither more nor less than the future President Riché—the predecessor of Soulouque, and the man of adoption by the enlightened class of the country, who have wept him, (we can say without metaphor,) with tears of blood.

A class so indulgent to the fanaticism of servility was evidently capable of experiencing it, more or less, on their own account. This predisposition did not, even, await the stimulus of fear, to be revealed in them: thus, under the régime of an ultra-democratic constitution, whilst Soulouque was only President, the warmest advocate of equality, thought it very natural and regular, that, at the formal dinners, he should have himself served by Generals, placed behind his chair. Among the penitent revolutionists, who, moreover, exalted the principle of authority, were there not many of them that pushed their sincerity, even, to changing his plates? Terror has, therefore, done no more there, than stimulate a tendency inherent in the public mind of Hayti; and whose outward manifestation does not imply any inward revolt. His black Majesty has even subjected, with impunity, the monarchical sentiment of his subjects to some very rude tests. To conceal nothing—Soulouque, (in comparison with whom the chaste Hippolyte was, not long before, open-breasted; and whom we have seen, up to 1849, especially in his bloody expedition to the South, repel, with virtuous horror, the female enticements, which enthusiasm and often, alas! fear excited, on his march) —Soulouque, since he has become Emperor, seems quite decided to take, literally, the intrepid rhetorical figure, by which certain official addresses have designated him—*the father of his people*. No lady of the court, they say, will be long sheltered from the formidable attentions of Faustin. And if I reveal these intimate details, it is only properly to state that this is not vice in his estimation. The idea of domination, especially of royalty, being inseperable in the African mind, from that of discretionary* power, Soulouque really only sees in this matter one of the thousand superb privileges, belonging to his position as Emperor; and he exercises this right, with the double security, of a pure conscience, and an iron-constitution; another guarantee of stability, which we must take into account. Those who speculate, on the natural death of Faustin, risk having to wait so much longer, because he practices a proverbial sobriety, with regard to rum—that slow poison of the negroes, which kills them toward the hundreth year.

From all these guarantees of security and durability, there would have resulted anywhere else a reaction of clemency: unfortunately, Soulouque continues to show himself, as inexorable and suspicious, as in the very height of the crisis of 1848. On the occasion of his accession to the throne, a proclamation, made the *fusion of all hearts* the order of the day, and advised the citizens, to *join the hand of reconciliation over the altar of their country*. Some persons ventured to take the thing literally, and timidly expressed to His Majesty, that, at least, in carrying the altar of the country from prison to prison, their bolts and walls would be an

---

* Here is another shade of this negro interpretation of the right of domination. After the scenes of April, the friends of Similien, would occasionally through idleness drop into the shops, and say to the merchants wives, with the most natural tone imaginable: "You, please me; and when we shall have killed your husbands, you will become our wives."

insurmountable obstacle, to the required hand-shaking. But at this simple mention of an amnesty, Soulouque exhibited the angry horror of a miser, upon whom they prevailed to expend, in a day, the patient savings of a year. Since then, let us remark, he has been so much the less able to entertain the idea of clemency because his deference for monarchical modes and precedents seem to dictate to him, that he would have the benefit of it, without the cost. In fact, there is not a single official repast given at the palace, at which Faustin Ist does not bridle up, during dessert, to such toasts as the following: *"To the magnanimity of the hero! To the clemency of the great man!"*

Reaction could, scarcely, be produced in Hayti except from Rome. But for the audacious deception practiced, by the Abbé Cessens, it, assuredly, only depended on the Holy See, to take advantage of the ardent desire, this negro monarch felt, to be crowned, to benefit the innumerable *suspects* confined, without trial, in the prisons; it was only necessary to have made an amnesty the first condition of this coronation. Even now, if a *concordat* should put an end to the monstrosities above described—if in place of the scandalous adventurers, who, in order to have their irregularities tolerated, are often the first to flatter the fantasies of Soulouque—a real clergy, so much the more respected because it would have the benefit of the contrast, should make the counsels of humanity and good sense heard by this brute, but not depraved nature, it would not be necessary to despair, perhaps, of clemency. The character of Soulouque offers, in fact, resources valuable to every civilizing influence, which will be in a situation to profit by them. I will put in the first rank, an extreme respect for foreign opinion;—a respect, which penetrates the natural dissimulations of his black majesty; which renders it sensitive beyond all expression, to the pleasantries of the French and American journals; and which has often succeeded in controlling him, even, in his most sanguinary transports of rage; as witness the success, with which our Consul-General touched this spring in 1848.

Soulouque has, (which I believe I before stated,) in addition to the good traits of natural suspicion, an instinctive deference for all advice, the disinterestedness of which, he cannot suspect; and hence, again, the ascendency of the French consul, when pleading the cause of a class, which, with a small number of exceptions, had previously set up as a matter of policy, hatred to France and Frenchmen. The influence then, a foreign agent, whose interference in their domestic affairs, loyal and well conducted as it may be, must always produce some umbrage, has been able to obtain accidentally, might not a serious clergy—a body whose intervention would not be offensive, because it would be exclusively moral, and moreover, anticipated and accepted,—obtain more easily still, and in a measure more lasting?

The day, that a steady light of humanity shall penetrate this darkness of savagery—when Soulouque shall be able to comprehend, that to breathe and walk are not political crimes, and that the only ambition of the class he fears, is neither to be imprisoned, nor shot—on that day, all things considered, Hayti will be, theoretically, nearer to civilization, than it has ever been. Let us not forget; although he may have sprung from the midst of the mulattoes, only to enter among the ultra-blacks, and hence has not ceased to suffer from the contact of anti-French influences, Soulouque is, with Riché, the only Haytien chief, which has, if not understood, at least felt the necessity of encouraging, and retaining our countrymen.* But it was because of its hatred and distrust of Frenchmen, that Hayti refused the right of property to the

---

* He has even more merit in this particular than Riché, who was not beset like him, by the ultra-black minority, and who was encouraged in his civilizing tendencies, on one side, by a few men of the young mulatto generation, who, in this respect, were much more intelligent than their predecessors; and on the other hand, by some enlightened blacks, among others, his minister, M. Larochel. The opposite happened to Soulouque. If some men secretly deplored that their country was not open to white civilization, they concealed it, or even pretended to join the clamors of the ultra-black party, in order not to attract upon themselves the suspicions of this terrible party. Soulouque, besides, had to struggle, in his own council, against the anti-French objections of his minister of finance, M. Salomon, a well-instructed and very able black.

whites; and, if our old colony, which "exported annually four hundred millions of pounds of sugar, no longer makes more than enough for the wants of its sick;" if, after having given to its metropolis, an annual excess of near twenty-two millions of francs, it now returns, with great difficulty, to its own treasury only six to seven millions; if its money, only, circulates for the *fifteenth* of its nominal value; if the little coin, which, usury causes to circulate on the sea-coast, is burdened with an interest varying from 36 to 365 per cent; if, finally, near the middle of 1847, before the ultra-black panic, and under the influence of a complete reaction of security, a plantation of fifty *arpents*, well situated, and in great part set with coffee-trees—that is, in full operation—was found only to realize *a thousand francs*—it is to the ridiculous and savage exclusion, of which I have spoken, that this relapse into barbarism must be above all attributable.

The black insurrection inherited only the waste it had made. European immigration could alone replace, in old Saint-Domingo, the elements of labor and commerce, which disappeared from it, with our colonists. It, alone, could bring back there capital, the proceeds of cultivation and manufacturing, the experience and the commercial relations necessary,—to revive the sugar-houses,—to place local production in a situation to contend with the increasing competition, which was caused, by the agricultural and mechanical ameliorations introduced, by European activity, in the other Antilles—to restore to this production its former outlets—to substitute, in fine, for the fatal expedient of a continued emission of notes, the normal resources of an increase of revenue. The disposition, which Soulouque exhibited with regard to the whites, in general, and the French in particular, would have been, therefore, an augury of veritable regeneration to Hayti; if in this, as apropos of the *piquets*, as apropos of the amnesty, and always for the want of an enlightened and acceptable arbitration, which might have rescued at the proper time, the civilizing purpose or instinct, from those savage prejudices which neutralized them, it would not have been necessary to be satisfied, again, with the rule without the application—with the principle without its consequence. Although, it was only necessary for him to frown, to destroy this combination of savagery and fear, which perpetuated, twenty-five years after the foreign recognition of Haytien independence, an isolation thenceforth without pretext, Soulouque made, or allowed to be introduced into his imperial constitution, the article prohibiting whites from acquiring real estate in Hayti.

Soulouque had not even the logic of his despotism. This strange constitutional Emperor would, most certainly, have had shot, and with the best faith in the world, whosoever had dared to assert, that the Goverment was not Faustin Ist; and it is not too much to wish, that he would carry his imitation of Christophe, in this respect, even to the end; who, setting out from the same idea, believed that it was his interest, at least, to administer the finances of the Government, as a good proprietor; but no. Jealous of accumulating in this, as in all other cases, the profits of the most contradictory situations, Faustin Ist, carried into the administration of the country, which he considered as his perpetual patrimony, the improvident greediness of a transient revolutionist.

The Government is charged with clothing the troops; and, under this pretext, Soulouque, who is awarded the office of furnisher-general, purchases constantly, hundreds of pieces of cloth at fictitious prices—often double, and even triple, their real value; which (to use a common expression), is equivalent to saying, that his black Majesty makes the goose jump from his own basket. The military stores are filled with cloth, which they constantly offer, (and it is always accepted, thanks to the allurement of this profit,) at *from one to two hundred per cent.* It is well known that, notwithstanding this profusion of cloth, the formidable Empire of Hayti continues to exhibit the bizarre phenomenon of an army dressed in rags. The favorite officials of the day, naturally have their share in the plunder, which includes all the Government supplies. At first, Soulouque, alarmed by the invasion of this famished band of highest bidders, who followed on his steps, repelled them *en masse;* but since, he has allowed himself to be bent,—and is satisfied to levy a profit, of from thirty to forty per cent., on every transaction of the kind he permits.

Besides, he has rather gained than lost, by this division of profits; because the *piquets* in favor, and their friends, have become so many courtiers, whose inventive avidity is able to ferret gold out of transactions, in which His Majesty, often thought, he had made a clean sweep. Some individuals found out the secret, of stealing from the plunder itself. We will cite, for instance, that such supplies, as have to pass through three or four hands, are sold each time at a profit of eighty to one hundred per cent., before reaching the military stores. Soulouque levied, as his share, 60,000 francs, in that cause, decided in favor of a lady of his acquaintance; and who had to pay, in consequence, fifteen francs to the Goverment for what was only worth four.*

---

* The ramifications of public peculation did not always stop there. Rather than permit these fabulous supplies of cloth to rot, some Generals found it logical to resell them, for their own benefit, to the retailers of Port-au-Prince, below the market price of the fabric; which had the triple effect—of depriving the treasury of the duties, it would have received upon the same quantity of cloth, delivered to consumption, in the regular way; of creating a ruinous competition, with the houses, which had supplied themselves, with similar merchandise, in this way; and finally, of diminishing the quantity of goods exchanged with those abroad;—that is, the ex-

If Soulouque would employ the sums, he annually monopolises, to create plantations and sugar manufactories, he might, perhaps, congratulate himself, on this concentration of capital, in one hand; *for, it is by the absence, or dispersion of productive energy, that the richest and best situated of the Antilles, has become the most uncultivated and abandoned of all.* These millions, unfortunately, only enter the imperial money-chest, to be sent directly out of the country; and, go to Paris, London, or New York, to pay for the splendid caprices of His Majesty's toilette. Let us add; in his incorrigible mania to steal himself, Soulouque, not satisfied with disposing of the public revenues, at pleasure, also, smuggles, like any other common mortal, in order that, the articles purchased, for his own use, may enter without paying duties.*

---

portation of domestic products suffered by the legal importation, in proportion to the deficit, and causes of depression.

Since this was written, M. Maxime Raybaud has, moreover, succeeded in imposing upon Soulouque an arrangement, which has the result on one part, of protecting, the payment of the colonial indemnity, from the fraudulent tricks that the interpretation of the convention of the 15th of May, 1847, excited;—on the other part, to secure the payment of interest, and the extinguishment of the Haytien loan. The financial wants, which this double obligation has created, will put a stop to the unreasonable wastes, of which I have spoken. If he is wanting in all foresight, and capability of generalization, Soulouque knows how, on the contrary, to yield to the pressure of an immediate necessity.

* To the passion for fine clothes, and handsome decorations, Soulouque, has latterly added the mania for building. His great de-

Soulouque's official receipts go abroad, like his private revenue, and are, besides, worse employed there. All, he does not retain for his personal expenses, is spent in preparations for exterminating the Dominicans; especially in buying American vessels, often out of service, which he loads with artillery, as though he desired to render them still more incapable of sailing; and which his negro sailors blow up, from time to time, body and goods, either by carelessness, or in breaking into the powder-magazine to steal the wherewith to make fusees and crackers. It is useless to show that such purchases, besides being the occasion of ruinous armaments, are of a nature, too unusual to encourage the current of exchanges; and constitutes a wasting loss to the Haytien treasury.

A system, in which every thing combines, on one hand to increase the expenses, and on the other to reduce, at once, the receipts, and the capital circulating in the interior, the primary cause of these receipts,—this system has, necessarily, but one consequence: the continued emission of notes. And accordingly, in manufacturing them almost

---

sire is to possess a house in each of the squares of Port-au-Prince. He has also turned his attention a little to agriculture, and actually seeks to improve a considerable plantation, in the vicinity of the Capital, which the nation made him a present of. Unfortunately, he has impressed *en masse* for this operation, and in the name of military service, all the cultivators of the banks of the *Artibonite*, the only part of the Empire, where agricultural labor is not entirely abandoned.

without intermission, at from *fifteen to twenty-five thousand gourdes* a day, is displayed in all its *éclat* the financial genius of Soulouque.

What sustains, as I have remarked, the circulation of this fabulous paper-money is the fact, that the foreign importers have still the goodness to receive it only upon the *sine-qua-non* condition of, immediately, exchanging it, and on the spot, for products of the soil, especially coffee and dyewoods—which are now almost the only remaining branch of Haytien export. Simple good sense would, therefore, counsel the encouragement, at any price, of the export of coffee, in order to counterbalance as much as possible the causes of depreciation, with which, a continued and unlimited emission of notes burdens the representative expression of this production. Soulouque has done just the contrary.

The socialist experiment of monopoly having resulted in destroying, or nearly so, the metallic receipts of the treasury, by putting to flight foreign importation, which alone nourished them, Soulouque imagined in 1850 to replace them, by natural resources. The enticement was so much the more tempting, as by a very rare coïncidence, it happened that very year, on one hand, that the crop of coffee was of extraordinary abundance in Hayti—and on the other, that coffee was very much in demand, and consequently very dear in the markets of Europe. At the same time, that the monopoly laws were repealed, the Haytien government awarded itself, therefore, the right of taking for its own benefit, at the merchant-consignee's, the *fifth* of the coffee designed for exportation, at the rate of fifty *gourdes* the quintal—that is, nearly forty per cent. below the current price. This loss of *forty per cent.*, assessed on the five-fifths, was explained, as to the mass of exported coffee, by a former over-tax of eight per cent.; but this was not all.

The government is privileged to pay for this fifth monopolized by it, at forty per cent. below the current price in custom-house goods, which it agreed to receive in payment of the export duties due on the four-fifths remaining; but, as the merchant in possession of a thousand quintals, for example, received in payment for the two hundred quintals taken away by the government, 10,000 gourdes in custom-house goods, then, by the terms of the tariff, it was only entitled to 6,400 gourdes, as the export duty of the remaining eight hundred quintals, and there remained some 3,600 gourdes of unemployed goods. By one of those curiosities of credit, only to be met with in Hayti, these unemployed goods, and hence without value, lost in the transaction only about fifty per cent.; which, on a thousand quintals of coffee, worth in the producing market 80,000 *gourdes*, reduced this new loss to 1,800 *gourdes*, or to a little more than two per cent.

This two per cent. added to the eight per cent.,

above-mentioned, increased to more than ten per cent. the over-tax, with which, this new financial combination of M. Salomon has oppressed the whole exportation of coffee.*

But, in ordinary times, the coffee of our old colony, although of excellent quality, was formerly placed, with some difficulty, in European markets; which was attributed to the imperfect manner of cleansing it. What would then happen when, being no longer sustained,—at the place of production, because of low rates resulting from the excess of the crop,—and at the place of consumption, by the fluctuation of the prices,—these coffees, besides, are offered in European markets, with an additional charge of from *ten* to *eleven* per cent.? The consumer would not wish any more; the exporter would not demand any more; and the cultivator, (of course,) would not produce any more.†

---

* This financial expedient was, to be sure, the occasion of new intrigues. It was thus, for example, that the sale of the fifth of the crop of 1850–'51 was burdened with two good-will presents of five francs each per quintal of a hundred pounds.

† To speak correctly, they did not gather it any longer. The cultivation of coffee is now reduced, indeed, in Saint-Domingo to the gathering of the grains which, periodically, fall from the old coffee trees, not a single one of which is renewed. The blacks even allow to be lost on the spot, a portion, more or less considerable, of this precious product—according as it sells, more or less well, in Europe, and as there is wanted, a greater or less quantity, to represent the few yards of cottonades and some pounds of salt meats, required by each family, from foreign commerce. It is by favor of the margin left by this excess, that the export of the coffee of the country can

Sooner or later, the situation of things, which I have described, must produce its extreme consequences; but they are inevitable, if this partial monopoly is maintained. Coffee failing, importers will stop their shipments; for it is not probable that they will consent to exchange cargoes of provisions, (meal, fabrics, &c.,) for cargoes of dye-woods, which vessels never take, except by engagement, and often only as ballast. Importation being arrested, the circulation of the *paper-gourde*, which is sustained by it alone, would cease also; so much the more, that the three or four elements of interior trade which Hayti possesses, proceeds from the soil, and is found (considering the extreme division of property) almost always reunited in the same hand; which is sufficient to paralyze barter.

Deprived, by the same blow, of the receipts from

---

still resist the factitious enhancement of price, with which the monopoly of the fifth has affected it. But the miracle of fertility, of which I speak, cannot continue indefinitely. The old coffee-trees, and their young shoots, are gradually stifled by the formidable power of the vegetation of the forests, which formerly gave them shelter; the excess in question will disappear; production will cease, even by becoming insufficient, whence a double cause of real rise in price, which being added to the economical consequences of the monopoly of the fifth, will close European markets to Haytien coffee. Only one method will then remain to regain these markets: the renewal of the plants. But the blacks, whom the prospect of an immediate, and certain, profit cannot now recover from their apathy, will not issue from it for a stronger reason, before the prospect of a hypothetical and remote profit.

importations, of the revenue from exportations, and the territorial tax, which the contributor could no longer pay, but in rags of dirty paper, His Majesty, would have but one resource left to sustain, for a short time longer, the splendor of his throne: namely, *to sell his counts, dukes, and barons to the planters of Cuba and Porto-Rico.* As to the black peasants, from the moment the cessation of these commercial transactions shall have taken from them, all chance of increasing their means of living by labor, they will not be slow to shut themselves up, in this problem: to obtain the necessaries of life at the least fatiguing price possible.

This problem, nine Haytiens in ten have already proposed to themselves; and the bananas have resolved it. I have heard many individuals assert, that this solution was the best; and rejoice over the happiness of a people, which would only have to sleep, two or three years in succession, to wake up in the midst of the golden age. There is in this opinion, all things considered, some truth. The only inconvenience of this happiness is, that it will suppress, with the necessity of labor, the feeling of social solidarity; destroy with this sentiment the respect for property; introduce want thenceforth by the gradual disappearance of the bananas, which the stronger will steal from the more feeble, and for the reproduction of which, the latter will have more reason to care; and bring man, finally, to consider his fellow-man as a repast served by nature. Certain oceanic peoples, not less privileged than the subjects of Soulouque with respect to climate, justify this disgusting hypothesis.

Indeed, the more we contemplate this living enigma, called Soulouque, the more gloomy it becomes. Never were such numerous energies, guarantees, and civilizing aptitudes, found accumulated in the same hand; and never was there made a more gratuitous recoil towards barbarism, with a mind more reckless of consequences. According as this inexplicable monarch shall be pleased to enter on the path, his interests and instincts direct him—or, to remain in that, I cannot say what hidden impulse drives him,—Hayti will be prosperous in ten years, or cannibal in twenty. Does Soulouque conceal his game? He almost explained it, one day, when he said to some one: "In order to tear from me my secret, it would be necessary to open me like a mackerel!" This operation would expose his black Majesty, too much. Let us endeavor to seek the secret elsewhere:—in that little Dominican Republic whose obstinacy, in continuing republican, costs so much sleeplessness and grief to Faustin Ist.

XV.

The Dominican Republic.

The social condition of the Spanish part of Saint-Domingo presented at the epoch of the first revolution, a complete contrast with that of the French portion of the Island. Whilst here, principles, truly christain, contained in the edict of 1698, gradually gave place to a legislation, which branded mixed marriages, embarrassed emancipation, and openly established the prejudice of color, as a means of police—there, all was organized to facilitate the fusion of the two races. The code of the Indies recognized marriages between master and slave; permitted emancipation, in an absolute manner; allowed to the slave, in fact, the power of redeeming himself, by recognizing him the owner of the revenue acquired outside the labor, due to the master; and assimilated, almost entirely, the enfranchised class to the whites. Spanish customs, with their tendencies to practical equality, which did not exclude subordination, but gave it a patriarchal character, also favored intermixture; and local circumstances facilitated this influence of manners.

At the very time the labors of the mines had exhausted the few aborigines, who escaped from the ferocity of the first *conquistadores*, the occupation of Mexico and Peru opened, to the spirit of adventure, an illimitable field. The want of laborers, on one hand, and the allurements of the unknown, on the other, caused the most enterprising portion of the population, to emigrate to *terra-firma;* and planting on a large scale, which prevents all contact between the master and the slave, remained almost unknown, in the newly settled Spanish colony. The servitude of the blacks, who were about to replace in Hayti the Indians (declared free by repeated edicts of the Metropolis) was changed into domesticity. Besides, the greater number of the colonists had adopted, the favorite occupation of the Spaniards of that period ; they became herdsmen. And, the isolation, which this kind of life produced,—the community of ideas, education, necessities, and the relations of equality, nearly absolute, which was brought about, in the long run, between the master and the slave,—did the rest.

The double stratum of free blood, which the conquering race, and the last remnant of the indigenous race, mingled* with the African blood, was so little distinguished from it in the second generation —the bronze tint of the Spaniard, the copper hue

---

* Four thousand natives rallied around the *Cacique Henri*, with whom Spain finally treated as power with power. Their descendants, though considerably mixed, are still recognized by the beauty of their hair, which both men and women take great pride in wearing smooth and flowing. Some connoisseurs pretend to distinguish the women of Indian origin by the following sign: that the veins, instead of being designated by blue lines under the skin, appear red.

of the Indian, and the bistre color of the mulatto, tended so much to blend together, under the influence of a common hygiene, and climate,—that the closest observers (if there were any) would have been, often, very much embarrassed to discover, in their faces, the secret of a lineage, lost in the savannahs and forests.

This work of fusion, which, neither European immigration, under its moral relation, nor African immigration, in its physiological relation, could lessen, was summed up, at the period of the revolution, in the following figures: 25,000 whites of the pure Spanish race;—15,000 Africans which, by their distribution, escaped every insurrectionary propagandist, and, moreover, were too proud of the social superiority, which a daily contact with their masters gave them, over the slaves of the French part of the Island, to consent to imitate those, whom they scornfully called "negroes;"—and, finally, 73,000 *sang-mêlés*, who styled themselves *volunteer whites;* and who, there being no injurious objection raised against them, were at length considered as such.* The dissolving element of the French colony, had thus become the conservative element of the Spanish colony. Vanity, which there dug an abyss of hate between the three classes —here, produced their cohesion.

The troubles of the French portion of the Island

---

* We borrow these figures from the book of M. Lepelletier de Saint-Remy.

only served to render this cohesion closer. Hostilities having broken out between Spain and France, the Spanish Governor committed the error, of attracting and enrolling the bands of Jean-Francois, and Biassou. They entered the East, as into a conquered country, exacting titles, cordons, a pension of a hundred thousand livres each, and massacred, occasionally, the royal emigrants—of whom they had declared themselves the protectors. Jean-Francois slew a thousand* of them at Fort Dauphin, under the eyes of the Spanish authorities, who did not dare to protest, although they had given them an asylum. Whilst the slave minority, comparing the mildness of its servitude, with the strange liberty enjoyed by the soldiers of Jean-Francois, who were mutilated, killed, or sold, at the least caprice of their masters, were strengthened more and more, in its contempt of the "negroes" and the revolution—the white minority, and *sang-mêlé* majority, experienced a common indignation, and a common terror, in seeing themselves at the mercy of these savage masses, whose every step had been marked on the frontier, by the massacre of whites or mulattoes.

When the peace of Bâle gave us the whole Island, and Toussaint, being disposed to deceive the Spanish portion, as he had done that of the French section, indicated that he was about to take posses-

---

* Histoire d'Haïti, par Madiou.

sion of the East, *in the name of France*, this accord of repugnance and fear was still more energetically manifested. A deputation, from the parishes, went and supplicated the two Metropolises to concert together, so that the cession of the East might be delayed, until France was prepared to take possession of it, instead of her *soi-disant* delegate. But, before the response came, Rigaud, who alone held Toussaint in check, was defeated; and the latter, leaving Dessalines to complete the massacre of the colored men of the South, abruptly returned towards the Spanish part of the Island. The mulatto, Chanlatte, and General Kerverseau, who served under his orders, vainly endeavored, at the head of a hundred and fifty French, and a handful of Dominicans besides, to stop the passage of the black army. As to the Spanish Governor, he limited himself to a show of defense; and Toussaint remained master of this magnificent territory, which his approach made a desert. All who could fly, had fled!

These events transpired in 1801. The following year, two frigates appeared on the horizon of Saint-Domingo. At this mute signal of deliverance, without even knowing whether a landing was possible, (the condition of the sea not permitting it) a hundred and fifty créoles, aided by a few Frenchmen, seized one of the forts, by massacring the garrison, and being compelled by the want of succor, to seek the open country, propagated the revolt.

At the end of twenty days, the whole East had submitted to its new Metropolis. After the disaster, which smote the army of Leclerc, and when our flag, surrounded by only a few hundred soldiers, seemed rather to compromise, than to protect, the population which it sheltered, the East, alone, had the courage to continue French ; preferring, the danger of fidelity, to the risks of negro rule—and, even, to the guarantees of material security, offered by the British protectorate. Their invincible horror of the negro yoke, and their confidence in the French flag, have continued until now, the two distinctive traits of popular opinion in Dominica. Dessalines, coming a short time afterwards, at the head of twenty-two thousand negroes, spread massacre, pillage, and devastation to the very gates of Santo-Domingo; and General Ferrand being obliged to retreat before him, they proved this double tendency. The devotion of the Dominicans to France did not depreciate for a moment.

Under the able administration of Ferrand, the ancient *audiencia*, not long before the most desolate of the Spanish colonies, rapidly changed its aspect. Public offices were organised, roads opened, and outlets abroad established. But, four years had already passed away, and France, who was absorbed in her Continental struggle, seemed not to remember, that, in the midst of the Gulf of Mexico, a handful of French citizens were abandoned to themselves, between an enemy six times more numerous, and the Ocean, which was ploughed by the cruisers of another enemy, awaiting, from the Metropolis, a sign of encouragement, or, at least a verbal pledge of protection. A gloomy disaffection began. In the meanwhile, the unjust invasion of Spain by Napoleon took place, and the Castillian citizens of Saint-Domingo were touched to the heart, by that electric thrill, which, from the Pyrenees to Cadiz—from Cadiz to the Antilles—from the Antilles to the Vermillion sea—excited the Spanish race against us. These two wrongs were easily set to work against the French by the Governor of Porto-Rico, and especially by English agents; who did not cease to show to the Dominicans, on one hand, an innumerable army of negroes ready to profit at any time, by the desertion of France, to invade them—and, on the other, a British squadron, determined to protect them against the hatred of France, until the old mother country was prepared to succor them. An insurrection broke out, in the Canton of Seybo; and the leader of the insurgents, a Spanish créole, Juan Sanchez Ramirez, soon gathered about him two thousand men. Ferrand attacked them, with five hundred; who, after a combat of four hours, were overwhelmed and put to flight. Ferrand blew out his brains on the field of battle, and the few French detachments, distributed through the colony, fell back towards Santo-Domingo;—a place which was only protected by a dilapidated wall, and without a ditch, but which

Brigadier-General Barquier took it into his head to defend, against the combined efforts of the insurgents, and the English cruisers.

The small supply of provisions, which were found in the place, or which the corsairs succeeded in throwing in, were soon consumed, and they ate boots, harness, and their buffalo skins; these, likewise, were soon consumed. It then became necessary to make a sortie, and gain a battle, every time they desired to dine. In war they must do as in war; this dinner was composed, almost entirely, of poisonous roots, called *gualliga;* which grew, fortunately, in abundance in the vicinity of the city, and whose venomous properties, were a little abated, after six hours of very complicated manipulations. At the end of eight months,— and, after eleven sorties, and as many battles and victories, each of which cost the enemy very dearly —destiny interfered decisively: the *gualliga* failed. And as difficulty never comes alone, the English cruiser, having become by degrees a squadron, prepared a landing. Barquier, who had refused, to the last, to treat with the insurgents, resigned himself, therefore, to propose to the commander of the British forces, an honorable capitulation, and such, as could be demanded by brave men, still supplied with *gualliga*. I know but one thing quite as sublime as this super-human heroism, and which had the consciousness of its obscurity: it is the address made by Major General, Sir Hugh Lyle

Carmichaël, to his troops, in taking possession of the place:

"Soldiers!" said Sir Hugh, "you have not had the glory of vanquishing the brave garrison, which you replace; but you are about to rest your heads upon the same stones, where these intrepid soldiers are about to cease their glorious labors, after having braved the dangers of war, and the horrors of famine. May these grand souvenirs impress your hearts, with sentiments of respect, and admiration for them; and remember, that, if you follow some day their example, you will have done enough for our glory."

Barquier, with his diminutive garrison, marched out with the honors of war, and were taken to France, at the expense of Great Britain.

These are some of the magnificent souvenirs, which close the history of our brief domination at Santo-Domingo. To the involuntary respect, which they left, in the hearts of the inhabitants, the regrets of contrast—the first effervescence of past *Espagnolisme*—were added. The treaty of Paris confirmed the retrocession, which operated, in fact, in favor of Spain; and this beautiful colony—to which a French administration of four years duration, working under the most unfavorable circumstances, was sufficient to reveal the secret of its riches,—found its old metropolis poorer, feebler, and more incapable of resuscitation than ever. The memory of General Ferrand became, and continues to this day, in the Spanish portion of the Island, an object of real worship.

In 1821, an advocate, named Nunez Caserés took advantage of the reaction, produced by the discontent, or indifference, which was produced under the Spanish flag, to raise at Santo-Domingo the standard of Columbia, and proclaimed himself President. But an old municipal rivalry existed, between Santiago, an important town of the interior, and Santo-Domingo. A schism almost instantly, took place, and a fourth of the pillage of Christophe's treasury, saved by Boyer, they say, in one way and another, played an important part in the affair. Considered from a distance, the movement, which was about to subjugate the entire French portion of the Island, to the successor of Pétion, would pass for a mulatto reaction : and the latter, who ardently coveted the East, had easily sown division among its subjects, hoping that by favor of a kind of sympathy which his color, and his recent triumph over African influence, established between the sang-mêlée majority of the Spanish part of the Island and himself, he would be easily accepted as mediator. Indeed one of the two factions called him. Under the impression of the relative security he inspired, there was no defence organized ; and his army divided into two bodies, one of which, penetrated by the north, the other by the south, reached Santo-Domingo, without striking a blow ; where he had nothing to do but proclaim the Constitution of the West, (February the 9th, 1822).

The Castillian portion of the inhabitants had, however, neither shared this security, nor indifference. Foreseeing what Boyer contemplated in coming, and not being able to expect, the least help, from the Goverment at Madrid, they were reminded of the flag, which, twice before, had saved, the Spanish part of the Island, from an invasion by the West; and a deputation of notables, secretly, visited the Governor of Martinique, to solicit the protection of France. A fleet, under command of Rear-Admiral Jacob, was quickly dispatched towards Saint-Domingo; but in the meantime, the annexation deception of Boyer was accomplished. The negro troops, which already inundated the whole country, were restrained, by fear of an explosion of French tendencies, and Rear-Admiral Jacob arrived, only in time, to receive those of the inhabitants, who were more openly compromised by our intentions.

The ability, of which Boyer began to give proof, abandoned him in the administration of this easy conquest. In a country, where the fourth of the population was of white derivation,—and half of the *sang-mêlés* claimed this origin,—it was impossible to dream of, openly, applying that article of the constitution, which prohibited the whites from holding real estate. But Boyer applied it, in an indirect way; either, by obliging the whites to be naturalized as Haytiens—French as well as Spanish—who should continue to reside in the country, as proprietors;*—or, by confiscating the effects of the absent proprietors, who should not come forward, and make good their rights, after the expiration of a year, (which was prolonged four months in order to preserve the hypocrisy of forms);—or finally, by requiring the production of title-papers in a country, where the right of property, often, only rested upon oral tradition. If any white person protested, he was imprisoned, persecuted, and even sometimes shot; and this discouragement, or fear, drove off, one after another, the few important families, who had succeeded in avoiding the banishment, with which, these iniquitous fiscal regulations smote the European race. With it, disappeared from the soil, day by day, " talents, riches, commerce, and agriculture."† In a few years, the enormous accumulations, of money, which, the former descendants of the first colonists, allowed

---

* Those whites who did not wish to renounce their nationality, and swear allegiance to Boyer, had, it is true, the right of selling their lands; but a system, which drove away the whites established in the East, kept away, for a stronger reason, European emigration, which could only furnish them purchasers. The people of the country possessed a hundred times more land, than they could cultivate. This right was therefore simply ridiculous.

† Manifesto of the Dominican insurgents.—At the fall of Boyer, the figure of the Eastern population, which, twenty years before, rose to about 125,000 souls, was found reduced to about 85,000—a loss of nearly fifty per cent.

to accumulate in their coffers, from generation to generation, had disappeared; and the invasion of Haytien paper-money ended, in paralyzing the feeble commercial circulation, which the slow distribution of this coin had kept up.

The roads, opened by Ferrand, were no longer passable; and, by the gradual disappearance of foreign flags, agricultural production, had nearly descended to the level of domestic consumption. The old University of Santo-Domingo, which formerly, attracted the Spanish youth of the Islands, and the neighboring continent, no longer even opened its vacant halls, to the youth of the country, who were condemned to the weak intellectual broth, of a board of public instruction, which was organized, for the whole Republic, at a cost of *fifteen thousand francs*. It was not so, as to the architectural remains of the ancient Castilian magnificence which, by a frightful symbol, was unable to crumble down under this breath of barbarism.

Boyer did not even leave to the Dominicans, the privileges of a barbarous condition. The two great resources of every imperfect social organization—raising cattle, which in this propitious climate, and on the immense plains of virgin fertility, required neither money nor care—and cutting the precious woods, a labor which brought an immediate remuneration—did not escape any more than the rest, from the covetous greediness of the Port-au-Prince Government. The vast domains of land, granted to the first colonists, were almost everywhere changed into *hatos* (pastures) which the descendants of these colonists enjoyed in common.

Under the pretext, of applying to the East, the land system of the West, Boyer required, that the *hatos* should be divided between the occupants; and, as these had not been careful to preserve their titles to a joint property, which no one before denied them, this requirement, apparently so inoffensive, ended in the pure and simple confiscation of these common pastures. The division of these pastures, alone, would have been, besides, sufficient to ruin cattle-raising. The operation of this measure met with so much resistance, in its application, that it did little more than oppress the *hattiers* with a state of menace; but this was sufficient, to render the yoke of Port-au-Prince odious to them. An intolerable fiscal system, a little later, paralyzed the cutting of mahogany; and, finally, extended to the country, the discouragements and hatreds, which the destruction of commerce, and the material or moral proscription, which oppressed the *élite* of the population, had scattered through the towns. Let us add that, not content with associating the inhabitants of the East, with its present barbarism, Hayti made them responsible for her past, by making them pay their quota of the French indemnity, which they did not owe.

The blows, given by Boyer, to the Catholic sentiment of the Dominicans, who continue religious like the Spaniards of the XVth century, would have been a sufficient cause to band together, in a common antipathy, the different elements of that population.)

I have remarked, that, (with regard to religion, the old mulatto party still entertained the ideas of the revolution and the Directory. From the conflict between that bigoted philosophy, which only believed in compere Mathieu, and that ardent Catholicism, which believed alone in miracles, there was obliged to spring up mortal offences; and the Government of Port-au-Prince made the wound bleed at pleasure. The treasures of the Church, more than once, satisfied its financial penury. The presbyteries, chapters, and convents, were deprived of their lands and rents, for the benefit of the public domain. Cheats, and humiliations, of every kind, were no more spared that all-powerful Dominican clergy, which has personified, since the first days of the conquest, the supremacy of the Indies, than to the conventional priests of the French portion of the Island. (The Archbishop, primate of Santo-Domingo, who, nevertheless, was thought to have taken a hand in the annexation, rendered this antagonism more striking still, by refusing to extend his jurisdiction over the West, and, finally, astonished the masses, by deserting his See to go and die in a convent of Cuba.

The systematic exclusion, which, gradually drove

them from the public employments,—the presence of numerous black garrisons, in each of these towns,—the daily insults to which this contact exposed them, under a *régime*, where partiality in favor of the blacks, was established, by means of government,—all, concurred to give the Dominicans that *rôle* of the vanquished, which, in the absence of any other wrongs, justified revolt. At the first news of the insurrection of Cayes (1843,) the old Spanish *audiencia*, with Santo-Domingo in the lead, rose, *en masse*, against Boyer.

The idea of a separation did not, however, predominate on the first uprising ; for, the Spanish part of the Island sent deputies, to the Constituent Assembly, at Port-au-Prince. But, even there, the definitive rupture happened to be accomplished.

The Dominican deputation, nobly, prefered its own soil. The East consented, not to separate from the West—but upon condition, that the west would, no longer, persist, in separating itself from civilization,—and, that white immigration should cease to be prohibited. Either the threatening condition, which this last effort at reconciliation implied, was not understood,—or, that they thought the menaces of a population, six times less numerous than that of the French portion of the island might be disdained,—the exclusion of the whites was maintained. Absolute equality of worship was, besides, introduced, for the first time, in the fundamental faith ; and this innovation, in which the spirit of imitation had, probably, more share, than the spirit of system, (was perhaps considered by the Dominicans) as its legal approval, and in consequence, an aggravation of the blows given, under Boyer, at their religious sentiments. "If, when Catholicism was the religion of the State, its ministers were scorned, and vilified, what will it be now, that it is about to be surrounded by sectaries, and enemies?" (Manifesto of the Dominican insurgents.)

From this moment, all the districts of the East prepared for insurrection, whilst the Dominican deputies, who kept their seats, for the sake of form, in the Constituent Assembly, took secret measures, with Rear-Admiral Mosges, commanding the French naval forces,—with M. A. Barrot, envoy to Port-au-Prince, to negotiate the question of the indemnity—and with M. Lavasseur, our consul-general. The Dominican deputies asked, the concurrence of France, to the separation, which was being prepared; offering us, in exchange, either the sovereignty, the protectorate, or the cession, pure and simple, of their territory. Our agents refused to decide, confining themselves to transmitting these overtures to the French Government; but between the oppressors and the oppressed—between Port-au-Prince, which repelled civilzation, and Santo-Domingo, which invited it—between those Haytiens who, as a recompense of the generous abandonment of our rights, and of our systematic patience, in the indemnity affair, established hatred to the name of France in a constitutional principle,—and those Dominicans who, not owing us any thing after all, invited, for the fourth time in fifty years past, that French flag, they were the last to defend, in the Island,—could the sympathies of our Government be questioned? The deputies of the East, therefore, thought, it unnecessary to dissemble their hopes; and, one fine day, Hérard had them arrested.

M. Levasseur obtained their liberation; and the Dominicans only saw, in this measure, a formal pledge of our protection. The arrival, at Santo-Domingo, of M. Juchereau de St-Denis, the consul designed for Cap,—and who, in consequence of the destruction of that city, was allowed, by the Haytien Government, to transfer his residence to the eastern capital—the presence of French ships, which had transported M. Juchereau de St-Denis, and the Dominican deputies, liberated by M. Levasseur —and the undiplomatic, but ardent sympathy of our sailors—all, contributed to strengthen the Dominicans, in this conviction. Although, our agents might kill themselves, saying, that France had not decided; although, the chief of the Dominican deputation, M. Baëz, advised them, the very first, to await this decision before acting; Santo-Domingo gave the signal of revolt (27th February, 1844), which was propagated, with the rapidity of light, over the whole Spanish portion of the Island.

M. Juchereau de St-Denis could, at least, have prevented the consequences of an impatience, which it was not in his power to comprehend. The Haytien garrison of Santo-Domingo was perfectly prepared, to batter down the city; he obtained its capitulation. The chancellor of the consulate, M. Terny, even took it upon himself to overcome the last hesitations of the Haytien commander, by going, all out of breath, to tell the latter, that an innumerable body of insurgents would, in a few moments, come to slay him—him and his soldiers. "But I do not see any one," said the commander, putting his nose against the window. "It is true beyond question; *they are at dinner . . !*" replied M. Terny, with great composure, whose observation produced the greater effect, because he had the merit of the local color. "I did not think of that!" said the commander in reply; and the Haytien garrison embarked.

The insurgents published a long manifesto, intended to assert their wrongs and rights, with those civilized nations to whom they opened the Island. The Dominicans declared they revolted, in virtue of the principle, which had justified, some months previously, the fall of Boyer. This indirect sanction was even perfectly useless.

"Because the natives call the Island, Hayti, it does not follow, that the western part of it, which was first erected into a Sovereign Government, has the right to consider the territory of the East, as an integral part of that Government. . . . If the eastern portion ever belongs to any other domination, than that of its own sons, it will appertain to France, or Spain, and not to Hayti. . . ."

Do you object the tacit agreement of 1822? The existence of that compact is more than doubtful; and you have released us from it, at all events, by violating it outrageously. "We owe no duty to those who deprive us of our rights." Do you consider, on the contrary, the East as conquered by force? very well! Let force decide. Such is the substance of this long document, in which Spanish fatalism, and the *scholastic* wrangling of the old Metropolitan university, reveals itself, sometimes, in a piquant manner: as in this phrase: "*Considering*, that a people, which is condemned to obey by force, and obeys, does well;—but that as soon as it can resist, and resists, it does better. . . ."

And here this generous diminutive of a nation, for the past twelve years, has been strutting from battle field to battle field, mounted on its *considering*.

We have not related, here, the romantic episodes of this struggle; the useless attempts made, for eight years, by the English and Americans, to assume for Saint-Domingo, the interested part of saviors; the touching obstinacy of the young Republic for French tendencies, which refused, in the most desperate situations, to yield the right of offering itself to us, and which, in awaiting the reply of

France, was reduced to fight with only swords as a matter of economy. Let us confine ourselves to stating, that the Haytiens taken, *en masse*, would not have asked anything better, than to let the Dominicans alone. The rupture of the national bond, as they say at Port-au-Prince, was certainly the least regret of a revolution, which, a few days afterwards, detached, for its own advantage, the North and the South from this bond. But for Acaau—who frightened everybody a little, and appropriately rallied the different parties on the neutral ground of Guerrier's candidature,—Hayti would, probably, now be divided into four distinct Governments; two monarchies, and two Republics. The Haytiens have moreover exhibited, at all times, an invincible repugnance to being garrisoned at Saint-Domingo ; and the levies *en masse*, of which, the war in the East was, and is still, the pretext, opposed it for a stronger reason. Let us add that this war has frequently threatened the French part of the Island with famine, whose inhabitants supplied their stock of provisions, from the cattle of the Spanish part, and left them, in exchange, its coffee. If, finally, fear of the whites, made the submission of a country desirable, which invited white immigration—these very jealousies contributed, also, by reaction, to render odious a war, which, in prolonging itself, might substitute for this peaceable immigration, an armed intervention.

Guerrier and Riché seemed to share, in this repect, the general impression; and their attainment of power was marked, by a tacit truce, between the East and West. Soulouque, himself, seemed disposed, upon principle, to let the Dominicans alone; but M. Dupuy, and Similien became, the one, minister, and the other, intimate counsellor;—M. Dupuy, who was interested in military supplies, and Similien, who looked to the Presidency, were skillful enough, without their knowledge, to push him into a war, which, ensured to the one very handsome profits, and furnished the other Dominican balls as accomplices. Soulouque yielded, with so much less mistrust, to these suggestions, because they proceeded at the same time, from two opposite sides—from two rival influences,—from two sworn enemies. From 1847, the subjugation of the East, became the fixed idea of the future Emperor; and since—even among those, who deplored this mania —there were some who flattered it, in order not to be shot. The favorite delusion of Soulouque—that which his courtiers caressed the most,—consisted, a long time, in believing that the Dominicans sighed after Haytien rule; and, that the fear of punishment, which they deserved for revolt, alone restrained this impulse of submission. Therefore, he never ceased offering them a magnanimous pardon. One of the ministers, more honest than his colleagues, tried to give another direction to the President's ideas, and pronounced the word *federation*. "What is it, this federation?" said Soulou-

14

que, frowning at this word, so entirely new to his mind and ears. "Mr. President, it is—it is what you wish"—stammered the minister. "Then it is good," said Soulouque, tranquilised. "I do not retract it ; I promise the *federation;* I will even consent to recognize the grades, created by the insurgents!" In fact, amnesty, and federation were synonymous to Soulouque ; and this *qui-pro-quo* continued several months.

I have related, what misrepresentations Soulouque reported of his expedition in 1849 ; deceptions so much the more cruel, that after these repeated assurances of an amnesty, he expected to be received in the East with open arms. Enmities of skin, were added to the exasperation of being beaten, to poison the wound, with which, this savage pride bled. The victors were, not merely rebels, but also *mulattoes*, as he called them ; and his fixed idea of conquest was changed, into a fixed idea of extermination. The thirst for gold, which equaled, in Soulouque, the thirst for blood, had its part, also, in the preparations of destruction, which he never ceased to make against the "Spaniards ;" for the idea of Spaniards was always associated, in that part of the world, with the idea of *quadruples,** precious relics, and virgins of massive gold. This was the allurement, which, from a distance, fascinated Toussaint ;—which, had attracted Dessalines

---

* A Spanish gold coin valued at two *pistoles.*

up to the gates of Santo-Domingo;—and which, more recently still,—at the time of the African reaction, between the death of Guerrier and the accession of Riché,—invited Pierrot to the East, where he was as badly received, as his Emperor was later.

Have we not touched, decidedly, on the secret of Soulouque? If the negro tyrant continues the pressure of 1848, against the prostrate mulattoes, is it not from fear, (otherwise very chimerical) of seeing them, at the time of the general killing of the Dominicans, which he projects, develope the solidarity of despair, which unites them to the *sang-mêle* majority of that population? If, on the contrary, he caresses the *piquets* so much, it is because he, no doubt, thinks them indispensable to this work of extermination; in which, they would display, with a science, and aplomb of cruelty which they, alone, still possess, in the country of Biassou, those furious antiphathies of color, of which they are the last depositories. Does not the invasion of the Spanish part of Island, (if so be that this part may suffer itself to be invaded) offer, moreover, an easy solution of the unexpected difference, between the government and the *piquets*, on the question of pillage? This question may be put off, as long as the fabrication of paper money, and the prices of provisions, will help them to wait; but, which will be inevitably renewed, when this paper money is no longer worth anything, and the foreign merchants refuse to deliver their goods. This probably explains, also, how Soulouque, after being so much alarmed, by the attitude of these dangerous creditors, as to have the most pressing of them shot, nevertheless, continued to fill the administration, and the army staff, from their ranks. The hour of settlement having come, that would be the time to pay off the hatred of the West. Is it not, in short, in these expectations of a pillage whose riches are exaggerated, that it is necessary to seek the secret of that frightful improvidence, with which, His Majesty scatters and wastes, interest and principal, the last resources of the country? I have not invented these suppositions; they are current in Hayti,—and figured, not long ago as we said, in Europe, among the constitutional previsions of the time.

The last campaign against the Dominicans, brought a new and cruel disappointment to these expectations, (December, 1855). Only one of the two Haytien *corps d'armée* was engaged, by its advanced guard; which disbanded at the first fire, on this reflexion being uttered in a loud voice by one of the Generals: "the Emperor has *deceived* the common people, by assuring them, that the Dominicans would surrender, without striking a blow!"

This imprudent General was, no less a person than His Excellency, the Count de l'Ile à-Vache, alias the abominable Voltaire Castor; who, upon this remark being proved against him, was shot, with several Colonels, his friends.*

This was also, after all, a method with Soulouque of settlement, with the *piquets*.† The second corps did not even attack the enemy, and were remanded to general quarters, in consequence of a council of war; at which, it was decided that the troops manifested suspected dispositions. Hence, a new investigation, and another *fusillade*, in which General Dessalines, son of the Ex-Emperor of that name, and Colonel Belliard, son of the Ex-King Christophe, were associated. No rival dynasty will, therefore, have to congratulate itself upon the bad-luck of that of Faustin. After these acts of authority, Soulouque marched, in person, upon Santiago; but was stopped, some leagues from the frontier, by the Dominicans, who,

---

* In order to harmonize everything, after his fashion always, Soulouque sent to execution, with the friends of Voltaire Castor, many honest people.

† After the last news this settlement would have been more urgent than ever. The *piquets*, among which, for a year past, fearful impatience was exhibited, at length (in 1856) revolted in the plains of Cayes; and, now, the peninsular of the South may be, in blood and flames. Will His Majesty arrive in time on the spot? For himself, and the country, the whole question lies in this. Free to choose, the yellow and black *bourgeoisie* will range themselves, certainly with fear, on the side of Soulouque, on seeing the *piquets* on the other; but if Soulouque does not go in person, to rally these fears about him, the cities will be inevitably drawn into the insurrection. The *bourgeoisie* would rather howl in consequence of blows, than be eaten up by the *piquets*.

however, only remained masters of the field, after a furious combat of six or seven hours.

The manager of the pages to the Empress, a certain General Toussaint, who only held in common the name of the *first of blacks*, in spite of the pathetic appeals, made by several journals in his case, paid the penalty of this third misfortune. The Emperor, who had had him put under arrest, from the *début* of the campaign, as guilty of having censured the expedition, had him shot on his return. Soulouque reëntered his capital, on the very evening of *Saint-Faustin*, which, for the first time in eight years, passed without illuminations, and a salute of cannon. This sudden humiliation of defeat necessarily concealed formidable storms.

Besides, victory would have been more dangerous to Soulouque, on this occasion, than defeat; for a new element had appeared in the Dominican question.

A furious hatred had succeeded, in 1852, to the almost proverbial friendship, which had, for so long a period, united the acting President, Santana, with Ex-President Baëz. In 1853, the first banished the other, whom he accused of conspiring against him; and concluding, from certain manœuvres, in which, the name of France was improperly mixed up, as premeditating the violent restoration of Baëz, Santana entered into negotiations with the Americans. The most unforeseen chances conferred upon upon us, the mission of dissipating this mistake; and M. Maxime Raybaud, soon after, came to restore all to order, at Santo-Domingo. But the annexation glue was not detached, so easily, from whomsoever it touched; and the threats of a Haytien invasion helping, American influence seems to have gained ground in the councils of Santana.

Once well convinced, on his part, that he could only expect from France a friendly neutrality, Baëz threw himself back entirely on England; which was not sparing, however, in advances. Here then, the young Republic was condemned to oscillate, between the two influences, which repelled, so energetically, its interests and instincts. The question was thus reduced to know which, a British agent, or a *fillibuster Yankee*, should have the honor, and the profit, of relieving this patient sentinel, who, to the *qui-vive* of barbarism, had, for so long a time, responded: " France !"

England and the United States would bring, without doubt, strength, security, and riches; but the English protectorate, would be that of Protestantism—and the American, with the invasion of Protestantism, would be the tyranny of that inexorable prejudice of color, which spares, neither soul nor body—neither Christian nor citizen—neither talent nor fortune—neither the cradle nor the grave. We can understand the repugnance, which such an alternative inspires, in a country, whose religious wrongs have, perhaps, contributed more, to raise its indignation, than its national injuries; and where, the majority of the population belong to the *sang-mêle* races.

But, naturally, the greatest number of chances are in favor of the Yankee, whose covetousness has a more powerful impulse; and to whom, the proximity of the coveted territory, on one part, and the commodious irresponsibility of the Government at Washington, on the other, allows exceptional means of action.* But, if the least military success of Soulouque should furnish the American annexationists, who keep themselves on the watch, a pretext of *saving* the Dominican Republic, the following is the way the question would be presented to His Imperial Majesty. We borrow this citation from the *Weekly Herald* (New York) of the 28th of April, 1850:

" . . . . But if at this time, there is no movement with regard to the annexation of Cuba, there have been many made, concerning the Island of Hayti. His Excellency, B. B. Green, has been sent out to that country, for the purpose of making a report on its actual condition, its population, soil, climate and other matters; and Mr. Green is,

---

* Besides, that it enters into their avowed system of the absorption of all the Gulf of Mexico—the occupation of Hayti would have a very special interest for the American annexationists; because, from thence, they could descend, in a few hours, upon Cuba. This last consideration has been many times set forth, by the American press.

probably, at this moment in Washington, preparing and setting forth the result of his labors. We should not be at all surprised, from the information we have received, to see an expedition, (with the sanction of the Government at Washington) soon, leave some Southern port, to go to the assistance of the Dominican, or Spanish portion of the inhabitants, against the blacks; and, in the end *to invade the island and annex it to the United States.* A *projét* of this kind may be openly sustained, in the United States, and the organization of an expedition, with this view, would experience obstacles from no quarter. It would be a glorious thing to overthrow those horrible pirates—the worst of pirates and coal black bandits—the negro population called the Empire of Hayti, and to *reduce Faustin Ist to the condition, for which nature has designed him.*"

Whence it appears, that victory would have been a veritable misfortune to Faustin 1st; and that, in going to gather laurels at Santo Domingo, His Majesty would have run great risk of going, all of a sudden, to cut sugar cane in Louisiana. May this illustrious existence not terminate, where ends this modest book!

SOUTHERN BOOK PUBLISHING HOUSE,

Established 1833.

J. W. RANDOLPH,

Bookseller, Publisher, Stationer

AND

MUSIC DEALER,

Offers on the best terms for cash or approved credit, the largest *assortment* of goods in his line to be found south of Philadelphia.

THE STOCK EMBRACES

LAW, MEDICINE, THEOLOGY, HISTORY, BIOGRAPHY, POLITICS, SCHOOL, CLASSICS, JUVENILE, NOVELS, POETRY, and MISCELLANEOUS BOOKS, in English and other languages.

Particular attention given to the collection of Rare Works. Books imported to order.

AMERICAN, ENGLISH AND FRENCH STATIONERY

Of the best quality.

A large stock of STANDARD MUSIC, and all the New Popular Pieces are for sale soon as published.

BLANK BOOKS made to order, and all kinds of BOOK-BINDING executed in good style.

Catalogues will be mailed to all who send a stamp to pay the postage.

OLD BOOKS

Taken in Exchange for New Works.

J. W. RANDOLPH,

121 MAIN STREET, Richmond, Va.

BOOKS!

CFFERED TO THE TRADE AND FOR SALE BY

J. W. RANDOLPH,

121 Main street, Richmond, Va.

LAW.

HALL'S (EVERARD) DIGESTED INDEX OF THE VIRGINIA REPORTS, containing all the points argued and determined in the Court of Appeals of Virginia, from Washington to third Leigh, inclusive, with a table of the names of cases reported, 2 vols. 8vo, sheep, Richmond, 1825 and '35.................................... $3 00

HENING & MUNFORD. REPORTS OF CASES argued and determined in the Supreme Court of Appeals of Virginia, with select cases relating chiefly to points of practice decided by the Superior Court of Chancery for the Richmond District, by W. W. Hening and W. Munford, a new and *only complete* edition, with memoirs of the Judges whose decisions are reported; the present rules of the Court of Appeals, and of the Chancery Court in Richmond; references to subsequent decisions of the Court of Appeals, and to existing statutes in *paria materia*, with the points herein reported, and a list of the cases overruled. Edited by B. B. Minor, L. B., 4 vols. 8vo, sheep, Richmond, 1854.............. 20 00

JEFFERSON'S (THOMAS) REPORTS OF CASES determined in the General Court of Virginia from 1730 to 1740, and from 1768 to 1772, half calf, Charlottesville, 1829, 2 50

LAWYER'S GUIDE. THE AMERICAN PLEADER AND LAWYER'S GUIDE, in commencing, prosecuting and defending actions at common law and suits in equity, with full and correct precedents of pleadings in the several cases which most frequently occur, adapted to the practice of the United States, by W. W. Hening, 2 vols. 8vo, sheep, New York, 1811 and '26............................... 8 00

MATTHEW'S (J. M.) GUIDE TO COMMISSIONERS IN CHANCERY, with practical Forms for the discharge of their duties, adapted to the new Code of Virginia, 8vo, sheep, Richmond, 1850................................. 2 50

MATTHEW'S DIGEST OF THE LAWS OF VIRGINIA, of a civil nature and of a permanent character, and a general operation, illustrated by judicial decisions, to which are

prefixed the Constitutions of the United States and Virginia, by J. M. Matthews, 2 vols. 8vo, sheep, Richmond, 1856-7, 12 00
THE SAME INTERLEAVED WITH WRITING PAPER FOR N'TES, 2 vols................................. 17 00
MUNFORD'S (WILLIAM) REPORTS OF CASES argued and determined in the Supreme Court of Appeals of Virginia, 6 vols. 8vo, sheep, Richmond and New York, 1812, &c.. 36 00
PATTON & HEATH. A GENERAL INDEX TO GRATTAN'S REPORTS, from second to eleventh, inclusive, by J. M. Patton and R. B. Heath, 8vo, sheep, Richmond, 1856.................................... 3 50
PATTON & HEATH. REPORTS OF CASES decided in the Special Court of Appeals of Virginia, held at Richmond, and a General Index to Grattan's Reports, from 2d to 11th vol., inclusive, by J. M. Patton and R B. Heath, vol. 1, 8vo, sheep, Richmond, 1856.................... 6 00
PATTON & HEATH. REPORTS OF CASES decided in the Special Court of Appeals, held in Richmond 1855-6-7, by J. M. Patton and R. B. Heath, 2 vols. 8vo, sheep, Richmond, 1855-7............................ 7 00
QUARTERLY LAW JOURNAL, A. B. Guigon, Editor, vol. 1, 1856, vol. 2, 1857, vol. 3, 1858, vol. 4, 1859, 8vo, sheep, Richmond, per volume........................ 5 00
RANDOLPH'S (PEYTON) REPORTS OF CASES argued and determined in the Court of Appeals of Virginia, 6 vols. 8vo, sp. Richmond, Va., 1823, &c................... 24 00
RITCHIE'S (THOMAS, Jr.) TRIAL. A full report, embracing all the evidence and arguments in the case of the Commonwealth of Virginia vs. T. Ritchie, Jr., for the killing of John Hampden Pleasants, to which is added an appendix showing the action of the Court in relation to the other parties connected with the said case, 8vo, paper, New York, 1846.. 25
VIRGINIA. PAY AND MUSTER ROLLS OF THE VIRGINIA MILITIA IN THE WAR OF 1812, 8vo half calf, Richmond, 1851-2............................. 15 00
VIRGINIA CASES. A Collection of Cases decided by the General Court of Virginia, chiefly relating to the Penal Laws of the Commonwealth, commencing 1789 and ending 1826, copied from the Records of the said Court, with explanatory notes, by Judges Brockenbrough and Holmes, second edition, with abstracts prefixed to the cases, 2 vols. in 1, 8vo, sheep, Richmond, 1826 and 1853 .... 6 00
VIRGINIA LAW OF CORPORATIONS, ACTS OF THE GENERAL ASSEMBLY compiled from the code of Virginia, together with an act passed in 1837, relating to Manufacturing and Mining Companies, 8vo, paper, Richmond, 1853.. 50

WYTHE'S (GEO.) REPORTS. Decisions of cases in Virginia of the High Court of Chancery, with remarks upon Decrees by the Court of Appeals, reversing some of those decisions, by George Wythe, 2d and only complete edition. With a Memoir of the author, Analysis of the Cases, and an Index, by B. B. Minor, L. B. And with an Appendix, containing references to cases in *pari materia*, an essay on lapse, joint tenants and tenants in common, &c., &c., by Wm. Green, Esq. 8vo, sheep. Richmond, 1852........ 4 00
WHITE ACRE *vs.* BLACK ACRE, a Case at Law, reported by J. G., Esq., a retired barrister of Lincolnshire, England, 18mo, mus., Richmond, 1856................. 75
VIRGINIA. RULES OF THE COURT OF APPEALS from its establishment to the present time. Also, Rules of the District Courts of Fredericksburg and Williamsburg. 8vo., paper. Richmond............................. 10
GILMER'S (F. W.) VIRGINIA REPORTS. 8vo., calf. Richmond, 1821...................................... 2 00
GRATTAN'S (P. R.) VIRGINIA REPORTS. 15 vols., 8vo, calf. Richmond, 1845-60. Per volume........... 4 00
LEIGH'S (B. W.) VIRGINIA REPORTS. 12 vols., 8vo, calf. Richmond, 1830-44. Per volume................ 4 00
ROBINSON'S (C.) VIRGINIA REPORTS. 2 vols., 8vo, calf. Richmond, 1843-4. Per volume................ 4 00
HENING (W. W.) & SHEPHERD'S (S.) STATUTES OF VIRGINIA from 1619 to 1807. 16 vols., 8vo, sheep. Richmond, 1823-36.................................... 13 00
VIRGINIA ACTS OF ASSEMBLY from 1808 to 1860. 8vo, half sheep. Richmond ....
SELECTIONS OF THE MOST IMPORTANT PORTIONS OF THE REPORTS OF THE REVISOR'S OF VIRGINIA CODE. With notes by A. H. Sands. 8vo, sheep. In press..................................

POLITICS.

TUCKER'S (H ST. GEORGE) LECTURES ON NATURAL LAW, also Lectures on Government, 12mo, muslin, Charlottesville, 1844................................ 75
ANTICIPATIONS OF THE FUTURE, TO SERVE AS LESSONS FOR THE PRESENT TIME. Extracts from letters written from Washington to the London Times during the years 1864-5-6-7-8. 12mo, mus., Richmond, 1860... 1 00
TUCKER'S (H. ST. GEORGE) LECTURES ON CONSTITUTIONAL LAW, for the use of the Law Class of the University of Virginia, 12mo, mus., Richmond, 1843.. 75
VIRGINIA POLITICS. A History of the Political Campaign in Va. in 1855, to which is added a review of the position of parties in the Union, and a statement of the political issues distinguishing them on the eve of the Presi-

dential Campaign of 1856, by J. P. Hambleton, M. D., 8vo, mus., Richmond, 1856..... 2 50
VIRGINIA CONVENTION. Proceeding and Debates of the Va. State Convention of 1829-30, to which are subjoined the new Constitution of Virginia, and the votes of the people, 8vo, calf, Richmond, 1830.................. 5 00
VIRGINIA STATISTICS. Documents containing statistics ordered to be printed by the State Convention sitting in the city of Richmond, 1850-51, 8vo, calf, Richmond, 1851............ 2 50
VIRGINIA CONVENTION. Journal, Acts and Proceedings of a General Convention of the State of Virginia assembled at Richmond 1850, 8vo, half calf, Richmond, 1850. 5 00
VIRGINIA CONVENTION 1850-51. Register of the Debates and Proceedings of the Virginia Reform Convention, (imperfect,) 8vo, half sheep, Richmond, 1851............ 3 00
VIRGINIA. Journal of the Senate and House of Delegates for various years. Richmond.
VIRGINIA. Journal of the Convention of 1776. 4to, half sheep. Richmond, 1816........ 2 00
ELLETT'S ESSAYS ON THE LAW OF TRADE, in reference to the Works of Internal Improvement in the U. S. 8vo, mus., Richmond, 1839.................. 1 50
LETTERS OF CURTIUS, written by the late John Thomson, of Petersburg; to which is added a Speech delivered by him in August, '95, on the British Treaty; to which a short Sketch of his Life is prefixed. 12mo, paper. Richmond, 1804.................. 1 00
JEFFERSON. Memoir, Correspondence and Miscellanies from the Papers of Thomas Jefferson. Edited by Thomas Jefferson Randolph. 4 vols., 8vo, boards. Charlottesville, 1829.................. 5 00
JEFFERSON. Observations on the Writings of Thomas Jefferson, with particular reference to the attack they contain on the Memory of the late Gen'l Henry Lee. In series of letters, by H. Lee. 2nd edition. With an Introduction and Notes, by Charles C. Lee. 8vo, mus. Philadelphia, 1839.................. 1 75
LONDON (D. H.) ON THE COMMERCIAL, AGRICULTURAL AND INTELLECTUAL INDEPENDENCE OF VIRGINIA AND THE SOUTH. 8vo, paper. Richmond, 1860.................. 25
VIRGINIAN (THE) HISTORY OF THE AFRICAN COLONIZATION. (This contains, among other documents, portions of the Debate on Slavery in the Virginia Legislature of 1832.) Edited by Rev. P. Slaughter. 8vo, mus., Richmond, 1855.................. 1 00
RUFFIN'S (EDMUND) AFRICAN COLONIZATION UNVEILED. Slavery and Free Labor described and

compared. The Political Economy of Slavery; or, the Institution considered in regard to its influence on public wealth and the general welfare. Two Great Evils of Virginia, and their one Common Remedy, 8vo, pa. Richmond, 1860. The four pamphlets, each.................. 10

HISTORY.

BEVERLY'S (ROBERT) HISTORY OF VIRGINIA. In four parts. I. The history of the settlement of Virginia, and the government thereof, to the year 1706. II. The natural productions and conveniences of the country, suited to trade and improvement. III. The native Indians, their religion, laws and customs, in war and peace. IV. The present state of the country, as to the polity of the government, and the improvements of the land, to 10th of June, 1720. By Robert Beverly, a native of the place. Re-printed from the author's second revised London edition of 1792, with an introduction by Charles Campbell, author of the "Colonial History of Virginia." 14 plates, 8vo, mus. Richmond, 1855......................... 2 50

AN ACCOUNT OF DISCOVERIES IN THE WEST until 1519, and of Voyages to and along the Atlantic Coast of North America from 1520 to 1573. Prepared for the Virginia Historical and Philosophical Society, by Conway Robinson. 8vo, mus. Richmond, 1848. (Published at $5.) 2 50

JEFFERSON'S (THOMAS) NOTES ON THE STATE OF VIRGINIA. A new edition, prepared by the author, containing many new notes never before published.

It is printed from President Jefferson's copy (Stockdale's London edition of 1787) of the Notes on Virginia, with his last additions (they are numerous) and corrections in manuscript, and four maps of Caves, Mounds, Fortifications, &c.

Letters from Gen. Dearborn and Judge Gibson, relating to the Murder of Logan, &c.

Fry and Jefferson's Map of Virginia, Maryland, Delaware, and Pennsylvania—very valuable on account of the Public Places and Private Residences, which are not to be found on any other Map.

A Topographical Analysis of Virginia, for 1790—a curious and useful sheet for historical reference.

Translations of all Jefferson's Notes in Foreign Languages, by Prof. Schele de Vere, of the University of Virginia.

8vo, mus. Richmond, 1853......................... 2 50

SMITH'S (M.) GEOGRAPHICAL VIEW OF THE BRITISH POSSESSIONS IN NORTH AMERICA. 18mo, sheep. Baltimore, 1814...................... 35

VIRGINIA CONVENTION OF 1776: Historical and Biographical. By H. B. Grigsby. 8vo, mus. Richmond, 1855.   1 50

OREGON, OUR RIGHT AND TITLE: containing an account of the condition of the Oregon Territory, its soil, climate and geographical position; together with a statement of the claims of Russia, Spain, Great Britain, and the United States. Accompanied with a map prepared by the author. By Wyndham Robertson, jr., of Virginia. 8vo, paper. Washington, 1846......................   50

HOT SPRINGS. The Invalid's Guide to the Virginia Hot Springs, with cases illustrative of their effects. By Thos. Goode, M. D. 32mo, cloth. Richmond, 1846..........   25

VIRGINIA. Report on the Soils of Powhatan County. By W. Gilham, Prof. Va. Military Institute. With a Map. 8vo, paper. Richmond, 1857.......................   35

BIRD. WESTOVER MANUSCRIPTS, containing the history of the dividing line betwixt Virginia and North Carolina. A Journey to the Land of Eden, A. D. 1733; and A Progress to the Mines, written from 1728–36, and now first published. By W. Bird, of Westover. 8vo, boards. Petersburg, 1841. New edition in press...............   3 00

BLAND PAPERS, being a selection from the manuscripts of Col. T. Bland, jr., of Prince George county, Va.; to which are prefixed an Introduction and Memoir edited by Charles Campbell. 2 vols. in one, 8vo, h'f ro. Petersburg, 1840...   3 00

VIRGINIA POLITICS. A History of the Political Campaign in Virginia in 1855; to which is added a review of the position of Parties in the Union, and a statement of the political issues distinguishing them on the eve of the Presidential Campaign of 1856. By J. P. Hambleton, M. D. 8vo. mus. Richmond, 1856............................   2 50

VIRGINIA CONVENTION. Proceeding and Debates of the Virginia State Convention of 1829–30, to which are subjoined the New Constitution of Virginia, and the votes of the people. 8vo, calf. Richmond, 1830.............   5 00

VIRGINIA. Pay and Muster Rolls of the Virginia Militia in the War of 1812. 8vo, half calf. Richmond, 1851-2.   15 00

VIRGINIA STATISTICS. Documents constaining statistics ordered to be printed by the State Convention sitting in the city of Richmond, 1850–51. 8vo, calf. Richmond, 1851...   2 50

VIRGINIA CONVENTION. Journal, Acts and Proceedings of a General Convention of the State of Virginia, assembled at Richmond, 1850. 8vo, half calf. Richmond, 1850...   5 00

VIRGINIA HISTORICAL SOCIETY COLLECTIONS, ADDRESSES, &c. (Contents: Stuart's Indian Wars, 1763; Grace Sherwood's Trial, 1705; Address in 1833 by

J. P. Cushing; in 1851 by W. H. Macfarland; in 1852 by H. A. Washington; in 1853 by H. B. Grigsby; in 1856 by R. M. T. Hunter; in 1856 by J. P. Holcombe.) 8vo, half turkey. Richmond, 1833-56........................ 5 00

VIRGINIA CONVENTION, 1850-51. Register of the Debates and Proceedings of the Virginia Reform Convention, (imperfect.) 8vo, half sheep. Richmond, 1851........ 3 00

VIRGINIA. A Comprehensive Description of Virginia and the District of Columbia, containing a copious collection of geographical, statistical, political, commercial, religious, moral and miscellaneous information, chiefly from original sources, by Joseph Martin; to which is added a History of Virginia, from its first settlement to the year 1754, with an abstract of the principal events from that period to the Independence of Virginia, by W. H. Brockenbrough, formerly Librarian at the University of Virginia, and afterwards Judge of the United States Court of Florida, 8vo, sp. Richmond........................... 2 00

MAURY. Paper on the Gulf Stream and Currents of the Sea, read before the National Institute at its annual meeting in 1844, by M. F. Maury, Lieut. U. S. Navy. 8vo, pa. Richmond, 1844........................ 13

BURKE. The Virginia Mineral Springs, with remarks on their use, the Diseases to which they are applicable, and in which they are contra-indicated; accompanied by a Map of Routes and Distances. A new work—2d edition. Improved and enlarged. By W. Burke, M.D. 12mo, muslin. Richmond, 1853................................ 75

COTTOM'S EDITION OF RICHARDSON'S ALMANAC. 24mo, paper, 6c. Per dozen, 25c; per gross, $2.50. Containing, besides the twelve calendar pages and astronomical calculations, a Jewish Calendar, Gardener's Monthly Instructor, List of the Virginia Senators, Members of Congress, Senate and House of Delegates; Virginia and North Carolina State Governments; State and Federal Courts of Virginia, North Carolina, Maryland, and the District of Columbia; Conjectures of the Weather, Equation or Time Tables, Receipts, Anecdotes, &c. Published annually.

JEFFERSON & CABELL. Early history of the University of Virginia, as contained in the Letters of (during the years from 1810 to 1826) Thos. Jefferson and Joseph C. Cabell, hitherto unpublished; with an Appendix consisting of Mr. Jefferson's bill for a complete system of education, and other illustrative documents; and an Introduction, comprising a brief historical sketch of the University, and a biographical notice of Joseph C. Cabell. 8vo, muslin. Richmond, 1856........................ 2 50

JUBILEE AT JAMESTOWN, VA. Report of Proceedings in Commemoration of the 13th of May, the Second

Centesimal Anniversary of the Settlement of Virginia, containing the Order of Procession, the Prayer of Bishop Madison, the Orations, the Odes and Toasts; together with the Proceedings at Williamsburg on the 15th, the day when the Convention of Virginia assembled in the old Capitol, declared her Independent, and recommended a similar procedure to Congress, and to the other States. 8vo, paper. Petersburg, 1807........................ 1 00

VIRGINIA. Journal of the Senate and House of Delegates for various years. Richmond.

VIRGINIA. Journal of the Convention of 1776. 4to, half sheep. Richmond, 1816..... .... 2 00

JEFFERSON. Memoir, Correspondence and Miscellanies from the Papers of Thos. Jefferson. Edited by Thos. Jefferson Randolph. 4 vols., 8v, boards. Charlottesville, 1829.. 5 00

JEFFERSON. Observations on the Writings of Thomas Jefferson, with particular reference to the attack they contain on the Memory of the late Gen'l Henry Lee. In series of letters by H. Lee. 2nd edition. With an Introduction and Notes, by Chas. C. Lee. 8vo, mus. Philadelphia, 1839. .... 1 75

AGRICULTURE.

RUFFIN'S (EDMUND) FARMER'S REGISTER. 10 vols., 8vo, half roan................................... 30 00

RUFFIN'S (EDMUND) PRIZE ESSAY ON AGRICULTURAL EDUCATION. 2nd edition, 8vo, paper....... 10

RUFFIN'S (EDMUND) AGRICULTURAL ESSAYS: Containing articles on the theory and practice of draining (in all its branches:) advantages of ploughing flat land in wide beds; on clover culture and the use and value of the products; management of wheat harvests; harvesting corn fodder; on the manner of propagation and habits of the moth or weevil, and means to prevent its ravages; inquiry into the causes of the existence of prairies, savannas and deserts, and the peculiar condition of soils which favor or prevent the growth of trees; depressed condition of lower Virginia; apology for "book farmers;" fallow; usefulness of snakes; embanked tide marshes and mill ponds as causes of disease; on the sources of malaria, or of autumnal diseases, and means of prevention; on the culture, uses and value of the southern pea, (Ruffin's Prize Essay of November, 1854,) and especially as a manuring crop. 12mo, half bound. Richmond, 1855............ 1 25

RUFFIN. An Essay on Calcareous Manures. By Edmund Ruffin, a practical farmer of Virginia from 1812; founder and sole editor of the Farmer's Register; Member and

Secretary of the former State Board of Agriculture; formerly Agricultural Surveyor of the State of South Carolina; and President of the Virginia State Agricultural Society. 5th edition, amended and enlarged, with plates. Fine edition, 8vo, library style, $2; cheap edition, 12mo, half roan or mus. Richmond, 1852...................... 1 25
PLANTATION AND FARM INSTRUCTION, Regulation, Record, Inventory, and Account Book, and for the better Ordering and Management of Plantation and Farm Business in every particular. By a Southern Planter. "Order is Heaven's First Law." *New edition printing.*

THEOLOGY.

MAGRUDER & ORVIS' DEBATE on the Punishment of the Wicked, and on the Kingdom of God. 12mo, muslin. Richmond, 1855.................................... 75
WALSH'S (REV. J. T.) NATURE AND DURATION OF FUTURE PUNISHMENT. 12mo, muslin. Richmond, 1857...................................... 50
MEMOIR AND SERMONS OF THE REV. WILLIAM DUVALL, City Missionary. By the Rev. C. Walker. With a portrait. 12mo, mus. Richmond, 1854......... 50
STRINGFELLOW'S (T., D.D.) STATISTICAL AND SCRIPTURAL VIEW OF SLAVERY. 4th edition, 12mo, mus. Richmond, 1856......................... 50
FAMILY CHRISTIAN ALBUM. Edited by Mrs. E. P. Elam. 8vo, mus. Richmond, 1855.................... 1 50
FLAVEL'S WORKS. Balm of the Covenant. View of the Soul of Man, &c. 8vo, half roan. Richmond, 1828.. 60
BLAIR. Sermons of Rev. John D. Blair, collected from his manuscripts. 8vo, sheep. Richmond, 1825............ 50

POETRY.

BARTLEY'S (J. AVIS) POEMS. Lays of Ancient Virginia, &c. 12mo, mus. Richmond, 1855.............. 75
MOCK (THE) AUCTION. Ossawatamie Sold! A Mock Heroic Poem; with Portraits and Tableaux, illustrative of the character and actions of the world-renowned Order of Peter Funks. By a Virginian. 12mo, mus. 10 tinted plates. Richmond, 1860........................... 75
CARTER. Mugæ, by Nugator; or Pieces in Prose and Verse. By St. Ledger L. Carter. 24mo, half roan. Baltimore, 1844..................................... 75
BETHEL HYMNS. A Collection of Original Spiritual Songs. By Mrs. Elizabeth Sowers, of Clark county, Va. 48mo, sheep. Richmond, 1849....................... 25
FARMER'S (C. M.) FAIRY OF THE STREAM, and other Poems. 12mo, boards. Richmond, 1847.......... 50

COURTNEY'S (REV J.) SELECTION OF HYMNS. 24mo, sheep. Richmond, 1831..................... 35

SCHOOL.

VAUGHAN'S (S. A.) ABECEDARIAN; OR, FIRST BOOK FOR CHILDREN. Designed to render the learning of the Alphabet, and of Elementary Spelling and Defining, pleasing and intellectual; and to fix in the mind habits of attention to the force of letters in the formation of words, and to the meaning of words, and through their application to their appropriate objects, to inculcate the love of Nature and reverence of Nature's God. 12mo, roan back. Richmond.. 15
YOUNG (THE) AMERICAN'S PRIMER, OR FIRST BOOK. 24mo, paper. Richmond, per dozen.......... 25
SCHOOLER'S (SAMUEL) ELEMENTS OF DESCRIPTIVE GEOMETRY, the Point, the Straight Line, and the Plane. 4to, mus. Richmond, 1853................ 2 00
    The paper, type, and plates, are in the finest style of the arts; and the book, altogether, has been pronounced equal, if not superior, to any English, French, or American work on the subject.
GARNETT'S (JAMES M.) LECTURES ON FEMALE EDUCATION, AND THE GOSSIP'S MANUAL. 3rd edition, 18mo, sheep. Richmond, 1825............ 50
CÆSAR, with English Notes. By Samuel Schooler. *In preparation.*

SLAVERY.

STRINGFELLOW'S (T., D.D.) STATISTICAL AND SCRIPTURAL VIEW OF SLAVERY. Fourth edition, 12mo, mus. Richmond, 1856....................... 50
FLETCHER'S (JOHN) STUDIES ON SLAVERY. 8vo, sheep. Natchez, 1852............................... 2 00
DEW. An Essay on Slavery. By T. R. Dew, late President of William and Mary College. 2d edition, 8vo, paper. Richmond, 1849.................................. 50
RUFFIN'S (EDMUND) AFRICAN COLONIZATION UNVEILED. Slavery and Free Labor described and compared. The political Economy of Slavery; or the Institution considered in regard to its influence on public wealth and the general welfare. Two Great Evils of Virginia, and their one Common Remedy. 8vo, pa. Richmond, 1860. Each................................... 10
UNCLE ROBIN IN HIS CABIN IN VIRGINIA, AND TOM WITHOUT ONE IN BOSTON. By J. W. Page. 2nd edition, plates, 12mo, muslin. Richmond, 1853..... 75
WHITE ACRE *vs.* BLACK ACRE, a Case at Law, reported by J. G., Esq., a retired barrister of Lincolnshire, England, 18mo, mus. Richmond, 1856................ 75

MASONIC.

DOVE'S (JOHN) VIRGINIA TEXT BOOK OF ROYAL ARCH MASONRY. Plates, 12mo, mus. Richmond, 1853, ... 1 25
DOVE'S (JOHN) HISTORY OF THE GRAND LODGE OF VIRGINIA, AND ANCIENT CONSTITUTIONS OF MASONRY. 18mo, muslin. Richmond, 1854..... 75
DOVE'S (JOHN, M.D.) MASONIC TEXT BOOK. 2nd edition. Plates, 12mo, mus. Richmond, 1854.......... 1 25

NOVELS.

REMINISCENCES OF A VIRGINIA PHYSICIAN. By Prof. P. S. Ruter. 2 vols., 12mo, paper. Louisville, 1849, 50
SOUTHERN AND SOUTH-WESTERN SKETCHES. Fun, Sentiment and Adventure! Edited by a Gentleman of Richmond. 18mo, mus. Richmond................ 60
TUCKER. Gertrude. A Novel. By Judge Tucker, Professor of William and Mary College. 8vo, paper. Richmond, 1845.................................... 35
UNCLE ROBIN IN HIS CABIN IN VIRGINIA, AND TOM WITHOUT ONE IN BOSTON. By J. W. Page. 2nd edition, plates, 12mo, mus. Richmond, 1853........ 75
SKETCHES OF CHARACTER, (Randolph, Wirt, Kenton, &c.) AND TALES FOUNDED ON FACT. By F. W. Thomas. 8vo, boards. Louisville, 1849......... 25
MICHAEL BONHAM, OR THE FALL OF BEXAR. A Tale of Texas. In five parts. By a Southerner. 8vo, paper. Richmond, 1852............................ 25
EDITH ALLEN, OR SKETCHES OF LIFE IN VIRGINIA. By Lawrence Neville. 12mo, mus. Richmond, 1855... 1 00

MUSIC.

EVERETT'S (DR. A. B.) ELEMENTS OF VOCAL MUSIC; including a Treatise on Harmony, and a Chapter on Versification. Designed as a text-book for teachers and pupils in Female Seminaries, Male Academies, Singing Classes, etc., etc., and for private study and reference. 2nd and enlarged edition. 18mo, mus. Richmond, 1860, 50
EVERETT'S (L. C. & DR. A. B.) NEW THESAURUS MUSICUS, OR U. S. COLLECTION OF CHURCH MUSIC; constituting the most complete variety of new Psalm and Hymn Tunes, Sentences, Anthems, Chants, &c. for the use of the Choir, the Congregation and the Singing School, ever offered to the American people. Comprising also all the popular old choir and congregational tunes in general use. Music, 8vo, boards. Richmond, 1860...... 1 00

WINKLER'S HINTS TO PIANO-FORTE PLAYERS.
12mo, boards. Richmond, 1847...................... 25

MISCELLANY.

LUMBER (THE) DEALER'S ASSISTANT, OR COMPLETE TABLES OF THE MEASUREMENTS OF TIMBER, &c.—showing the quantity in feet and inches in any number of plank or scantling, from one to fifty; of any length in feet or half feet, from eight to twenty-two feet long; of any width in inches and half inches, from three to twenty inches wide. By George S. Sutherlin. 12mo, half sheep. Richmond, 1849.................... 50
VIRGINIA JUSTICE'S RECORD BOOK OF JUDGMENTS. Cap size, half bound...................... 1 50
PAJOT'S OBSTETRIC TABLES, translated from the French, and arranged by O. A. Grenshaw, M. D., and J. B. McCaw, M. D. 4to, boards. Richmond, 1856....... 1 25
PHYSICIAN'S TABULATED DIARY, designed to facilitate the study of Disease at the Bedside. By a Physician of Virginia. Pocket size. Muslin. Richmond, 1856.... 50
SOUTHERN LITERARY MESSENGER. 29 vols., 8vo, in numbers. Richmond, 1834-59......................100 00
☞ Most of the volumes or numbers are for sale separate.
RANDOLPH'S POCKET DIARY AND DAILY MEMORANDUM BOOK. Richmond, 186—. 18mo, half bound, 35c.; tucks... 60
RANDOLPH'S POCKET DIARY, DAILY MEMORANDUM AND ACCOUNT BOOK. Richmond, 186—. Half bound, 75c.; tucks....................................... 1 00
LIBRARY CASES, OR BOXES, in neat book form, very convenient and useful for preserving valuable pamphlets and magazines. 8vo. roan back........................ 60
SKETCHES OF CHARACTER, (Randolph, Wirt, Kenton, &c.,) AND TALES FOUNDED ON FACT. By F. W. Thomas. 8vo, boards. Louisville, 1849......... 25
EDGAR'S SPORTSMAN'S HERALD & STUD BOOK 8vo, sp. New York, 1833........ .... 1 50
WATER CURE. By Dr. J. B. Williams, and others. With comments and explanatory remarks on bathing for invalids, &c., by J. Timberlake. 18mo, paper. Richmond, 1853.. 25
THE PRACTICAL MINER'S OWN BOOK & GUIDE. By J. Budge. With additions by J. Atkins. Plates, 12mo, muslin. Richmond, 1860............................ 2 00
THE CARPENTER'S GUIDE IN STAIR-BUILDING AND HAND-RAILING, based upon Plain and Practical Principles, with sufficient explanations to inform without confusing the learner. By Patrick O'Neill, Practical Stair-Builder. Folio, mus. Richmond................. 2 00

www.ingramcontent.com/pod-product-compliance
Lightning Source LLC
Chambersburg PA
CBHW030006240426
43672CB00007B/849